Digital Marketing for Business 2021

3 Books in 1

Exceed 2020 With the Step-by-Step Guide for Beginners, Make Money Online Using the New Strategies to Win in The Digital World, and The Ultimate Tips and Tricks.

Christopher Clarke & Adam Preace

© Copyright 2020 by Christopher Clarke, Adam Preace. All right reserved.

The work contained herein has been produced with the intent to provide relevant knowledge and information on the topic on the topic described in the title for entertainment purposes only. While the author has gone to every extent to furnish up to date and true information, no claims can be made as to its accuracy or validity as the author has made no claims to be an expert on this topic. Notwithstanding, the reader is asked to do their own research and consult any subject matter experts they deem necessary to ensure the quality and accuracy of the material presented herein.

This statement is legally binding as deemed by the Committee of Publishers Association and the American Bar Association for the territory of the United States. Other jurisdictions may apply their own legal statutes. Any reproduction, transmission or copying of this material contained in this work without the express written consent of the copyright holder shall be deemed as a copyright violation as per the current legislation in force on the date of publishing and subsequent time thereafter. All additional works derived from this material may be claimed by the holder of this copyright.

The data, depictions, events, descriptions, and all other information forthwith are considered to be true, fair and accurate unless the work is expressly described as a work of fiction. Regardless of the nature of this work, the Publisher is exempt from any responsibility of actions taken by the reader in conjunction with this work. The Publisher acknowledges that the reader acts of their own accord and releases the author and Publisher of any responsibility for the observance of tips, advice, counsel, strategies, and techniques that may be offered in this volume.

BOOKS INCLUDED:

Affiliate Marketing 2021
Exceed 2020 With the Step-by-Step Beginner's Guide to Make Money Online, Passive Income and Advertising for Your Blogging Profit (The Most Effective New Mastery Secrets)

Digital Marketing for Beginners2021
Exceed 2020 Generating Passive Income with The Ultimate and Most Effective New Social Media Strategy, Using the New Proven Tips for Business and Personal branding.

Social Media Marketing 2021
Exceed 2020, Become an Able Influencer Using Instagram, Facebook, Twitter, and YouTube with the Ultimate Mastery Workbook for Success Strategies.

Table of contents

Digital Marketing for Business 2021 1
Affiliate Marketing 2021.. 18
Introduction 19
Chapter 1: What is Affiliate Marketing? 23

    The Basic Set up 24
    The Potential 24
    The Reality of Affiliate Marketing 25
    Get Educated 28
    Paid or Free? 28
    The Importance of Choosing the Right Niche . 30
    Where You Go is Up to You 30

Chapter 2: Choosing a Niche 31

    Market Size and Trends 31
    Keyword Planners 36
    Note your Keywords 37
    Demographics 40
    Finding Offers 43

Chapter 3: Finding the Best Offers 45

    Finding Specialty Websites 45
    Evaluating Websites 46
    Types of Affiliate Programs 49
    Affiliate Programs 53

        JV zoo 53
        ClickBank 53
        Others 54

    Evaluating Affiliate Offers 55
    Website Evaluation 56
    Conversion Rates 58
    Product Pricing 59

Selling Physical Products 61

Chapter 4: The Right Mentality for Affiliate Marketing 63

It's not a get rich quick scheme 63
Be persistent 63
Stay Focused 64
Be disciplined 64
Don't be afraid to lose money 65
Act like there is no Plan B 65
Don't get emotional 65
Don't make excuses 66

Chapter 5: Building a Marketing Base 68

A Website 68
A Blog 69
A YouTube Channel 70
A Facebook Page 70
Email List Builder 70
Landing Page 71
Instagram Account 71
Other Social Media 72

Chapter 6: The 4 Golden Rules of Profits 73

Focus on a Small Number of Products 73
Never Cut Corners 73
Review, Don't Sell 74
Test, Retest and Adapt 76
Bonus – Avoid Make Money Online 76

Chapter 7: Driving Free Traffic 79

A blog to Target Keywords 80
Incorporating SEO 81
Post Regularly 82
Collect Emails 83

Create backlinks 84
Robots and Crawling 84
YouTube Channel 84
Using Your Facebook Page 86
Landing Page 87
Instagram 88
Email Marketing 92
Summary 95

Chapter 8: Social Media Advertising 96

Facebook Campaigns Overview 97
Types of Ads 99
Where to Advertise 100
Pinterest Advertising 101
Twitter Advertising 102
YouTube Advertising 102
Linked-In 105
WhatsApp 106

Chapter 9: Other Advertising Methods 107

What a Pay Per Click (PPC) Ad Is 107
Effective PPC Ads 109
Budgeting and Keywords 110
Network Advertising 111
Solo Ads 111

Chapter 10: Ten Most Common Mistakes 115

Thinking people will just arrive at your website
.... 115
Not providing enough content 116
Hard selling your audience 117
Too Many Products 118
Not Enough Products 119
Failing to Know Your Products 120
Falling Victim to Shiny Object Syndrome 120
Spending money when you don't have to 121

Not putting in any time 122
Failing to track campaigns effectively 123
Focusing only on price 124
Being cheap 124
Failing to adjust the copy 125
Sticking to a bad product too long 125
Paying too much attention to gravity 126

Chapter 11: Ten Tips for Success 128

Learn from others 128
Remember the mobile space 129
Focus on profitable products 129
Focus on products you can believe in 130
Do head to head comparisons 130
Pick a mid-range niche 131
Always add value 133
Add your own bonuses 133
Use multiple traffic sources 134
Give a thumbs down 134
Pay attention to call to action buttons 134
Use varied price ranges 135
Use time limits 135
The Rule of Seven 136
Don't use canned material 136
Banners rarely work 137
Don't obsess on followers 137
Make a business plan 138
Opt for Income Streams 139
Utilize PLR products 140

Chapter 12: Platforms to Use in Affiliate Marketing 141

Take into account age 141
Consider making apps 142
Who the customer determines where to advertise 142

Refine the target audience as much as possible 143
Use surveys 143

Chapter 13: Creating A Cohesive and Compassionate Presence 145

Understanding Parasocial Relationships 146
The Power Of Your Voice 148
Compassionate Marketing 150
Supporting Your Audience 152
Maintaining A Consistent Approach 154
Building A Sense Of Community In Your Community 155
Reviewing Your Vision For The Future 157

Chapter 14: Affiliate Marketing Trends of 2021 159

Push Updates Are Still Useful 160
Run Compliant Campaigns 161
Try Unusual Placements 163
Quality Must Be Your Priority 164
Whitehat SEO Matters 167
Market For Transparent Brands 169
Get On Facebook And Instagram 172
Focus Largely On Single-Conversions 174

Chapter 15: The 2021 Affiliate Marketing Forecast 177

Affiliate Marketing Has Not Reached Its Peak Yet 177
Quality Marketers Will Earn, Low-Quality Will Not 178
Your Website Strategy Needs To Change 179
Push Traffic Will Change In Nature 180
New Affiliate Programs And Agencies Will Come Out 180

Conclusion 182
Digital Marketing for Beginners 2021 183
Introduction 184
Chapter 1: What Is Digital Marketing? 188

    How Did Digital Marketing Begin? 188
    What Does Digital Marketing Require? 190
    Who Can Use Digital Marketing? 190
    How Will I Make Money with Digital Marketing? 191

Chapter 2: Identifying Income Channels 194

    Selling Products 194
    Selling Services 196
    Affiliate Marketing 197
    Dropship Marketing 199
    Choosing the Right Income Channel for You 200

Chapter 3: Tapping into a Global Audience 202

    Why You Need a Clearly Defined Audience .. 202
    How to Identify Your Custom Audience 203
    Discovering Where Your Audience Is 205

Chapter 4: Interacting with Your Audience 208

    Hanging Out with Your Audience Online 209
    Creating a Relationship with Your Audience . 211
    Building Trust and Credibility 215
    Gaining and Maintaining Positive Momentum 220

Chapter 5: Digital Marketing Delivery Channels 223

    Search Engine Optimization (SEO) 224
    Content Marketing 225
    Social Media Marketing 226

Pay Per Click (PPC) 227
Affiliate Marketing 228
Native Advertising 229
Marketing Automation 230
Email Marketing 231
Online PR 233
Inbound Marketing 234

Chapter 6: Using Social Media for Marketing .. 236

Why Social Media Marketing Works 236
Who Should Be Using Social Media Marketing
.... 239
Creating Your Social Media Presence 239
Engaging with Your Audience on Social Media
.... 243
Combining Social Media Marketing and Other
Marketing Strategies 245

Chapter 7: Creating Organic Content 247

What Counts as Organic Content? 248
Who Should Be Using Organic Content
Creation? 248
Creating Social Media Content 248

    Written Content 250
    Graphic Content 252
    Video Content 253

Creating Email Content 255
Creating Blog Content 259
Creating Video Content 261
Combining Organic Content with Other Digital
Marketing Strategies 262

Chapter 8: Targeted Paid Advertisements 264

Why Targeted Paid Advertisements Work 265

Who Should Use Targeted Paid Advertisements 267
Where You Can Use Targeted Paid Advertisements 268
Targeted Paid Advertisements That Are Right for Your Business 269
Creating Pay Per Click Advertisements 271
Creating Native Advertisements 275

    Promoting Your Profile 276
    Sponsoring a Post 277
    Selling A Product or Service 277
    Creating a Video Advertisement 278

Combining Targeted Paid Advertisements with Other Digital Marketing Strategies 279

Chapter 9: Online Marketing Events 280

    Why Online Marketing Events Work 281
    Who Should Be Using Online Marketing Events 282
    Types of Online Marketing Events to Consider 283
    Hosting a Webinar 285
    Hosting Product Demonstrations 287
    Hosting Courses 288
    Online Marketing with Online PR 290
    Combining Online Marketing Events with Other Digital Marketing Strategies 292

Chapter 10: Tips to Help You Succeed 293

    Keep Your Website Up to Date 293
    Design and Evolve Your Customer Experience 295
    Get Your Business on Google 296
    Master Your Call to Action 296
    Track Your Performance With Analytics 297

Chapter 11: Mistakes to Avoid 299

   Avoid Outdated Marketing Tactics 299
   Avoid the "Abandoned Profile" Effect 301
   Avoid Going into Digital Marketing Without a Plan..301
   Avoid Underestimating the Importance of All Devices 302
   Avoid Not Diversifying Your Approach for Greater Reach.. 304

Chapter 12: The Power of Staying Relevant Through Conflict and Disaster 305

   Staying Relevant During Regular Times Vs. Peculiar Times... 306
   Leveraging Trends to Stay Relevant 309
   Avoiding Tacky or Insensitive Campaigns...... 311
   Deepening the Sense of Community Within Your Brand...313
   Engaging in the Way Your Audience Is Engaging 315
   Keeping Up with the Changing Times.............317

Chapter 13: The Latest Trends in Digital Marketing 320

   Facebook Is Losing Grounds with the Younger Demographic 321
   Instagram Is the Most Popular Platform for Younger Kids 322
   Properly Designed Chatbots Are Excellent for Customer Service... 324
   Messaging Apps Are Excellent Tools for Marketing Through... 325
   Video Content Must Be Used for Your Brand to Stay Relevant 326

Context In Your Content Matters As Much As
Quality Does 327
Email Marketing Campaigns Should Be More
Personalized 329
Interactive Content Is the Mainstream
Marketing Strategy of Choice 330

Chapter 14: The 2021 Digital Marketing Forecast
.... 332

Automation Meets Personalization, and the
Balance Matters 333
Non-Linear Advertising Captures Attention . 334
Marketing Automation Is a Powerhouse, and It
Must Be Used Correctly 335
Voice Search Marketing Is an Essential 336
Content Marketing Should Be Content Selling
.... 337
Hyper-Targeted Advertising 338
Maximizing Your Digital Marketing Budget
Will Matter 340
Streamlined Marketing Strategies Will Change
The Game 341

Conclusion 343
Social Media Marketing 2021 346
Introduction 347
Chapter 1: Introduction to Social Media 351

How Social Media Works for Business 351
Choosing the Right Niche on Social Media 354
Creating Your Profiles and Pages Properly ... 357
Identifying Winning Strategies for Marketing
on Social Media 359

Chapter 2: Becoming an Influencer 363

Who Should Be an Influencer? 365
Finding Your Unique Edge 367

Setting Yourself Apart from the Rest.............. 368
Creating Consistency in Your Presentation .. 370
Ditching Marketing Gimmicks........................... 371
Building Follower Relationships with
Boundaries 373

Chapter 3: Facebook Marketing 375

Who Should Use Facebook, and Why? 375
Leveraging Facebook in Your Marketing
Strategy 377
Marketing on Facebook in 2021........................ 378
How to Monetize Your Facebook Page 381

Chapter 4: Instagram Marketing 386

Who Should Use Instagram, and Why?.......... 386
Leveraging Instagram in Your Marketing
Strategy 387
Marketing on Instagram in 2021...................... 389

 Instagram Stories and Story Highlights 391
 IGTV 394
 Customizable Buttons...................................... 396
 Shopping Features... 396

Monetizing Your Instagram Page 397

Chapter 5: YouTube Marketing 401

Who Should Use YouTube, and Why? 401
Leveraging YouTube in Your Marketing
Strategy 403
Marketing on YouTube in 2021....................... 406
Monetizing Your YouTube Channel 413

Chapter 6: Twitter Marketing 419

Who Should Use Twitter, and Why?................ 420

Leveraging Twitter in Your Marketing Strategy 421
Marketing on Twitter in 2021 423
Monetizing Your Twitter Page 431

Chapter 7: Mistakes You Must Avoid 435

Not Being Personable Enough 436
Thinking You Don't Need A Strategy 437
Not Targeting Your Audience Effectively 438
Improper Management of Negative Feedback 439
Using Promotional Tools in a Poor Manner . 440
Posting Low-Quality Content to Meet Quantity Goals 442
Not Focusing on Your Analytics 443

Chapter 8: Tips to Guarantee Your Success 444

Take Advantage of Video Marketing 444
Get More Social with Your Audience 446
Research Your Market Frequently 447
Highlight Your Products on Social Media 448

Chapter 9: How to Create Your Strategy 450

Outline Your Brand and Goals 450
Create the Bridge Between Your Audience and Goals 452
Begin to Take Action 453
Review and Revise Your Approach as Needed 453

Chapter 10: The Power Of Paid Advertising 455

Paid Advertising Leads To Rapid Results 456
Targeting Your Paid Campaigns 457
Creating A Cross-Promotional Campaign Strategy 459

Monitoring the Performance Of Your Ads 461
Using Your Results to Amplify Your
Performance 463

Chapter 11: The Need for Community-Oriented Brands 466

Step 1: Recognize That Building A Community Takes Time 467
Step 2: Start By Building A Community Within Your Team 468
Step 3: Passionately Embrace A Relevant Social Cause 469
Step 4: Use Video To Involve Your Customers 470
Step 5: Drive Your Social Media Presence with Value 472
Step 6: Develop Educational Content For Your Audience 475

Chapter 12: The Latest Trends in Social Media Advertising 478

Ephemeral Content Is Expanding In Popularity 478
Niche Social Platforms Are Gaining Popularity 479
Video Content Is A Non-Negotiable Marketing Tool 479
Social Media Is Often Used For Customer Service 480
Personalization Is The Key To Success 480
Social Media Communities Are On The Scene 481
Local Targeting Is Gaining In Popularity 482
Social Listening Is A Strategy You Must Be Using 482

User-Generated Content Is A Marketing Powerhouse 483

Chapter 13: The 2021 Social Media Forecast 485

Regulatory Control and Legal Scrutiny Continues 485
Influencer Marketing Continues To Rise In Success 486
Social Commerce Continues To Expand 486
Voice Search Is Becoming Increasingly More Popular... 487
Intuitive Content Is Skyrocketing 487
AR And VR Are Finding Their Way into New Industries 488
Company-Specific Device Apps Will Be Trending 488

Conclusion 490

Affiliate Marketing 2021

Exceed 2020 With the Step-by-Step Beginner's Guide to Make Money Online, Passive Income and Advertising for Your Blogging Profit

(The Most Effective New Mastery Secrets)

Christopher Clarke & Adam Preace

Introduction

Congratulations, and welcome to Affiliate Marketing 2021!

This book will introduce you to the powerful world of affiliate marketing, which may have just become one of the most influential models of the present and the coming years . I don't think anyone has expected this year to turn out the way it did. Yet, it turned affiliate marketing into a robust business model that enables those who are willing to speak up and promote their voice to use it for a myriad of incredible things. More than ever before, consumers are looking for a sense of camaraderie and community, and they will find that in affiliate marketers.

Since the model's conception, affiliate marketing has given a significant voice to individuals so that individuals can connect with consumers, cultivate healthy relationships, and use those relationships to sell products. While modern affiliate marketing is a newer model, it is based on the original form of marketing, word-of-mouth marketing. Mostly, one person is paid to use word-of-mouth marketing to tell many people to purchase a product from a specific company.

These days, affiliate marketing is just as powerful as it ever was. Only those who undertake the role of affiliate marketers are given an incredible opportunity to do something even more significant than just market products. The result? *Your audience grows wildly abundant, and you sell even more products*. That's right; by broadening your marketing scope beyond just marketing products, you manage to exponentially increase your sales and earn a killing through affiliate marketing.

In *Affiliate Marketing 2021,* we will introduce you to the powerful world of affiliate marketing so that you can produce passive income, hedge yourself against the tumultuous economy that we have come across in 2020, and fulfill your dreams of being a well-paid affiliate marketer. Even during our current economic climate, you can make hundreds, thousands, and even tens of thousands of dollars as long as you play your cards right. Plus, it is a low-commitment model that does not require you to maintain your own product, inventory, employees, or even your own website. Most people barely work part-time hours at their affiliate marketing business, and they *still* make incredible profits off of their time. It is a killer business model, from the ground up.

I know that during tough times you might be skeptical, and you may want to brush this off as being some sort of fantasy dream business. The truth is, this is 100% real, and many people are actively doing this *right now* and have become very wealthy in the process. Yes, you really can start your own online business, with zero product, and make it big. And no, the internet is not too crowded and the market is not over-saturated. We are always waiting for the next big thing to come around, and right now is the time for you to position yourself as being that next big thing.

For you to succeed with affiliate marketing, you must be ready to take action, invest energy into your business, and make it work for you. This is key. Too often, people claim they want to be affiliate marketers. Still, they do not take the time to research the power of community, understand the importance of connection, or leverage their role in parasocial relationships. You *must* be willing to understand the "job description" that comes with affiliate marketing and do it well, just as you would with any other business.

The only time people fail in affiliate marketing is when they fail to read the job description or fail to fulfill their duties. They didn't take action, so they failed! You will not be one of them.

Inside *Affiliate Marketing 2021*, we have laid out every step in a clear, easy-to-follow action plan that you can use to help you develop the most reliable business plan for your affiliate marketing brand. The process will include defining your brand, growing your brand, and growing yourself to be the type of person who can sustain and deliver on that brand. The result will be people happily connecting with you, engaging as a part of your community, and consuming whatever you market to them.

The amount of income you earn through affiliate marketing is entirely up to you and the action you are willing to take. The more you give to your brand, the more you will get out of it. If you only want to make a few hundred dollars a month, you can go ahead and make some extra cash through a side hustle. If you want to earn tens of thousands of dollars every month, you can certainly do that, too. The key is putting into your business what you want to get out of it, and stay committed until you see the results you desire.

I want to make it clear right now; affiliate marketing is not a get-rich-quick scheme. Yes, you can become massively wealthy through this marketing method. However, you are not going to become wealthy overnight. It takes time to build up a community that trusts you and to leverage that community to create deals with brands who want to access the community you have developed. You must be willing to be patient, consistent, and committed to growing that community if you are going to establish a level of trust that will turn you into a successful affiliate marketer.

If you can remain committed, though, which I have no doubt you can, you will have the power to create anything you want through your affiliate marketing business. So, what do you think? Are you ready to get started? If so, let's begin!

Chapter 1: What is Affiliate Marketing?

You've probably heard all the buzz, maybe you found out about affiliate marketing searching about starting an online business.

Simply put, affiliate marketing is doing online and social media marketing to sell other people's products.

But let's be clear about what affiliate marketing is not. First off it's not an MLM scheme. When you do proper affiliate marketing, you are not trying to recruit new members to any kind of system that makes its money through recruitment of sales people that spend all their time recruiting other salespeople (or any time, for that matter). If you find some kind of program like that – run!

Affiliate marketing is about selling genuine products. They can be physical products, they can be websites, it could be something like driving traffic to Amazon, or it could be selling a digital product (a video course, on some niche topic, software, or digitally downloaded book, something of that nature). A good affiliate marketing program does not involve any kind of MLM or Ponzi scheme type set up and is based on moving products to the buying public. When the product sells, you get paid a commission.

The Basic Set up
When you get right down to it, affiliate marketing involves two things. The first is that you're pre-selling potential customers on the product. We will explore how to do this in detail later, but you're going to create reviews or websites or email campaigns that gently persuade people that the product is right for them. Of course,, it's not going to work all the time or even a large percentage of the time. But all you need to do is get some of the people you are coming in contact with, whether it's through a blog, Facebook, or Instagram – to be interested in the product. For some products, it's going to be easy, and there are ways to tap into people who are online already looking for the products you're selling. Other times it's going to take a little more work but the rewards may be outsized.

The second step is to send that traffic to the product owners website. Any traffic you send will be tracked using time-tested technologies that have been working online for more than twenty years, and so when there are sales you'll get a commission!

The more traffic you send, the more money you make. It's that simple!

The Potential
The sky is the limit with affiliate marketing. Many people have become multi-millionaires just using affiliate marketing alone. Others use affiliate marketing as a stepping stone, building a six-figure business and learning how to do online marketing in the process, and

then launching their own products later down the road, where the big money is. If you take that path, you can make a virtually unlimited income.

But we want to emphasize that's not really required. You can earn a very good income, anywhere from a few hundred dollars a month, all the way to high seven figures, doing nothing but pushing traffic for other people's products.

And after you have set up your sales machine, you can put as much or as little effort into it as you like. Imagine having a passive income generator that makes you money while you sleep, twenty-four hours a day seven days a week, all year long? You can spend time with family and friends, travel, engage with your passions, while your sales machine is driving income into your bank account!

Imagine having a side business that runs on autopilot that pays your car payment, or helps raise money for expenses like health insurance or the kid's food, entertainment, and clothing. Or imagine having a side business that ran on autopilot that made your house payment. Or maybe… in 1-3 years you'll make a million dollars or more!

The truth is how far you take this business is entirely up to you.

The Reality of Affiliate Marketing

Now that we've given you quite a pep talk, we're going to bring you back down to earth. In real life, most affiliate marketers fail. And that's part of the reason we wrote this book – because we don't want you to fail. Not having the right information is one of the main reasons that people don't earn any money doing affiliate marketing.

Later in the book, we're going to go into detail on the top mistakes made by new affiliate marketers so that you can avoid them by learning about them before getting started. But there are two big things that stand out and we're going to mention them repeatedly. We don't want to be boring or repetitive, but its important that you learn up front the biggest factors that determine success or failure in this business.

The first factor is simply not taking action. The reality is that most people that sign up as affiliates and take a course, or some other initial steps do not follow through with taking action. We can tell you what to do in this book, but the reality is you have to actually implement the steps. Sadly more than 90% of affiliate marketers fail to make substantial profits. But those that do, quickly earn very high incomes.

Part of that means having a realistic view of online businesses. We have hyped up the benefits of having a passive income, and many online marketers who train new affiliate marketers focus a lot on the vision of people having money streaming into their bank account while they travel and spend most of their time pursuing hobbies they are passionate about, surrounded by family and friends.

You can get there – but you aren't going to get there without putting the work in to build a foundation. Think of it this way, we could write the idea of Wal-Mart down on paper, and imagine the billions of dollars in sales it would generate. But without actually building the stores, nothing is going to happen. Once the stores are built, for the people that founded Wal-Mart, it basically runs on autopilot.

An affiliate marketing business isn't anywhere as near complicated as a brick and mortar retail business like Wal-Mart, but you have to build your own foundation and in the early months of your business that is going to take effort. But later, it will pay off if you take all the steps that we outline in the book.

The second problem that most affiliate marketers have is persistence. You aren't going to put up a web page or run one Facebook campaign and immediately start making $1,000 a day. You are going to have to learn how to write copy that converts, build the right advertising campaigns, and so forth. That might take some time, and some people are going to find it takes more time than others – but if you are persistent, you can get there.

The problem is most people actually give up, and do so very early. They run one Facebook campaign and then when it fails to make money, they quit. Or they put up a one-page website and tell themselves "see, it's not working".

We hope that you don't take that approach. You need to be persistent, and when something isn't working, keep trying and adjusting until it does.

Get Educated

Learning as much as you can about online marketing is an important step. And by downloading this book, you've taken the first step on that journey! That doesn't mean you should buy an endless array of $2,000 courses from all the online gurus that are out there, but you should put effort into learning what works. For example, learn how to write sales copy if you are not already a sales writing expert. There are many free resources, whether on YouTube or on blogs, that will teach you the steps you need to take to start building your online business. You can also find a low-cost course on Udemy that will help you learn the steps you need to get it set up properly. But no matter where you go for your education, the point is to keep learning – and be prepared to adjust. We live in an era of rapidly changing technology, so what works in 2020 may not work in 2022 or 2025, so it's important to stay on top of things and keep growing as things develop and change. New technology often means new opportunities, and far too many people fail to capitalize on them!

Paid or Free?

Many people ask if it's possible to earn big money without spending money on things like advertising and marketing.

The answer is a DEFINITE YES.

In fact, our opinion is that free is the way to go. But there is a price to pay for everything. We think it was Ben Franklin who said: "time is money". Well, that was true in 1776 and it's still true in 2021!

So if you want to go the free route, you are going to need to put more effort into building an infrastructure online that is going to drive traffic. You are also going to need some patience because that takes time to work. It also takes persistence, because you're going to have to work at it on a regular basis for many months. We are going to outline the steps to take in this book and show you what you need to do.

For the impatient, there is always the paid route which guarantees a flow of traffic. That can work right away – and it will for the traffic part – provided that you have everything perfectly set up. That means your advertisements have to be well designed, well targeted and have the right sales copy. It means your landing pages have to be perfect (don't worry if you don't know what a landing page is, we'll explain those to you later). If things aren't set up right, taking the paid route can cost you a lot of money. And that can make people give up too when they are on the verge of success.

You can also take a mixed approach which is what we prefer, do some paid marketing but also set up the "freebased" business infrastructure as well. That is the best way to generate traffic, and over time the free side of your business can take on an increasingly larger role. We'll explain why that works later in the book.

The Importance of Choosing the Right Niche

We are going to be talking about choosing a niche, but choosing the right niche is one of the most important steps you will take. First off, you want to select something you are passionate about. If you pick something you aren't interested in, then you aren't going to do well with it. The reason is that you're going to have to spend time building your business, and doing that for something that isn't of interest is going to be a drain on you, and your lack of passion is going to come through in your sales copy. Of course,, there needs to be some balance, if you are passionate about something that people aren't willing to spend money on, you're not going to succeed at affiliate marketing either. So it needs to be something you're interested in that also drives people to spend money. Fortunately, there are many choices!

Where You Go is Up to You

In the end, where you go into this business is entirely up to you. There is a minimal effort you need to put in, so even if you are only hoping to make $300 or $500 a month, you'll still need to put some work in. But if you want to earn seven-figures, its entirely possible, provided you take the right steps. So let's get started and get into the details!

Chapter 2: Choosing a Niche

The first all-important step in affiliate marketing is choosing a niche.

In the beginning, you might want to concentrate on having a single niche, so that you can devote time to building an online and social media following, and gain some expertise in marketing to one area. But there is no reason to be limited in your thinking, you can certainly build out businesses in multiple niches. It's often productive to do so in related niches so that you can cross-sell to different audiences, or upsell to the same audience. For example, if you were building a business based on a product that taught people how to trade on the stock market, you could also sell them products based on making money trading Forex, options, or Cryptocurrency.

Market Size and Trends

The first things to do when choosing a niche are to learn about it. You need to know the market size and trends in interest in the topic. If a particular diet was really popular three years ago but people are moving on, then marketing that diet probably isn't the most productive approach to your business.

Market size is something that doesn't really have a right answer. There are several factors that need to be taken into account. For example, a large market size means more customers. But it also means more competition selling. One example of this is the ketogenic diet. There are lots of ketogenic diet plans you can sell as an affiliate that is on the market. However, there are also lots of other affiliates out there selling the same products. So it might be hard to stand out against the competition.

Another factor is what are the pricing points for products aimed at a given niche. When you are marketing to large audiences, the pricing points might be lower. That can be bad, or good. You might only earn $5 a sale, but you might be able to generate large amounts of traffic so that those $5 sales add up to big money. On the other hand, you might do better in a smaller niche where you can charge $400 a sale. Then you don't need many sales to start making a full-time living from your business.

One tool that can be really useful when doing your analysis is Google Trends. You can find it here:

https://trends.google.com/trends/

Let's see the kind of information that you can get from Google trends. I am going to use it to study some trends in popular diets. So the first thing I'm going to do is enter the phrase "ketogenic diet".

Now, this is interesting! Everyone has been talking about the ketogenic diet lately, but online searches for the term are on a definite, downward trajectory over the past year. Sometimes people refer to it with the slang term "keto", so let's compare that:

When you do that, you get an entirely different picture. This gives us some insight – when you are thinking about niches you need to consider all the different ways that people will be looking for information about it.

You should also keep a record of your results. Later, we are going to be using keywords to drive traffic to our business. So you should start keeping a list of promising keywords, either in a spreadsheet or even in a notebook. In this case, we've found that the phrases "keto" and "keto diet" are important.

The main thing to notice is that while the ketogenic diet was rapidly declining, keto and keto diet look steady, if not increasing a little. So interest in the diet hasn't waned, rather the jargon people are using to refer to it has changed. That's another thing to keep in mind as you market over the years, something that worked two years ago ("ketogenic diet") might not work now. You always need to be prepared to make adjustments!

When you are researching a niche, you are going to want to compare different angles. In this case, we are looking at diets. So we're going to want to see what diets are the most popular. For our example, we can check multiple diets, but just to illustrate we'll add "Mediterranean diet" and "Vegan diet".

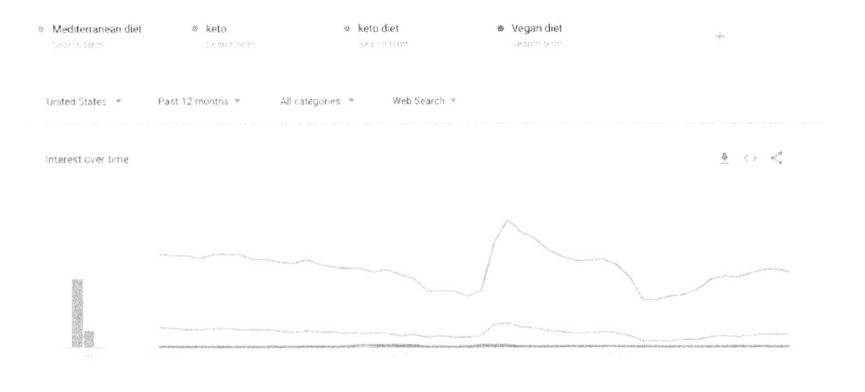

Keto and keto diet simply blow away the other choices. In January, most people are thinking about taking up a new diet:

jan 5 -11, 2020	
mediterranean diet	6
keto	100
keto diet	18
vegan diet	2

Those are pretty stunning results. What that tells you is for every person that searched for a vegan diet, 18 people searched for keto diet and 100 for "keto." Only six searched for the Mediterranean diet. Put another way, 100 times as many people are looking into keto compared with the vegan diet.

Of course,, we'd have to dive in more deeply to see if that was really true, like with "ketogenic diet," phrases like "Mediterranean diet" or "vegan diet" might not be the ideal phrases – but what we've found out so far is pretty noteworthy.

Keyword Planners

One of the most important tools for affiliate marketers is to have a keyword tool. Google offers a free tool which you can find here:

https://ads.google.com/aw/keywordplanner/home

There are many other keyword tools that are frankly a bit better, but Google Keyword Planner can give you the information you need. Google Trends only gives us relative volume, it doesn't actually tell us how many people are searching on different topics.

Keyword tool io is a good tool that also lets you do keyword analysis for other platforms like YouTube:

https://keywordtool.io/

We can check the keto diet, for example, and it will give us results like this:

Keywords	Search Volume	Trend	CPC (USD)	Competition
ketogenic diet food list	6,600	-76%	$1.04	45 (Medium)
ketogenic diet foods	8,100	+50%	$0.68	49 (Medium)

Notice that these tools not only tell us the search volume on specific keywords, they also pull up related keywords. This helps us accurately determine how large the audience size is in order to determine whether or not it's a niche worth pursuing.

Note your Keywords

We have to remind you again to keep track of all the keywords – and not just for advertising purposes. A large part of your online strategy will be keeping a blog or website of some kind, and the articles you post on the site need to target specific keywords. Using the example above – "ketogenic diet food list" is an excellent keyword to target in an article or blog post.

Trying this out with Google Keyword Planner, we enter:

Discover new keywords

ketogenic diet keto diet

GET STARTED

This is the result we get back:

Keyword (by relevance)	Avg. monthly searches	Competition	Ad impression share	Top of page bid (low range)	Top of page bid (high range)
Keywords you provided					
keto diet	1M – 10M	High	–	$0.39	$1.64
Keyword ideas					
keto	100K – 1M	High	–	$0.48	$1.42
keto diet plan	10K – 100K	High	–	$0.51	$2.61
ketogenic	10K – 100K	High	–	$0.28	$1.52
ketogenic diet foods	1K – 10K	Medium	–	$0.23	$0.97
ketosis	100K – 1M	Low	–	$0.06	$0.16
keto diet foods	100K – 1M	Medium	–	$0.23	$0.89
ketogenic diet menu	10K – 100K	Medium	–	$0.33	$1.48
the ketogenic diet	1K – 10K	High	–	$0.45	$2.08
keto meal plan	10K – 100K	High	–	$0.99	$8.19
keto diet meal plan	10K – 100K	Medium	–	$0.64	$3.96
ketogenic diet weight l	1K – 10K	Medium	–	$0.52	$2.06

Unlike the other site, it only gives average monthly searches. Personally, we don't find that as useful, which is why we opt for third-party tools. But when you are just getting started Google Keyword planner can be very helpful. It suggests a large number of related keywords – in this case, 918 – and you can download them into a spreadsheet. That would be useful for starting a business based on this niche because we could then use those keywords to create dozens of articles to drive traffic.

Another thing to note is the bid range. Keyword Planner is really there for people that advertise on Google and so they want to know the bidding prices to get on the top of the page. You can compare bidding prices for each niche you are interested in so that you can determine how competitive the niche is.

What you want to avoid is a niche that is small and nobody is interested in marketing to. You should sell things that are already selling.

You are going to find that some ideas have a very small niche size. One example is horse training. Relative to a niche like a keto diet, it's going to be very small. However, products for horse training might sell for $2,000, while products teaching people about the ketogenic diet might only sell for $35. Also, it might turn out that the ketogenic diet is a fad and doesn't last for five years, horse training is more evergreen, even though it's a narrow and small niche.

It's possible to get success either way, but it's going to be easier to attract attention when going for the smaller niche because there is less competition. While there are possibly hundreds of people searching for "keto diet" for every person that searches for "horse training", it's probably also the case that there are hundreds of websites promoting "keto diet" as compared to the number of horse training websites. That means if you started a horse training blog, you could probably rank for keywords faster and find it easier to generate free traffic.

But that should not dissuade you – the first and foremost consideration is your passion and interest – as long as you can find products that sell (and we guarantee there are training programs and books for the ketogenic diet that sell). If you are committed to a niche and can find a good affiliate program for it, then you can get success by taking the right steps even though there may be more competition. But these different factors can all weigh in on your decisions.

Demographics

How you market is going to depend in part on the demographics. This will not only help you target your advertising but you are also going to need to know who your ideal customer is. Of course, there are always variations, but just a guess, who is the average person who is interested in the keto diet?

One of your best friends in this regard is the Facebook ads manager. Even if you are not going to run Facebook ads, you should utilize the audience insights tool in order to get some idea of who the ideal customer is for a given niche. You can find it here:

https://business.facebook.com/ads/audience-insights/

To use one example, we searched on "keto diet app" as an interest on Facebook. Here are the results we got:

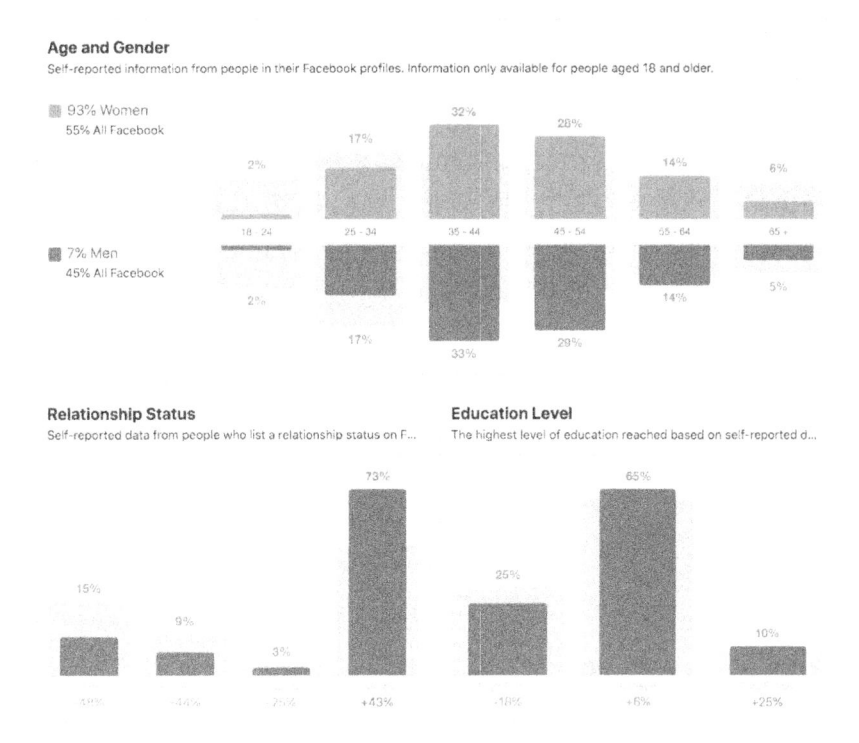

Age and Gender
Self-reported information from people in their Facebook profiles. Information only available for people aged 18 and older.

- 93% Women
  55% All Facebook
- 7% Men
  45% All Facebook

Relationship Status
Self-reported data from people who list a relationship status on F...

Education Level
The highest level of education reached based on self-reported d...

The first thing is the stunning gender differences. The audience is made up of 93% of women. Most are married and in the age range of 35-44. If we add in the more general "weight loss" the gender weighting adjusts to 80% female and 20% male. So the first item we searched on maybe a little bit misleading, but the point here is we want to show you the type of information that you can get from using this tool. So if you know ahead of time that most people searching for the keto diet are married women aged 35-44, aren't you going to use that information to tailor your marketing and design your website?

Financial products are great to use for affiliate marketing, and one of the most popular niches in the financial area is Forex. If you don't know what that is, it's "foreign exchange", and it's a market where people trade currencies. So it's like the Euro versus the dollar and so forth. Looking up some Forex related terms on Facebook Audience insights, we find that the makeup of the audience is extremely different from the one that we found for the Keto diet:

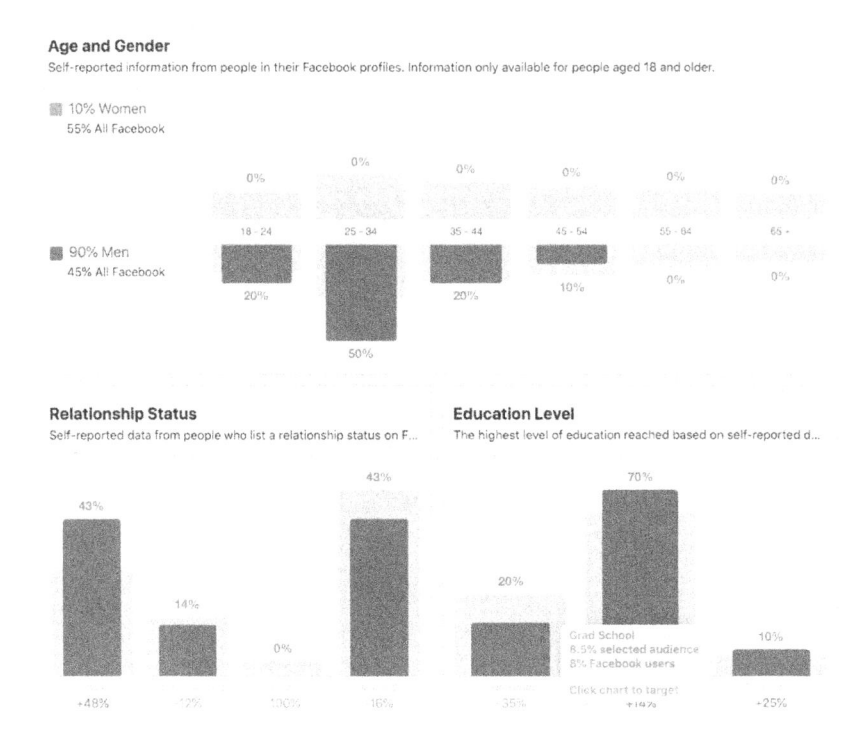

Age and Gender
Self-reported information from people in their Facebook profiles. Information only available for people aged 18 and older.

- 10% Women
  55% All Facebook
- 90% Men
  45% All Facebook

Age	18-24	25-34	35-44	45-54	55-64	65+
Men	20%	50%	20%	10%	0%	0%
Women	0%	0%	0%	0%	0%	0%

Relationship Status
Self-reported data from people who list a relationship status on F...

- 43% / 43% / 14% / 0%

Education Level
The highest level of education reached based on self-reported d...

- 70% / 20% / 10%

Grad School
6.5% selected audience
8% Facebook users

This time, the audience is 90% male. Not only that but its equally divided between married and singles.

The makeup of the audience and the ideal customer isn't just important for marketing your primary niche. You should think about other things that you can sell people. Knowing that most people searching for Keto diet are women, you might want to try getting them to sign them up on an email marketing list, which you can use to sell products. And you would then sell products specifically targeted at women since you know 9/10 of your prospects are going to be female.

This can have all kinds of implications, such as the colors you use on any websites you create, and what kinds of images you display. For instance, you are going to want to show before and after pictures of women on the keto diet more than you are going to want to show images of men developing muscular bodies after weight loss.

Of course, there are many men following diets, but you would have to find the specific keywords that would lead you to target men interested in the keto diet.

Finding Offers

In the next chapter, we are going to move forward to the next step. So far, here is what you need to do:

- Write down three subject areas you are interested in.
- Do research to estimate the size of the markets.
- Find important keywords and search volumes.
- Use Facebook audience insights to get a picture of your ideal customer.

In the next chapter, we'll move forward and find out the steps you need to take to find good offers.

Chapter 3: Finding the Best Offers

Once you've found your niche (and you should start with at least three) the next step is to do some research to find out if there are products selling in the niches that you've selected. There are many ways to go about it, and probably the best thing to do is to head to websites that already sell products geared towards affiliate marketers. There are many choices out there, so many in fact that we are going to have to ignore most of them because its very easy to get overwhelmed. In the beginning, it's best to focus on the top sites and use what other people have found already works.

Finding Specialty Websites

It's possible to find many websites that use affiliates to help drive traffic. You might already have some favorite websites in your niche. If you aren't sure, use some of the keywords you've found in order to see what websites selling products related to the niche come up. Then when you find websites, scroll down to the bottom where they have links to various administrative features related to the company. You will want to look for a link that says *affiliates*. If you can't find one, they may not have an affiliate program, but as a backup, you can search for the name of the company with "affiliates" or "affiliate programs".

For example, looking in the stock market trading niche, we find a site called "Raging Bull".

https://ragingbull.com/

They have an affiliate program and note their top affiliate makes $82,00 a year promoting their products.

https://ragingbull.com/affiliate/

The first things you are going to want to look for is the size of the commissions paid by the site. Also, you will want to look for information about any top affiliates and their earnings, and if they have any resources (graphics and so forth) that you are allowed to promote their site.

Evaluating Websites

One of the best tools around is similar web, which you can use to estimate website traffic for any site. The similar web is a tool that is available as a free web browser plugin. For Raging Bull, we find that they have 1.1 million visitors a month:

SimilarWeb

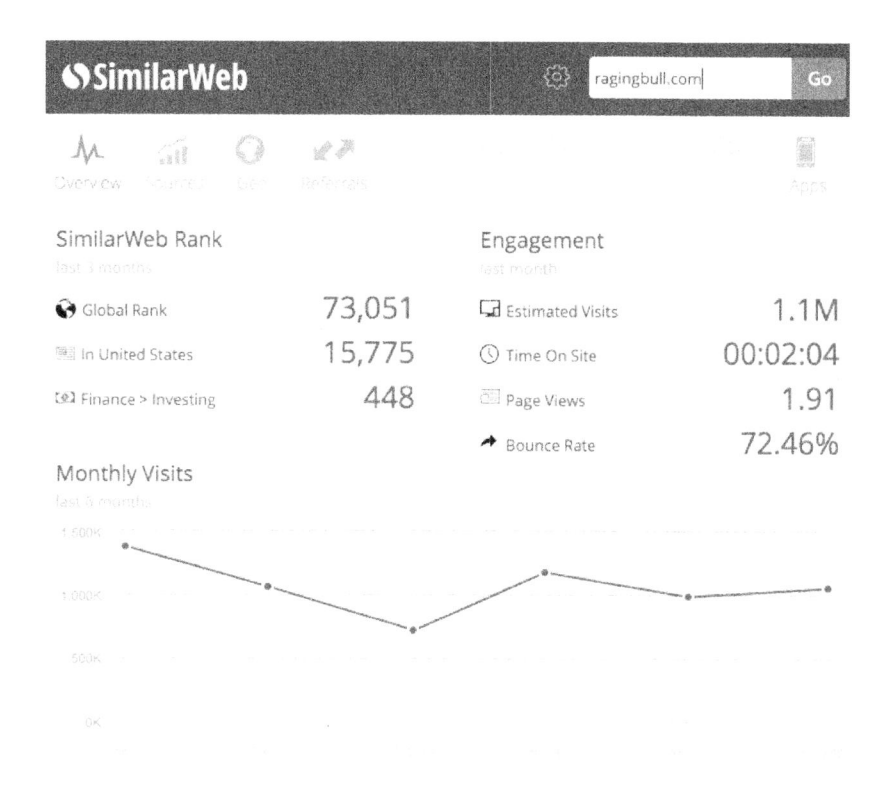

SimilarWeb Rank (last 3 months)	**Engagement** (last month)
🌐 Global Rank — 73,051	🖥 Estimated Visits — 1.1M
🇺🇸 In United States — 15,775	🕒 Time On Site — 00:02:04
💼 Finance > Investing — 448	📄 Page Views — 1.91
	➜ Bounce Rate — 72.46%

Monthly Visits (last 3 months)

Also note the bounce rate, which tells you the percentage of visitors that only visit one page before leaving the site. The lower the bounce rate the better, but you should compare with competing websites in the same niche rather than trying to find some absolute cutoff to use. Of course, if it's a site that sells products and has multiple product pages, a high bounce rate may not be a good sign.

Amazon, for example, has a bounce rate of 43%.

Another useful tool is spyfu.

https://www.spyfu.com/

Spyfu provides a wealth of information about keywords and possible pay per click (Google, Bing) advertising that the site is using, and they also give suggestions for competing websites (you will want to check them as well, for affiliate offers). As you can see, they even tell you how much the website is spending on PPC advertising – in this case, more than $16,000 a month. That's how they are getting a million visitors.

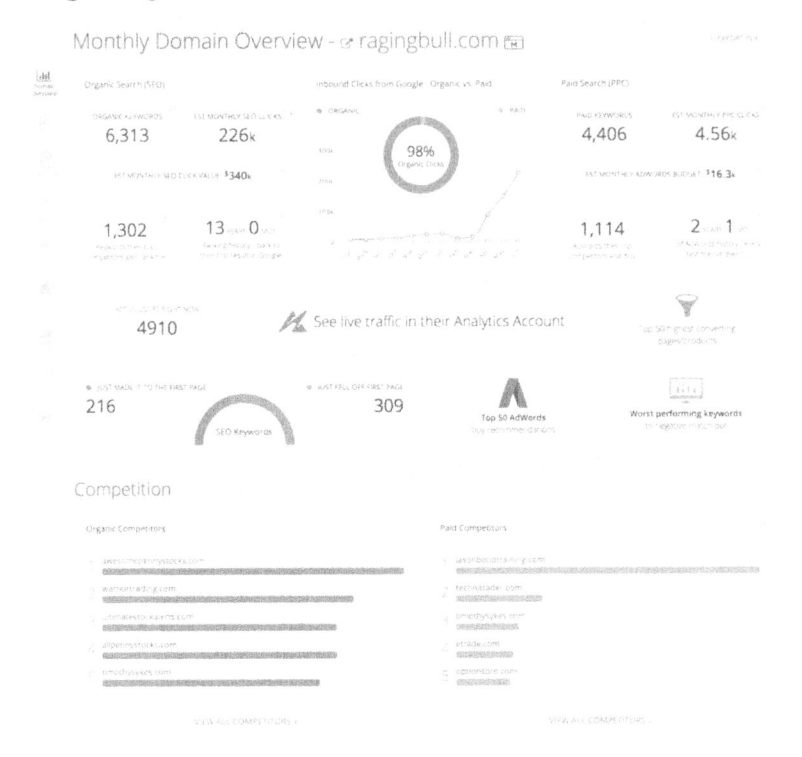

SpyFu can also be used to find even more keywords of interest. They offer some free features, but you can pay if you want and find it useful to access more tools.

Types of Affiliate Programs

There are many different types of affiliate programs that are available. Many people start by looking for well-known websites such as Amazon or eBay. These are certainly options that you can use in order to generate some affiliate income. One of the advantages of using a site like Amazon is that you are already promoting a well-known selling product. In that case, one of the best approaches is to actually buy the product and do real reviews of the product. You could either use these in paid promotions or better yet make free YouTube videos and blog articles reviewing various products. Then you link in the video or blog post back to the product in question, using an affiliate link that Amazon provides.

The downside of that approach is that the commission rates are going to be smaller in comparison to some other options that we are going to discuss. Again there are always trade-offs. Amazon or eBay has the advantage of being very well-known and trustworthy. When we are talking about marketing online, trustworthiness is always a huge factor. Contrast that to marketing for a relatively unknown product or website, having to build up trust is going to be one of the most important aspects of your marketing. With a website like Amazon, that is already done for you.

Another option to consider is being an affiliate for Shopify. In recent years this has become a very popular option to use. This can be combined with other efforts. For example, many people that are interested in starting a business where they use Shopify as their primary platform, are also going to be looking for other tools such as an email marketing builder. So you could also sign up as an affiliate for a program like Leadpages and also AWeber, which are platforms online marketers use to build email landing pages and lists of customers.

Therefore, the same customer that would be interested in Shopify is going to be interested in these other tools as well, and so you might possibly get referred repeat sales from the same customer. This is always a strategy that you should be using no matter which type of offer you go for.

Here are some of the options available among the top affiliate programs:

- Bluehost: this is a web hosting platform that is very popular. Many people use Bluehost to start blogs or other websites. They offer a very nice affiliate program and since it's a well-known product, it will be easy to sell. This is also something that's easy to promote because there is such a need for the service. However, remember that when you're promoting something of this nature, the competition is going to be very extreme simply because there are so many other people promoting it.

- Amazon: of course, everyone knows Amazon as the leading retail website in the world. One of the nice things about Amazon as far as being an affiliate is concerned, as we stated earlier the site is already well known and trusted. People go there for the simple fact to spend money in the first place, and they probably already have their credit card stored on the site. That saves you a lot of trouble, believe me. Second, every single niche is already represented on Amazon. So it will not be hard for you to find something that you're interested in promoting. The downside is that the commissions are going to be relatively small compared to some of the other options that we are looking at. You might consider using Amazon as a starting point to learn how to do affiliate marketing. But you will probably want to find something more lucrative in the future.

- eBay partner: Of course, eBay was one of the earliest websites that became very large and well-known. It still has huge amounts of traffic and everyone knows about it, and it also allows payment capability integrated with PayPal, which removes that barrier of the customer having to provide payment information. Remember that is something people always worry about. Another advantage of eBay is that people are constantly looking for things to buy including used products to save money. Like on Amazon, practically every niche under the sun is represented on the eBay. You could include eBay and Amazon as part of a larger strategy to get started. They could provide complementary ways to run your affiliate offers.

- Marketer tools: Believe it or not, one of the ways you can make money fairly easily is by promoting products useful to other marketers. Remember that there are many people starting online businesses all the time, and many of them are looking to sell their own products, but they have no online resources. They may need hosting, a place to have a membership site or courses post, and other resources like lead forms to collect email addresses of customers. Some of the tools you can market to these people include Bluehost as we already mentioned, AWeber, which is an email list marketing site, and you can also use a site called click funnel which lets people use drag and drop tools to create landing pages. Clickfunnels actually has a pretty lucrative affiliate program. However, it is competitive because many people are trying to sell it.

- Another option is Kajabi. This is the website that hosts video courses. Online video courses are a very lucrative business and marketers need a place where they can host their course, materials, otherwise, they would have to develop their own tools from scratch which would cost a fortune and take a long time. This website does everything for them and one of the nice things about this and some of these other affiliate programs is that they provide a monthly affiliate commission. So if someone signs up for the site and remains a member for 36 months, you get 36 months of payments in commissions.

Affiliate Programs

All of those options that we discussed above are viable. However one of the best ways to get into affiliate marketing is to join a program or website which specifically promotes affiliate products, rather than doing it as an afterthought. These have many advantages because they are totally geared towards promoting affiliate marketing. Typically, although not always, these sites are used to promote digital products. So it may be a video course, or a downloadable book or set of books. Sometimes physical products are shipped as well. But remember with physical products there is a chance of returns.

JV zoo

This website is useful for finding products or courses that can be used for joint venture marketing. In many cases, there will be very high priced products. The marketer might sell them using a webinar, and your job as an affiliate will be to get people to sign up for the webinar. So you simply drive traffic and earn commissions from the tracking of your affiliate links.

ClickBank

ClickBank was one of the original websites that offered affiliate products when the Internet became popular with the public. It's been around since the mid-1990s. ClickBank is one of the best sites - especially for beginners and we will focus a lot on ClickBank in the future parts of the book as a result.

One of the reasons that ClickBank is so nice is that it offers a wide range of products as far as pricing, and different niches. It's almost like a mini Amazon in the sense that you can find products for almost every niche. The quality of products on ClickBank is wide-ranging, and so you're going to have to do a little bit of research to find good products. But believe us, there are many good products that you can find on ClickBank. Many a millionaire was born marketing ClickBank products, and you can even take a course, taught by millionaire ClickBank affiliates called CB University. As you are evaluating products on ClickBank or other sites you will use the same tools that we described earlier like the similar web.

Others

There are many other affiliate oriented programs and websites. You should take a look at them all and select the one you like the best, or even use multiple programs. However, in the beginning, we recommend that people stay focused on one until they really learn how things work.

Some of the interesting programs that have generated a lot of success include wealthy affiliate, CJ affiliate, and commission junction. You will be able to find tools and products to sell using these programs. Some like *wealthy affiliate* have website building tools. However, we actually recommend a combination of a blog with click funnels to do your marketing rather than relying on canned programs like that.

Evaluating Affiliate Offers

So let's go through the process of evaluating products on ClickBank. The first step you should do is sign up for an account, but don't worry about it that's not necessarily a commitment and its free. Just go ahead and open an account so that you can do some research.

Once you have opened an account, go to the ClickBank marketplace. Then simply put in a keyword of interest such as keto diet, or dog training. Then go ahead and search. You will see a huge number of offers for most niches come up.

There are many ways to search such as keyword relevance, popularity, and a mysterious metric called gravity.

Gravity tells you the number of affiliates who have sold a product in the last 12 weeks. So if you see a high gravity, it's an indication that the product is selling. Gravity is a weighted number, so it's not an exact representation of the number of people promoting or selling the product. Another thing to consider is, it's also an indication that there is a lot of competition in the market, and it might be saturated with people promoting the product. Gravity can range from 0 to well over 200.

Many online marketers that have a lot of experience recommend that you select products with the gravity of 20 up to about 60. This is a good balance between a product that is selling and one that is oversaturated with promotion. Note that some products are good and selling even if they have a low gravity.

Also, keep in mind that gravity can be misleading in some cases. Affiliates can buy their own product and it's going to record a credit for the sale in the gravity. So if there is a product that has recently been launched by a popular online marketer, whether it's another online marketing course, or a diet product, A burst of new affiliates purchasing their own copies at a discount could over-inflate the numbers. So more evaluation is needed.

You might consider signing up for an account at CB engine.com. You can look up the history of gravity and other metrics for giving products that are for sale on ClickBank. Finding out if a given product has a long-term history of high gravity can give you an indication of what is really a good product and what is not. If a product has maintained a similar level of gravity for many months, that is a good indication that the product is actually selling well.

Website Evaluation

Once you find a product that is of interest, the first thing you're going to want to do is to look at their website. Do you want to be looking at the website from the view of a customer? Does the website look high-quality? Is it something that would make you want to spend money? Does it give the impression that the product is high-quality? All of these issues are important.

It is important to be a little bit flexible in your view. Often, websites have cheesy sales pitches. However, that in itself should not put you off. The reason is those kinds of sales pitches often work in some niches. So you want to be looking for the overall quality of the website rather than judging whether or not it's a totally cheesy sales pitch. Also if it looks cheesy and has a high gravity with a lot of web traffic, then you should not focus too much on your interpretation of the sales letter. Generally speaking, websites that have a video pitch or "video sales letter" are the best.

Second, always check the website using similar web. Remember that tool will tell us how many visitors per month the site has and what the bounce rate is. By checking those numbers you can get a reasonable idea of how well the product is selling.

Many products on ClickBank and other sites might not have much affiliate Traffic, and so on ClickBank for example, the gravity might be low. But you may find out that the website has huge levels of traffic anyway. So the product might be popular and selling. It's important to find out what the actual traffic to the site is.

Also, you are going to want to look for a low bounce rate. Remember this is always going to be relative, so you might want to compare the bounce rate between related websites rather than focusing on the absolute value.

Another thing that you want to look for is whether or not the website *leaks*. What that means is that the ClickBank vendor will have a sales page that you can find on the marketplace that they are using to collect email addresses or redirect customers somewhere else.

So, you want to make sure that the vendor is not trying to collect email addresses on that specific page. Of course, they are going to collect email addresses of their customers, but they should be doing it on another webpage and not the one that they are providing you in order to make sales. The reason that's important is that it can cause a loss of tracking of your affiliate link. So you want to make sure that you always get credit for the sale - so look for a pop-up email input box that comes up. Sometimes they come up when you move off a page, so check that by moving your mouse or clicking the back button. If you have a choice, opt for an offer that does not have one on their sales page.

Conversion Rates

It's impossible to know how many sales are actually being made. The only thing you can do is make a rough estimate. A typical conversion rate is 1 to 3%. So you can use similar web to estimate the traffic to the site, and then figure out a possible range of the number of sales per month the website is getting. Keep in mind this is only an estimate, some websites might have a much higher conversion rate, and some may only have a really low rate, like a 10th of a percent conversion rate. Generally speaking, a 1% to 3% range gives you a reasonable idea in most cases.

Product Pricing

When selecting a product based on pricing, there are many variables to consider. First of all, you want to make sure that the product pays enough that it's going to be worth promoting. Even if you are doing free promoting, you don't want to sell something that only gives you something low like a $7 commission. At the very least, look for something that is $30 and above or maybe around $27 at the lowest. ClickBank provides all the information on how much money you make including the average amount per sale and some other metrics that tell you the initial amount per sale, and if it's a subscription product it will tell you how much money you make from that as well. Many products offer upsells which can also increase the number of earnings.

Recurring billing products are also good to look for since as long as the customer stays subscribed, you can earn monthly commissions. ClickBank is very reliable for tracking affiliate links and making sure that you get all the commissions that are due.

So we want to aim for something that pays at least a $27 commission. However, there are products on ClickBank that pay much higher. You can go to $50, $100, and even several thousand dollars in commissions. Of course, the more expensive something is the more hard work you're going to have to put into selling.

However, one advantage is that in all cases, the vendor does most of the heavy lifting for you. Many products that cost $500 or more on ClickBank are driven by webinar sales and all you have to do is direct traffic to the webinar. Then the vendor does the rest.

When getting started trying to learn the ropes, it's probably best to start with a low to a mid-range product in a popular niche so that getting sales is relatively easy. You could even use the niche we talked about earlier, which was the ketogenic diet.

So you can research and find products on ClickBank that are aimed at the niche and then look for pricing in the range of $25-$50. Then check the websites and evaluate traffic levels and quality. Of course, you don't want to see a website that has traffic that is consistently declining. That might mean a dying product.

It can be possible to obtain a review copy of a product. You will have to email the vendor and ask. If they don't offer one, you can buy it using your own affiliate link to get a discount. It can be very helpful to actually buy the product -- remember this is an investment. So that way you can actually review the product for quality and know what's in it.

When you really know what is in the product then you can write effective and honest reviews about the product and post them online. It would also be helpful if you make YouTube review videos which is a great free marketing technique. But a YouTube video is only as good as the sincerity behind it, which is why it's good to actually get the product and look at what it contains rather than trying to fake it. Far too many people try to fake it and it comes off very badly.

Selling Physical Products

Drop shipping programs and Amazon FBA are also popular ways to market online. These programs have their advantages and disadvantages but can be effective ways to make money. Let us state right off the bat that its simply easier to sell digital products or act as an affiliate for someone who is going the shipping and product storage for you.

One of the nice things about Amazon FBA is that you can have a business selling physical products – even branded ones – without having to maintain your own inventory. You can approach things this way by having the manufactured products shipped to a company that specializes in getting them to Amazon for you, then once there Amazon handles the rest. Keep in mind you might be charged small fees for warehouse space, so it's important that your products actually sell.

To find products, you will want to start using a website called Alibaba, that you may have heard of. This is a kind of "Amazon" for businesses looking for products to sell. This allows you to directly connect with product manufacturers. Most of them are in China or India, so you are going to have to deal with things like long shipping times, customs and tariffs, and other issues.

You can find products you like and then have them ship you a sample. You will have to pay for the samples, but that way you can evaluate the product. They can be branded on your behalf, and possibly manufactured with your own custom designs and logos, and you can work out the details with the manufacturer once you settle on something. For example, you could launch your own branded line of cosmetics or sell guitars or drones.

Once everything is set up, then you can start ordering inventory and have it shipped to an Amazon FBA company that will take care of the rest for you, putting together good web pages on Amazon is going to be your next job. Once everything is set up, then from there it's going to be like any other online business, so you can use the other techniques that we discuss in the book.

Chapter 4: The Right Mentality for Affiliate Marketing

Not everyone is cut out to be an affiliate marketer. In this chapter, we are going to run through some tips and suggestions about the right mentality for affiliate marketing. Its important that you have the right mindset for success, otherwise you will end up quickly frustrated and more than likely just give up.

It's not a get rich quick scheme

If you are entering affiliate marketing looking for a get rich quick scheme, you are probably better off taking some of your hard earned money to a nearby casino. Affiliate marketing doesn't work that way. You wouldn't open a restaurant hoping to make $20,000 the first day, at least we hope not because in 99% of the cases that is not going to happen. So you shouldn't expect that with affiliate marketing either. Prepare yourself for a slow and gradual process where you build up income over time, rather than expecting a huge immediate payday.

Be persistent

When you start off affiliate marketing, you are going to have a lot of failures in the beginning. You are going to be trying things and they simply won't work. That is the nature of life and business. When it comes to online marketing, one of the biggest factors is getting enough eyeballs on your offers. That takes time and it also takes learning the right ways to present things to get people in a buying frame of mind. You are probably not going to hit home runs right away, so you need to be persistent to make adjustments and try again several times before you find success. If you are not persistent it's not going to work out for you.

Stay Focused

A lot of people, due to their impatience in wanting to make money, have trouble staying focused. They will try promoting a product for a couple of weeks, and if they don't get many sales, they'll run off and try another product instead of refining the approach they were using with the first one. You need to stay focused, and unless there is some flaw with the product you're promoting (and there could be at times), you need to look at what you are doing wrong rather than running off to make the same mistakes with a new product. When you have settled on a good product, stay focused and push until it gets sales.

Be disciplined

One of the upsides of online marketing is that you can make a passive income. But that possibility also attracts people that lack the discipline to build an online business. Just because at some point it can allow you to make money without having to be working on it all the time doesn't mean that it won't require any work. You put the work in upfront and then payoff from the business comes down the road. In the meantime, you need to have the discipline to regularly work on the business. If you are the kind of person that works hard for a while and then slacks off, you are not going to find success with affiliate marketing. You need to have a daily program where you put work in on a regular basis and don't stray from it.

Don't be afraid to lose money

The number of businesses that lose money at some point is endless. Consider Tesla, which has innovative and solid products, but they have yet to have a profit. You should not be afraid to lose money in your efforts to build an online business. Of course, you don't want to be reckless, so don't spend money you don't have. However, you should be ready to spend money to build websites or run ad campaigns and take losses as part of the learning and growth process. People who are too afraid of risk are not going to get anywhere. Part of your journey to success is going to include some inevitable failures which cost money. Learn from them and you will do better next time, eventually getting to profitability.

Act like there is no Plan B

A so-so approach to affiliate marketing is not going to work as well as one that you take very seriously and think in terms of a point of no return. Get committed to the attitude that there is no other option than to make your online business a success. You have to be totally committed in order to succeed.

Don't get emotional

People that get emotional will fail. Emotion can come into the equation in many ways, for example, you can panic if you lose money on an advertising campaign. It can also happen the other way, maybe you get euphoric with a couple of sales. That could turn into a problem if you suddenly veer from your plan and spend huge sums on advertising campaigns that may fail. Approach your business as if you were a detached scientist looking at a test tube or some data. Make your decisions based on what the real world is telling you and not based on your wishes. A successful business will grow gradually and doesn't get there on emotional outbursts.

Don't make excuses

One of the main complaints we hear from people who would like to get into affiliate marketing is it's too technical. That is nothing more than an excuse to justify your lack of taking action. There are many tools available that eliminate many of the technical hurdles, and you can always hire help if the technology is too much. Of course, that is only the first excuse we hear. The second which comes up just as frequently if not more so is "I don't have enough time". Everyone has time. Yes, some have more time they can devote than others, but complaining that you don't have enough time is just another excuse to do nothing and feel comfortable in the situation you're currently stuck in. Make time. Even if you only devote a half hour a day when starting out, that is going to make a huge difference down the road. You don't have to work on it full time to get started, although if you could it would help drive it faster. But working on it a half-hour a day is akin to someone who saves $10 a week. If you come back a few years later, they have a substantial bank account. Any work you put in now will pay off later.

People will also come around with it takes too much money to become an affiliate marketer. In fact, you can launch your business with $100. You don't have to spend large sums of money on expensive advertising campaigns. You can trade time for money and use free techniques to drive traffic. The payoff will come slower, but it's going to be stronger anyway. So a lack of money is hardly an excuse. If you don't have any capital available, maybe you should start looking around your house. Do you have anything you don't need that you can sell? Is it possible to take up a part-time job just for a month or two in order to raise some capital? We don't generally recommend debt, but you could look into personal loans as well. But again, you can build an online business using free tools once you've got a few basics in places like web hosting and a blog. So you don't even need a lot of capital unless a paid promotion is going to be the only strategy you use.

Making excuses is the biggest factor preventing people from having success online. If you are making excuses to yourself, then you need to change your thought patterns. The successful affiliate marketer looks for ways through problems, they don't let the excuses prevent them from taking action.

Chapter 5: Building a Marketing Base

Building a marketing base is going to be an important part of your affiliate marketing business. By this, we mean that you have a web presence in place. We are going to talk about driving free traffic later, but here we are going to summarize the elements that you should have in your business in order to succeed. You are going to need them no matter what, whether or not you are using free or paid traffic or some combination of them. So let's summarize them and then we will look at the details of how to use them in future chapters.

A Website

A website is not strictly required, but we are going to recommend one and make it easy on you. Many people try to run affiliate marketing businesses using only landing pages. This is definitely possible, but you are going to be more successful the stronger you make your web presence. Your goal as an affiliate marketer should be to be the best there is, and the best one is not someone who is just putting up one landing page and driving Facebook ad traffic to it. That is someone who is cutting corners. It might work for a while, but people that try to cut corners are generally not the ones that find the most success.

It doesn't matter where you get your website, but bluehost.com is a good option to consider, as is host gator or Go, Daddy. The main consideration is you're going to want to have a website where you can install and use WordPress to run a blog.

A Blog

This is the main purpose of your website. People often ask us if they can use a free site like blogger.com or wordpress.com. While you can, in theory, there are several reasons not to. We will just discuss the top two reasons to avoid doing that. The first is you want to be completely in control of your content. Don't put yourself in a position where a third party can take down your posts or close down your blog, and you lose all the content. You want to be in complete control as much as possible, and the best way to do that is to have your own website with your own blog. A service like wordpress.com might have their own rules about affiliate marketing. You might not find out until they shut down your site. Make your own rules. The way to do that is to take total control, so get your own site and put your blog there.

The second issue is that it comes across a lot better if you have your own domain name. Any domain name that is associated with some free hosting site will make it look like amateur hour marketing. You want to come across as professionally as possible, and part of that is going to mean having a domain name that identifies you as a business or is at least related to the niche you are promoting.

Also remember that if you are going to promote more than one niche, each niche is going to need its own website.

A YouTube Channel

Next, you should set up a YouTube channel for your business. Keep things separate, not only from your personal stuff but also by niche. If you are going to become an affiliate marketer for drones sold on Amazon but also for ketogenic diet books, you need to have those on different YouTube accounts. It would look really bad if you try and promote them both from the same account. That makes you look like a cheesy affiliate marketer, and people don't like that. Setting up multiple accounts is not very hard to do. Give the account a meaningful name that is associated with the niche.

A Facebook Page

A Facebook page is going to be required in order to run ads on Facebook, and even if you don't do that, you are going to want one to bolster your web presence.

Email List Builder

Having an email list of prospects is important. The service we recommend is Aweber, but you can also use Mail Chimp, Constant Contact, Get Response, and there are many others. It really doesn't matter which one you use, but you must collect email addresses and keep lists of customers from each niche in order to make money.

Landing Page

If you have a website, you could go through the hassle of creating your own landing pages, but these days there are many tools available that make it super easy and they work a lot better than anything you can create from scratch. A landing page is a simple web page used to collect email addresses. When advertising, you will drive traffic to a landing page and offer some free product (a video, book, or guide) in exchange for the email address. These days, you can't get around the need for a landing page, and the simple fact is they work. They will help you build a list of eager customers ready to buy products.

There are many options available, but one of the best around is called Click Funnels. It's a drag and drop platform, and it readily integrates with services like Aweber. They know what they are doing over there because the entire business was created by former affiliate marketers. So they know exactly what you need and they give it to you. It's entirely drag and drop and so easy to use, and you can integrate the pages it creates with your website. You can test it out using a 14-day free trial to see if it's too your liking, but we have yet to come across anyone who wasn't satisfied.

Instagram Account

An Instagram account isn't essential, but if you don't have one you're basically leaving free traffic on the table. It does take a little bit of additional work, but a half-hour per day or every other day can produce good levels of traffic to your site over time.

Other Social Media

There are other options to consider, such as Pinterest and Twitter. But we will place those in the optional category. If you have a blog, Facebook page, landing pages, and Instagram account, we believe you are pretty much set up for success.

Chapter 6: The 4 Golden Rules of Profits

In this chapter, we are going to focus on four golden rules that are necessary to follow in order to achieve profits.

Focus on a Small Number of Products

Keeping your business manageable is one of the most important aspects of getting off on the right foot. If you try and generate income streams from a wide array of products, it's going to be too difficult to devote the time and attention required to each product in order to make them successful. It's better to focus on getting 2-3 products successful and get them generating handsome levels of income than it is trying to get 20 things going that you can't wrap your mind around.

Never Cut Corners

Remember in the last chapter we told you that some people want to just have a one-page website or landing page, and drive traffic to it using Facebook advertising or some other method. That might work some of the time or for some people, but most marketers that cut corners don't win. The more effort you put into your business the more you are going to get out of it.

Also, remember that can lay a foundation for your own products later on. So if you have a niche you are passionate about and build up a blog with a nice following, you can smoothly transition from using it to promote other people's products into selling your own. Then instead of just getting a commission, you are the one in the driver's seat getting all the earnings, and even have affiliates working for you.

Review, Don't Sell

Even though people are being sold to all the time and they know it, one thing everyone seems to hate is a pushy salesperson. This can happen online just as well as it can happen at a used car lot. If there is one thing that people hate it's going to buy a used car and having some salesman chasing you down and trying to get you into buying a car right away. The same thing works online; people don't like someone who is pushy trying to hard sell them. Avoid salesy presentations and focus on talking about the niche you are in and the needs it has.

One of the ways to be really successful online, whether it's as an affiliate or selling your own products, is to become someone that people look to for solutions in the niche. So you need to start thinking about positioning yourself as someone who can do that for them. Start by looking at what the pain points are for people in the niche, and figure out ways those pain points can be solved.

In your writing, you can follow time-tested formulas that have been used with successful sales for decades. You can use this technique in emails, in blog posts, and on sales pages. Begin by stating problems that people in the niche are having. This immediately helps prospects see you as a real person who knows exactly what they are going through. If possible, you can frame yourself as having gone through the same situations.

Then you want to offer solutions to some of the problems. Of course, some kind of solution is going to be offered by any product, which is why they exist in the first place. A diet book is going to include recipes and instructions on how to follow the diet – but you want to offer people lots free solutions to some of their problems in order to build a trusting relationship with them. As part of this process, you want to avoid explicitly selling. Only on a rare basis do you really want to push a product, and you should never do that during the initial phases. In the beginning, you want to mention products in an offhand way, after having already provided people with a lot of free and valuable information.

That way, people are going to start viewing you within the context of being an authority figure in the niche as well as a trusted friend. So when you recommend that they buy a product, they are going to trust your recommendation. After all, you seem like you really know about the niche and you also are trustworthy since you're giving them free information that helps them.

That is one reason why finding a niche that you are passionate about can be really helpful. If you are interested in some subject, like fitness and weight loss or finance, it can really help propel things along. You will find yourself able to study the subject and it makes it easier for you to write about it. Something to keep in mind is that most people only have causal knowledge about different niche subjects. So if you put in a little bit of time studying, you are already ahead of 90% of people. That means its easy to put yourself in a position where you are viewed as an authority figure. And when you're an authority figure, you can solve some of their problems and they are going to be coming back to you for more information.

As an affiliate marketer, the hard lifting of closing the sale isn't up to you, it's up to the vendor. That means you should focus on explaining why a given product can benefit them, rather than trying to push people into closing the deal. Ultimately, the goal is to direct clients to the sales page when they are in a state of mind of having already been convinced about the product. That way conversion rates are going to end up being a lot higher.

Test, Retest and Adapt

Finally, be ready to change approaches that aren't working. You should test to get actual results, and when conversion rates aren't high, make improvements and test again. Change your approach if it's not working. If you run Facebook ads but don't get sales, maybe people seeing your offer aren't suitable prospects and you need to find customers somewhere else so adapt and try advertising on another platform.

Bonus – Avoid Make Money Online

It can be tempting for new affiliate marketers to try and promote make money online products. However, this isn't the best strategy for new affiliate marketers or even most experienced people. There are several reasons for this. Unfortunately, a lot of new affiliate marketers get drawn to these types of products because they often pay large commissions. But they can be and usually are hugely competitive. And the competition can be fierce, the niche is often dominated by long-term marketers that have large budgets for advertising. So it's going to be hard for you to claw your way through the noise to get noticed and earn money. Second, they are going to be very experienced and so your competition is going to be able to crush your efforts.

But another important aspect to consider is these products are often hard sold. They make absurd claims, like making $50,000 a week. Yes, it happens sometimes, but not usually. And most customers have a skeptical attitude about people sitting around with fancy sports cars, jumping out of airplanes, and claiming they are making millions while traveling with a laptop. We aren't saying that it can't happen or that some of the people aren't valid marketers, but it's not going to happen to most people and prospects are super skeptical of cheesy sales offers when the promise is that you are going to make a bunch of money.

Another issue with those types of offers is that many of the big websites like Facebook, Google, and Bing look down on them. They are often as skeptical of the claims as prospective customers are. Facebook even prohibits outright advertising for many online businesses.

So you are better off choosing affiliate offers that offer real solutions to niche problems, like learning to play piano, keto diet recipe book, Forex trading software, and so on.

Chapter 7: Driving Free Traffic

Believe it or not, this is one of the most exciting chapters for us. It's because we really believe in free traffic. Many people have the mistaken belief that the days of free traffic ended long ago, and worrying about things like SEO is a waste of time. Or they mistakenly believe that Facebook advertising is the gift of the ages and it's all you need. The fact is they are wrong on all counts. Think about Facebook – they are under a lot of scrutiny and prices are rising due to increased competition. Facebook users are also getting concerned about being manipulated by marketers, so it's not as easy as it was three or five years ago to show them an ad and get them signing up for your list or even buying products. So you don't want to be dependent on paid advertising, and we are talking about FREE traffic here, so why not take advantage of it?

In this chapter, we are going to give you an overview of a reliable process that can help you drive free traffic to your offers. Admittedly, this is not something that people looking to earn money fast are going to be happy with because it does involve a lot of upfront work and it takes time to start driving traffic to your site. But once it starts working, it can be like a snowball rolling downhill, gradually picking up momentum. Once it's going you will be generating long-term traffic that keeps coming without having to put more work in, and it can grow and grow if you keep up with the efforts, leading to more sales and higher levels of income.

With free traffic, it begins with blogging.

A blog to Target Keywords

The first step that you need to take care of is making sure that your blog looks good. While you can install WordPress and use a free template, the free templates don't look as good or as professional and that is going to hurt you in the long run. Invest the $45 to get a good template that you can use to make your blog visually appealing. Remember that in the affiliate marketing business information is king, so this is important.

Next, you are going to want to sign up for a service called Yoast. It's a plug-in that you install on your word press blog. While Yoast has a paid subscription you can get, they offer free tools and those are all 95% of people are going to need. Yoast will analyze your posts and help you optimize them. You will want to use its suggestions and incorporate them in your writing, and also use its capability to set up the headline and text that will show up in Google search for each individual blog post.

The next step is to follow a specific writing style. Each post you put up should have 2-3 images in the post. Break up text into chunks that are separated by h2 headlines and images. This not only helps make your blog more readable, but it's going to make Google look upon it more favorably. You can also help make your blog appealing by incorporating (via embed) related YouTube videos.

Don't put very many external links. What you don't want is people coming to visit your blog and then clicking off to go somewhere else. Instead, write a set of related posts on your blog, and then the link between them. Interlinking also helps drive traffic. As your blog develops, as random traffic comes to different blog posts, the links between them will help keep people on your site longer as they click through to read different articles.

Of course, you can incorporate your affiliate links to the products you are promoting. This can be done either implicitly, which means you link to the product in the text as a part of the conversation, or you explicitly in a product review or recommendation.

The focus of each blog post should be writing about real information on the niche, and not about doing hard selling.

Incorporating SEO

You don't have to be an SEO expert to benefit from it. Earlier in the book, we already gave you the first steps. Do your keyword research, and then compile a list of keywords. Each keyword (focus on long phrase ones) is then the anchor word for an article. It can be the basis of the topic of individual articles or part of the basis for it. For example, "keto diet food list" is one idea, and "cheap foods for the keto diet" would be another. Whatever niche you select, you can find many phrases like that which can easily be turned into articles.

Google loves content and it loves substantial content. Therefore you should avoid cutting corners by having blog posts that are short. Make your posts between 800-

1,500 words in length. They don't have to be super long, and you don't want to bore readers either – but you want readers and Google to see the site as one that is an information-packed authority site.

So you are going to want to use the keyword or keyword phrase for the article title and in one subtitle. Then have the phrase appear two to three times within the article itself. It can also help if one of your links is the keyword phrase or has it in it.

Make sure the "slug" which is the link created for the blog post includes the key phrase in it as well.

That is really all you need to know about SEO. You don't need to take an expensive class or do anything more than what we've described here.

Post Regularly

The bottom line is that you are starting a business, so you should not be afraid of putting some work in. That doesn't mean you have to work at it 60 hours a week. But the bottom line is the more blog posts you write, the more traffic you are going to be getting. And the more frequently that you post, the faster you're going to generate free traffic.

We recommend that you post at a minimum three times per week, and up to once per day. This pattern looks natural to Google. Unnatural patterns, like paying people on Fiverr or something to write hundreds of posts for you and then putting them up all at once, looks fake and

Google might actually penalize the site. Make it look like its real, genuine content that follows a natural posting pattern that someone genuinely interested in the niche would use. That guarantees long term success; again trying to cut corners does not and may even hurt you.

However, make sure each post is valid. Don't post about posting, post about topics that you've gotten from your keyword list. If you don't have time to write a valid and thorough post on one day, take a day off to make sure you get it right and don't post for the sake of posting. Remember to be patient, this is a long term process.

Collect Emails

You are going to want to collect the email addresses of people that visit your blog, and then sell to them using your email autoresponder. We aren't going to review the technical details of setting that up, but you want a popup that shows up when people click on the site, offering them something free in exchange for signing up with their email address. Many vendors on ClickBank or elsewhere offer free books or video courses that you can give away to people interested in the niche. Alternatively, you can write your own, and in this one instance, it might be something that you can hire outside help to create. But make sure its good quality, remember you want your prospects to associate you with good, reliable information so that when you recommend products they are likely to take your recommendation.

Create backlinks

After you have a few posts on your blog, you are going to want to start posting links to specific articles when relevant. This can be done on forums related to your niche or on websites like Quora. To avoid being banned, make sure there is some relevance to posting the link on the site. Also, do it as an afterthought and make sure you are participating in the form or on Quora and posting real responses to people's questions and commentary. Always remember the keyword is content! Posting backlinks to posts on your blog is going to help your blog get ranked higher on the search engines.

Robots and Crawling

After you set up your blog, be sure to submit the site to Google webmaster tools and Bing. While they supposedly automatically crawl the entire internet and so find things on their own, there is no sense in waiting and you are going to want to put yourself forward and submit it manually to speed things along. Also, check your robots.txt file. This is beyond the scope of the book, but you can look it up online and search for situations when robots.txt is keeping your site from being indexed. Make sure that is not happening in your case.

YouTube Channel

Having a YouTube channel for your niche is an important way to drive more traffic. It might not be essential, but with two affiliate marketers, if one has a blog but the other has a blog and a YouTube channel, the latter marketer is going to close a lot more sales.

You can make simple videos talking about your niche. You can even just summarize what you are talking about in your blog posts. It doesn't have to be a fancy video promotion; some of the most popular YouTube channels are those that have people simply talking on camera with self-recorded videos. You can even just use your smartphone to make and post the videos.

You aren't shooting for becoming a star, you are just looking for another way to provide good information to people and drive traffic. So the videos don't have to be perfect. Don't be camera shy, it's not that important. Being perfect or looking perfect isn't the goal here. When it comes to marketing a genuine presentation is going to go far. And something that seems like a regular person giving real information is worth more than gold.

A tool you should be aware of is VidIQ. It's free and you can install it in your browser, and find out what tags people are using on their videos that are related to yours.

In addition, we are going to want to use our YouTube videos to create more backlinks to the blog. That's why it's a good idea to connect the topics of your videos two topics of your blog posts. Then under each video in the description for the link back towards the blog. You can also do video reviews of affiliate products and put links including your affiliate link underneath your video descriptions. However, it's essential to make your reviews as authentic as possible. A good video review of an affiliate product can be extremely effective. There is nothing more successful than having a video of a person giving an authentic description of a product without using a hard selling technique, but giving the people the ability to link into the product and purchase it. So in that sense our YouTube channel we will have dual purposes. It will help put some backlinks to the blog to help bring those up in searches, and I will also help drive some traffic directly to the affiliate offers.

Using Your Facebook Page

A Facebook page is also an important part of your marketing. This can also be another tool that you can use to set up some backlinks that go back to the blog. One of the nice things about Facebook is that they allow you to create Facebook pages that are not connected directly to your personal profile. That information is kept a secret from your Facebook friends and personal connections. You can reveal it if you choose to but the idea here is that you can create Facebook pages that are often associated with the business, or even with pen names and personalities that you used to market products.

So in this context of trying to drive free traffic, one of the things that you will want to utilize is the ability to Post on the blog and then put a link back to the blog from the Facebook page. You can share the Facebook page on your blog. Later, if you do advertising on Facebook you can start to build up a Fanbase for the Facebook page. Now if you're going to do free traffic or rely entirely on advertising, it can help to have a Facebook page that has at least some content associated with it. So that's why we recommend that you start a blog and you have backlinks back and forth between the two. That way when people go to see your Facebook page there is going to be a wealth of information already on the page. Moreover, if you're posting good and useful content that can help get people curious and they may go back and check out your blog and sign-up for your email newsletters.

Landing Page

In most cases, your landing page is going to be part of paid advertising campaigns. That said, you can also utilize it when driving free traffic. So no matter what you're going to do you should get one set up. I encourage readers to do some research online to find out how to make an effective landing page. We can't go into the details here because there's not enough space. But basically, you're landing page needs to have a professional and clean appearance, with a good-looking photograph and a headline with some effective copy.

As we stated earlier, we believe that click funnels are by far the best tool that can be used to create landing pages. In fact, click funnels lets you do a lot more than that but that's that you can find out when checking it out for yourself. The important thing is to have a landing page ready before you go on and do things like start posting a lot to Instagram. You can also try to drive traffic from your Facebook page to the landing page. So the only purpose of the landing page is really to collect emails and then we are going to run email marketing campaigns to the people that sign-up on the email list.

Instagram

The next topic we're going to discuss is one platform that is often ignored. Instagram is a very powerful social media platform that you can use to promote your affiliate offers and drive a lot of traffic much of free traffic. For those who are not familiar with it let's describe what it is in a nutshell.

First of all, you need to understand that this isn't a website per se. Instagram is almost entirely a mobile application. So to create an account if you don't have one, you are going to want to download the app onto your mobile phone. Even if you already have an account, you are going to want to create a new one.

Instagram has three account types. The first is obviously a personal account. You don't want to be using your personal account to promote affiliate offers. For one thing, it's going to turn off your friends. Also, it's going to create confusion if you are using it to promote affiliate offers that belong to one niche or another.

They also allow the creation of a business account. This could be useful if you're going to be focused completely on one area. However, they also allow the creation of a niche account and for most affiliate marketers that are going to be the most suitable way to set things up. So keep in mind that you may want to have multiple Instagram accounts. You can have one for each one of your niches.

So where do you go from here? It's going to be like running a blog except this is going to be a visual blog. If you aren't familiar with what the app is it's basically an image sharing app. But you're going to make your images marketing images. So it will include a picture along with an important message that could be used to promote a product that you were using for your affiliate business. Recently, or maybe it's not that recently in social media time, Instagram also allows people to post short videos that are called stories. They are not very long, it's probably 15 seconds maximum. Even so, remember that for decades advertisers have been pushing products on television using 30-second spots. So that doesn't mean you can't do some very effective marketing with this tool.

To get started, you're going to want to start posting some nice images with text on them along with some occasional story videos. You can look in the app store and find Apps that are specially designed for use with Instagram. You don't have to use those but it's helpful to have some really nice text overlays without having to resort to using Photoshop or something like that.

Basically, you're going to treat this as if it was a blog. So you want to be putting up stuff aka content on your Instagram account, at least three days a week. Again, the more the better. You are also going to want to find other people on Instagram that are interested in the same niche. In fact, you might want to use this for spying purposes in the beginning so that you can get an idea of how to post effectively. But what you want to do is you want to start following people. The idea is to encourage them to follow you which some of them will.

Now, unfortunately, this is not something that's going to pay off overnight. It's probably going to take a few months just like blogging is. But in the end, it's going to be worth it.

Once again, this is going to work with a snowball effect and eventually, you're going to find that if you stick with it it's going to generate a lot of followers for you. But we are doing this just for fun. Instagram allows you to set up a profile page. You can have a link on your profile page, and what you are going to do is post a link to your landing page here. That way when people are curious after viewing your profile or some of your posts they will end up visiting your landing page. And this is all going to be free traffic and some of them are going to sign up for your email list. Once they have signed up you can then directly market to them.

Okay, so far we haven't talked about any paid advertising. And that isn't really the topic of this chapter but we are going to make a special exception for Instagram. The reason we are doing so is that this is not really advertising in the sense that most people are thinking about it.

Instagram is kind of a wild West unregulated environment. So what can happen is you can make trades with other people. There are two ways to approach this, one is a free way to do it, and you can also do it by actually paying someone. So let's take a look at how this will work.

For the first method, you want to find people in your niche that have a moderate amount of followers. They are also going to be interested in getting more followers and they may not want to spend a lot of money doing so. So you can contact them with an offer to make a trade. What you want to do in this case is to give a shout out and then have them give you a shout out in return. Basically what that means is that you can have them recommend to their followers that they follow you, and in exchange, you recommend to your followers that they fall this other account. This is probably not something you can do right out of the gate because you need to have some followers of your own. If you're trying to make a deal with other users that have larger accounts, in order to make it fair you can suggest that if they give you one shout out that you will put up three for them on your account.

Now let's look at the second way which is to actually pay to drive traffic. But like we said on Instagram this is not done in a formal way where you pay Instagram to run advertising campaigns. What you do here is you make deals with individual accounts. So you can contact people with large numbers of followers an offer to pay them to either give you a shout out or put a post up on your behalf. You might also be able to get people to temporarily link to your landing page. Or it could be possible to put the link in the post. So the way this is done is you need to contact them and ask them if they are interested in the promotion and what their charges are. Compared to most forms of advertising you are going to find that you are probably going to be able to get relatively low-cost deals that can help get you a lot of exposure. So for a mid-size account, you might be able to get someone to put up a post on your behalf for $35. It will cost more the larger the account is. We really can't give you specific numbers because everything is going to depend on the specific niche that you choose. But no matter how you look at it it's a very inexpensive way to get eyeballs onto your affiliate offers.

So that is Instagram in a nutshell. We recommend that you do more research into this topic and incorporate this exciting social media platform into your marketing efforts.

Email Marketing

One of the central components of any online business is having an email list. Before setting one up you need to sign up for a service each we discussed earlier. Then you're going to create a list for each niche. What we are going to do is create what's called an autoresponder. This is going to be a set of 5 to 10 or maybe 20 emails that are sent automatically on a schedule to people who sign up on your landing pages. So when they give their email address to submit the form they automatically start receiving these emails. In this book there's not enough space to discuss the technical details of setting it up, that is something that has to be researched elsewhere. What you need to know here is that this is going to be a vital part of all of your marketing efforts whether you are using paid advertising or free promotional methods.

The series of emails is going to be used too soft to sell

your audience on your product that you're promoting. So you want to send people emails that contain useful information about the niche. For example, if we were marketing a ketogenic diet book, we could send recipes to our audience. Or we could send dieting tips. The point is you're going to email your list useful information and give it to them for free. The point of doing this is the same point of having the blog. You are going to want to be giving them lots of helpful content to create a bond of trust and establish yourself as an authority figure in the niche. You should also link back to your blog from the emails in case people haven't seen the blog.

Of course, in your emails, you are going to promote your affiliate offers but you want to do it in a casual fashion. Only very rarely do you want to do a hard-sell in the emails? So your first email should take a structure like the following. In the beginning, you start off talking about some specific problem or a set of problems that the people who signed up for your email list are likely having. If you have the same problem in the past that's all the better because you can give it an authentic discussion. But that's not strictly necessary, so you can do some research to find out what the pain points are for your audience. Think of your emails as short blog posts.
So it's going to fall to the same structure that we discussed earlier. What we want to do is after describing pain points that the audience have, they want you to explain to them ways to solve the problems. By giving them solutions in the emails you continue to build up trust.

Then toward the end of the email, you can state that you have found this product which really helps solve whatever problems you've been discussing. Remember that not everyone is going to buy the product immediately. So that's why we are going to send a series of emails, and you don't have to worry about doing a hard sell on the first email.

You can send emails about once a day as long as they have relevant content. Keep it friendly and informative tone. At the end of each email, you can recommend the affiliate offer. When you are recommending the offer include the affiliate link directly in the e-mail.

This is an old and surprisingly effective method of marketing. All online marketers or should I save virtually all online marketers use email marketing in some capacity. Practically every website you visit these days has a pop-up form to sign up for their email list. They are using exactly this procedure in order to drive client traffic. If you end up evolving to the point where you sell your own product, you are still going to use email marketing in order to capture leads and sell to them.

How many emails you want to set up is up to you. The point is to keep the emails useful and informative. As people buy it's common to shift them to the new email list. A list of previous buyers is more responsive and they may be open to new products in the same niche. So just as an example using the ketogenic diet if we were selling a product that was a guide on how to get started following the diet when people purchased it we could move them to a secondary list that sold them through a set of new emails a cookbook for the ketogenic diet. Or maybe it would be a dessert recipe book or something along those lines. The specifics aren't important we just want to you to see the way that you can tap customers to sell multiple affiliate offers in the same niche. Using these techniques someone who was initially a $27 sale might end up sending you hundreds of dollars over time.

Summary

There're many social media platforms and we can't cover them all, but we have to stop somewhere. So let's take this as a starting point or an essential list. Remember that it's also important not to spread yourself too thin. Although we could talk about a lot of other social media platforms, it's more important to be spending your time building a solid blog then it is to be trying to post on every social media platform. So to summarize, in order to drive free traffic the first thing you need to do did you want to be creating a regular SEO posting on your blog. You also want to be posting videos on YouTube at least on a semi-regular basis and use them to both link to affiliate offers and also back to your blog. Then you want to have a Facebook page for the niche and post your blog posts on there. Next, you want to be posting on forums and message groups and answer sites including links back to your blog when they are relevant. From there we want to use an Instagram account. And finally, the anchor point of all of this is going to be the landing page and your email list. One of the most famous sayings online about running an affiliate marketing business is the money is in the list.

Chapter 8: Social Media Advertising

It's entirely possible to create a business that runs completely on free traffic. If you put in place all the elements that we discussed in the last chapter and keep posting on the blog and the other sites as we described over time, you are going to drive quite a bit of traffic and start earning a lot of money without having to spend any upfront cash on advertising. If you have hundreds of posts and you find that you're not getting any traffic, the problem is not with the method, which probably indicates that you are not writing about the right topics or not doing SEO correctly.

So now we're going to look at another approach of driving traffic which is to pay for the traffic. There are different ways to do this but these days using social media advertising is the most popular. Facebook is currently the king or queen if you want to put it that way of social media advertising. It has a lot of advantages and we already saw what those were when using the Facebook audience insights tool at the beginning of the book. Simply put, Facebook let you drill down big-time in a way that was never before possible.

Our recommendation is that you take a multipronged approach to your business. So although some people are going to be tempted to bypass the effort that we described the use to generate free traffic in the last chapter, we recommend that you do both free and paid traffic. That will give a more sustainable long-term business and you won't be depending on Facebook to keep it afloat.

Facebook Campaigns Overview
So let's talk about the basics of advertising on Facebook. The nice thing about this is that you can get instant traffic. However, you need to know one important rule. The first rule of Facebook advertising is that you never directly link to an affiliate offer. Facebook looks down on affiliate marketing. If they see that you are driving traffic directly to an affiliate offer they may ban your account. So you don't want to do that ever.

In this case, the landing page comes to the rescue. Facebook does allow you to direct people two an email sign-up form. So bad is the method that is used in Facebook advertising? You run an ad on Facebook, and then you drive traffic straight to the landing page. So when you create your ad, the type you want to use is website traffic.

One of the important things it comes up when discussing Facebook advertising is the budget size. You can do amazing things only spending a little bit of money at a time. So what's important to start off slow and be patient? When you first start a campaign, we recommend that you start with a budget of $10. You should also be ready to do A/B testing, and so you might want to have two or three variations of your landing page created to drive traffic to. On click funnels, you can create a large number of landing pages so that's not an issue.

So you want to start with a small budget of $10 dollars per day and then when you develop campaigns that are effective, then you start to increase ad spend on those campaigns. There is a little trick that you want to use when increasing your advertising spend. That is, do it very slowly. So if you find that you have a campaign that is converting very well don't immediately increase the budget to $200 dollars per day. Instead, take the approach of upping the budget by around two dollars per day.

So what are you going to look for? The main thing you want to look for is the conversion rate. You want to see at least 2 to 3% of the clicks turning into email leads. So if 100 people click on the Facebook and you want to see at least two of them sign up for your email list. Now if you get something like 20 or 30 that's great! But if you are not even getting two or three there is something wrong somewhere along the pipeline. It may be that your ad copy on your landing page is not good or there is a disconnect between what you are saying in the ad and what people see when they get to a landing page. Make sure that the message is the same on the landing page and on the ad on Facebook.

Something that you need to keep track of that as a technical issue that goes a little bit beyond the scope of this book, is the Facebook pixel. This is a bit of code that you can install on websites. It keeps track of people signing up on the page or visiting the page. So it will help keep track of your conversion rates and Facebook will also keep track of people who visited the page but didn't sign up. The reason that's important is that what you can do is run future advertising campaigns that only target the people that visited the page but didn't sign up. So that way you don't lose those prospects. When you run your second advertising campaigns which are called retargeting campaigns, you will find that you get a lot more people signing up for your email list. It's not really hard to do click funnels is actually set up to have that code put it right into your landing page. All you have to do is copy and pasted but you will have to look at their help section to get the instructions.

Types of Ads

So the next thing we want to look at is what type of ad do you want to run. There are basically four options. The first option is a simple photograph. As long as your headline and a couple of lines of text copy are effective, and the photograph is directly relevant to your niche, this type of advertisement can be very effective. So it's not necessary to use a video. That said, video ads and of course, can be very good so if you can produce a good video or have access to one that you think would be effective in getting people to sign-up for your email list that is certainly a possibility.

Facebook also has some intermediate options. These include a slideshow, and a carousel, which is a mixture of videos and still images. And also they have another option which we are putting separately which is you can upload some still images and Facebook will create a video out of them. They claim that those ads convert pretty well.

The specific media that you decide to include in the advertisement as far as the specific media types, is far less important than whether or not it conveys the message that you want to convey. So don't get too caught up on deciding whether or not to use a video or an image. Stay focused on getting something together that is going to convince people to go check out your landing page.

Where to Advertise

In the last chapter, we lied a small bit. We said that Instagram wasn't really a platform where are you directly advertised. That's actually not true because you can advertise on Instagram through Facebook. So what you can do if you want to advertise on Instagram as well, is you create an ad that is also associated with your Instagram account that you want to promote. It's not even necessary to have an Instagram account to advertise on it. When you're creating your Facebook ad campaigns you can specify which particular areas are used to show your advertisement. So that can include Instagram along with the other options if you want.

So I pretty much sums up all there is to know about getting started with Facebook advertising. Once you get a successful Stream going using Facebook advertising, from there it's only a matter of getting your budgets set at the optimal level and then letting everything flow. You can pretty much reach everyone on Facebook these days so it's not necessarily required that you even consider advertising elsewhere. If you want to you can run your entire campaigns just targeting Facebook users. The audience is certainly big enough in order to keep driving a lot of traffic.

The next thing we want to mention is whether or not you advertise internationally. In part, that is going to depend on the offer that you're promoting. But generally speaking, you are going to want to expand as much as possible. Typically offers that do well in the United States also do well in Australia, New Zealand, Great Britain, Canada, and also South Africa. So at the very least, you are probably going to want to expand your campaigns to those countries. It may be the case depending on your offer that you might need to specialize the messaging and copy used for each different country. So that might require that you create advertising campaigns that are separate for each country. Again, that is something you will have to look into for your specific affiliate offer but the first thing to do is expand whatever's working with your startup campaign and see what happens. Then if it doesn't work out in the new country create new landing pages and/or Facebook advertisements that are targeted to the specific country. We personally like to keep everything separate so that it's easier to keep track of how everything is doing in different countries and markets.

Pinterest Advertising

Let's shift gears and talk about some of the other platforms that you might use for advertising purposes. Interest is definitely something that you might consider. It's another visually oriented platform and you can think of it as similar in certain respects to Instagram. So it's basically a photography website and so you're going to want to have a compelling visual image perhaps paired up with a text message on it to help drive traffic. This can be extremely effective, but we don't believe that it's going to be nearly as effective as running advertisements on Facebook. However, it's something you can look into if you feel that you can promote your product using only an image. The jury is actually still out as to whether or not this is effective for affiliate marketing. These days most people are sticking to using Facebook.

Twitter Advertising

Twitter has actually been losing users of late, but it still has a massive amount of traffic. That said, at this time we actually don't recommend advertising on Twitter. The platform in our view anyway, is not entirely suitable for pushing affiliate marketing products. Our opinion of this may change in the future but this is where it stands at the present time.

YouTube Advertising

Next, we considered advertising on YouTube. This is actually a very good platform to use for advertising provided that you can create a compelling video. The first advantage of advertising on YouTube is that is one of the heaviest traffic sites in the world. Second, advertising on YouTube is a surprisingly low cost. You might even find that it's quite a bit cheaper than advertising on Facebook. Another advantage of advertising on YouTube is the way that they have their advertising system set up. You can even use it to basically hijack popular YouTube channels. We'll be mean by this is that you can specify that your ad is shown on specific YouTube channels and even specific

YouTube videos. So you can have it showing on videos they get millions of views.

So the first step in doing YouTube advertising is to make or obtain a video to use for the ad. You don't want to use a video that is too long when you're using it for an advertisement. Our suggestion is one to three minutes. Earlier we mention that just to post on YouTube you can make any old video, but for this purpose, you want to up your game a little bit. The purpose of the video is going to be actually pitching whatever free giveaway you are using on your landing page. So when you create your ad you are going to associate the landing page with the video ad that shows on YouTube. So hopefully if you want to try this route, you will have the capacity to make a fairly compelling presentation where you tell the prospects watching the video what they are going to get when they sign up with their email.

You want to make sure that the video looks good but it doesn't have to be perfect. Many people simply film themselves talking shooting the video with a mobile phone in the same way that they would make a regular video. That said, since you are going to be spending money to get views for the video, you want to make sure that it's a very good video.

What's going to happen typically is that you are going to have your video shown as an advertisement that pops up at the beginning of other videos. Set up is determined by the user of the channel so they may have ads showing up in the middle of their videos or something like that, it really doesn't matter. So if you were to make a video about the ketogenic diet the first step would be to make a good video and then upload it to your channel on this niche. Then it's time to do some research. What you want to do is find specific videos and channels where you think it would be the best place to show the video. Don't be shy about having your video show directly on competitors channels. Think about the way that gas stations, fast food outlets, and drug stores position themselves in the market. If you go to one street corner with the McDonald's, it's certainly not unheard of to see a Burger King or Taco Bell across the street. Or if you see at Walgreens, chances are there is going to be a CVS pharmacy right across the street.

What we want to take a vantage of in the situation is that people who are already interested in your niche are going to be watching these very popular videos. So this is a way to get your message and offer directly in front of them.

You can also have YouTube set up the campaigns so that they also run automatically on the other channels and videos as well.

The bottom line about YouTube advertising is that it's one of the best methods that are available in the present environment. It's a great way to reach a lot of people, it's cheaper than Facebook, and video is certainly one of the most compelling ways to get peoples attention.

Linked-In

Another very high traffic website that can be used for social media advertising is LinkedIn. The value of this is really going to depend on what you're marketing. In case you don't know this is basically a site which is designed to facilitate professional networking. So it's kind of a business-oriented website where people basically post their resumes. With that in mind, advertising on the platform can be very cost-effective and you can reach a large number of people without having to spend a huge amount of money. But the key here is determining whether or not your offer is going to be suitable for the platform. In many cases it's not going to be any also have to consider how often are people visiting the site in comparison to YouTube or Facebook. You also have to consider the mindset. Marketers often talk about whether or not hey prospect is in a buying mindset or not when they see an advertisement. This is actually one of the strikes as compared to search advertising. It's easier to convert a prospect who is already in the mind to buy something so maybe they are actually searching on Google for some type of product when your ad comes up. So that means they are already primed to buy something related to the niche when they first come in contact with you. Someone who sees your advertisement on Facebook or in this case LinkedIn isn't in that mindset at all. That doesn't mean the advertising can't work obviously, as we have said Facebook advertising can be extremely effective. But what it means is there has to be a little bit of extra selling on the soft Side in order to get people in the right frame of mind. Our general feeling is that if your product is more business or professionally oriented such as possibly helping people learn new skills or improve the resume or whatever, that might be something suitable for advertising on LinkedIn. But getting flat abs or losing weight may not be the best products to use on this platform for targeting. So what you need to do is carefully evaluate whatever affiliate offers you are promoting and whether or not they are suitable. In the case of YouTube, Instagram, or Facebook, the audience is more general and pretty much suitable for anything.

WhatsApp

There are many different platforms we can consider but we're going to have to put a stop to it here and the last one which might have some advertising potential going forward is WhatsApp. This is going to be on average, a younger audience. So that is something to consider whether or not you will use it when thinking about this as an advertising platform. If you have a product that can potentially target a younger audience, then this might be something to consider. Of course, the problem for the app is that they're so many options available to advertisers. In other words, you can also reach the same audience that is on this app using all the other platforms that we've discussed. So the same audience is obviously going to be checking out videos on YouTube. If you're targeting an older demographic our opinion at this time is that this would not be worth pursuing. You can better reach the older demographic and this is anyone over the age of 35, by utilizing YouTube, and Facebook.

Chapter 9: Other Advertising Methods

In this chapter, we are going to go back to the old school methods. Believe it or not, they are still alive and well. This is essentially talking about advertising networks and pay per click advertising. Of course, things have narrow down quite a bit in the last 20 years, so Google is pretty much the only game in town however Bing can also be used in order to reach millions of customers. Despite all the talk about social media marketing, people are still searching like crazy on the Internet. And they are going to be continuing to do so for the foreseeable future. Having your advertisement come up when someone is looking for a specific topic remains one of the most effective advertising methods that are available. So we can't have this book and have it be complete without discussing it.

What a Pay Per Click (PPC) Ad Is

So just in case you are new to affiliate marketing and don't really know how this stuff works, let's go ahead and discuss what a PPC ad amounts to. Certainly, you have at least seen these advertisements when you're doing your own web searching even if you haven't thought about them much, or considered using them yourself.

This type of advertising is basically an extension of an old classified newspaper advertisement. So it consists of a headline and 2 to 3 lines of text. If it's in naturally with the Internet searching because it's similar in appearance to all the listed webpages that come up in the search. And since you're paying to show up in the search, it's possible to get at the top spot on the page, or at least near the top. So if you're willing to pay for it, this can drive quite a bit of traffic. Something to keep in mind is that you don't need to show up at the top of either in order to drive big results.

One advantage of this type of advertising is that it's possible to target people who are already in the buying mindset for the niche. So continuing to use the ketogenic diet example that we've been following, somebody might be searching to purchase a recipe book. So if you have an affiliate offer that is a recipe book for the diet, you can offer it to him immediately in the advertisement.

Now, unfortunately, as we discussed earlier Facebook doesn't allow certain types of advertising, Google and other sites that would be used for the purposes of this type of advertising often don't allow direct affiliate links either. Recently we tried running some campaigns on Bing. To test, we set up the link to go directly to the sales page wish we were running the affiliate campaign for. The advertisements were rejected because they said the link has to be your link that the advertisement goes to. So that puts more restrictions on this type of advertising then there used to be. 10 years ago or more, you could certainly directly link to the affiliate offer and that often resulted in huge numbers of sales only spending pennies and advertising. So those days are over.
That doesn't mean that the advertising method doesn't work, it just has to be adjusted. This is a good example of the flexibility that you need when you're doing online

marketing. The situation and the technology are always changing and you have to be able to adapt to it and find success in the news situation.

So anyway to get to the point, in this case, we have to do what we do when advertising on Facebook or anywhere else these days, and that is what redo his link to the landing page in order to collect peoples email addresses. So instead of paying to directly link people to a sales page, we are paying to get them on our email list. At first, it seems to be a little bit unfortunate, but it's actually an advantage. In the end, as we said earlier, the money is in the list as everyone says. So what that means to us as marketers, is that this is money well spent because we are getting a list of prospects that we can sell too over and over.

Effective PPC Ads

In order to have good PPC ads that have good conversion rates, you are going to have to be able to write good copy. We can't use a photograph or a video, in this case, to get people to click on the ad. But Let's assume that you have mastered the art of copywriting. The first rule that we would advise in running this type of advertising campaign is that you tied together with the headline of your advertisements with the headline that is on your landing page. They should convey a similar message.

The second rule that we would like to apply with this kind of advertising is that you describe your free giveaway. So on your landing page, you should have some sort of giveaway which is either a free book of some kind or a free video course, Something along those lines. So in that copy and we are talking about the text underneath the headline now, you should refer to the giveaway which is also prominently mentioned on your landing page.

The key here is to keep everything consistent. Consistency is going to help improve your conversion rates. So I am personally interested in your book, let's say that you're giving away a book that teaches them how to do a certain type of trade on the Forex markets, you're going to mention that book specifically in your advertisement. Then on the landing page, you want them to see that same message spelled out pretty much exactly in the text on the landing page. So they clicked on the ad in order to get the book, and then when they see the landing page it's going to be immediately clear that they can download the book for free if they sign up for your email list.

So it's really that simple. If you have that consistency your ad will be effective with a good conversion rate.

Budgeting and Keywords

PPC advertising is primarily driven by keyword selection. One of the mistakes that people make is that they choose too many keywords. You want to have your keywords focused but we will say a couple of hundred keywords are good to target. So you want to do your keyword research at ahead of time and have a good listing of keywords to submit when you create your advertisements. Budgeting should be rather limited especially in the beginning. Now if you find out that you can spend $10 and generate $100, then, of course, you're going to want to scale up your ads.

However, in the beginning, we recommend that you set a $20 dollars per day budget and do a lot of testing. What you want to look for is how much does it cost to get someone to sign up for the email list. And then he wants to calculate how much money on average a customer brings in. If that's profitable then you can go ahead and start scaling up the ad, but do it slowly so you don't suddenly blow through a lot of money.

Network Advertising

Now we're going to consider what we're calling network advertising. If you start searching online you will find out that there're many options to run advertisements that show up on peoples websites. Our general belief about this type of advertising is that you probably want to stay away from it in most cases. The reason is that this type of advertising tends to show up on basically any website. So it becomes harder to target the audience that you're looking for. It's almost like it's the opposite of advertising on Facebook. So this kind of advertising can actually result in just throwing money away even if the cost per click or other metrics are low in comparison. It's more useful to drive money towards methods that actually produce paying customers then it is to have ads showing up on websites where people are not really interested.

Solo Ads

A solo ad is an advertisement which runs in someone's email. So basically the way this works is that somebody who has a large email list sells access to their list. You pay the person usually through a service, and then they recommend your link, which is going to be your landing page, in an email that they send out to their list. The advertisements are designed to deliver a specific number of visitors to your page. When you go to various websites, you'll be able to select among a wide variety of people that are selling access to their email list. This can be a very lucrative way of advertising if it's done correctly.

one of the advantages of this type of advertising is that these people have already garnered together a large list which is interested in the types of products you may be offering. Secondly, it cuts out any involvement of large websites such as Facebook, or Google. Instead, you were just dealing directly with another marketer and chances are they don't care about the kind of things that Facebook is going to worry about. So if you happen to be promoting some type of offer which would be banned on Facebook, chances are you can use a solo in order to promote it. The most famous website used for this type of promotion is called udimi.com.

Solo ads generally run from 100 up to 1000 leads at a time. The cost could be about $500 in order to get 1000 leads to your page. So the second advantage that this type of promotion has is that the cost per lead is a fixed quantity. If your page converts well, that could turn into a very profitable situation. Of course, you will have to actually test in order to find out if it works or not. Don't be discouraged if it doesn't work the first time, you might need to refine the messaging on your page in order to get conversions.

One thing to avoid when using solo ads is to make sure

that your double option for your email list is turned off. What that means is that normally honey email list company is going to send someone who signs up for your list a confirmation email before they start sending your emails. The reason this is used is as a spam reduction feature. It seems like a little bit of overkill though after all the people voluntarily signed up for your list in the first place. In any case, when it's turned on that can often reduce the number of people that actually open your emails by a large margin. So make sure you turn it off before trying this type of promotion.

It can be to your advantage to use a newer offer web promoting to a list on a solo ad. The main reason for this is that these lists have been marketed to quite a bit. So they may have already seen whatever offer you are promoting.

The other downside is that sometimes you can run into fraud. Some unscrupulous sellers may use bots and other unethical methods in order to make it appear that they're driving traffic to your site. In reality, they are just taking you for a ride. One way that you will notice is whether or not people actually open the emails that you send. You can also look for unusual patterns in the traffic.

So you need to be a little bit careful about who you deal with. Although these are taking place on brokered sites, these deals are arranged on an individual basis. One good thing about Udemy is people do leave reviews which help you evaluate a given seller. One of the things that you can notice whether or not they actually got people to get sales which people often indicate.

Chapter 10: Ten Most Common Mistakes

In this chapter, we are going to discuss the most common mistakes the new marketers make went taking up affiliate marketing. Mistakes can be costly of course, and one of the problems that happen is that people and up not getting the sales of their expecting because they been making mistakes, and then they end up giving up early. We hope that we can help you avoid this problem by 20 out some of these mistakes in the beginning so that you can avoid making them yourself. Many of us made these mistakes early in our affiliate marketing careers, so we pave the way for you so that you don't have to make the same mistakes.

Thinking people will just arrive at your website

We certainly hope that the readers of this book realize that if you just put up a website it's not going to get automatic traffic. Unfortunately one of the biggest mistakes that beginning affiliate marketers make is they assume that traffic just appears at websites. That is not the case at all. It might've been true in 1995, but these days there are so many websites on the Internet that's very hard to rank high in the search engines on virtually any keyword. You have to put the effort in order to obtain the kinds of rankings that you need in order to bring in traffic that leads to sales. So although there are our own preferences about how to get traffic, you've got to take want approach or the other. Or preferably use both. And that means you should set up your site in order to drive good quality, free, organic traffic. And then on top of that, you can advertise to drive more traffic. Simply expecting traffic to magically show up is not going to work.

Not providing enough content

One of the things about online marketing is that you have to have an inclination towards information. Just think about all the blogs and websites that you look at in your own browsing. Even though everyone says reading is dead, the truth is reading has simply moved onto the computer for the smartphone. People are actually reading more than ever. And one of the things about online marketing is that you need to be providing content to your users. If you're providing inadequate levels of content it's simply not going to work. There are multiple ways this can rear its ugly head in your business. The first is in your emails. It's easy to write emails that aren't long enough and don't provide the user with any benefit. Each time that you write an email you should be focused on one thing. First of all, try viewing the email from the perspective of the customer. Second, ask yourself if the email actually solves any problems that the customer might have. Every single time that you send any content out to prospects it needs to solve at least one problem that they have in the niche. Using our ketogenic diet example, one problem that people have is they get the so-called ketogenic flu. The details of this aren't important here, we are just using it to serve as an example. So if you were marketing a keto product our suggestion would be that you look up keto flu on YouTube, and on some blogs, and educate yourself about it. When you do this you're going to find a lot of suggestions from different people about how to solve it. So what she could do is write them up in an email. So you start the email out by stating the problem and in a compelling way. People on your email list that have experienced it are really going to resonate with that kind of content. Then later in the email, you provide the solutions that you found doing your research. And then after that, you suggested they buy the product that you are using in your affiliate marketing, mentioning that it really helps you get over your problems with the ketogenic diet.

So your emails have to be substantial and contain a lot of content. Secondly, and we already touched on this, your blog posts also need to have substantial content. Don't go and post three or four lines and call that a blog post. Remember what we said earlier, any post you put up on your blog should have at least 800 words. Secondly and this is very important and we should've mentioned this earlier, do not duplicate content. The search engines are not going to reward any website that duplicates content.

When it comes to YouTube, the same basic principle applies. A YouTube video doesn't need to be particularly long, but it does need to deliver something of value to the viewer.

Hard selling your audience

Hard selling your audience - we're constantly bombarding them with emails, isn't approach that Is doomed to failure. Often new affiliate marketers are anxious to get a sale and they mistakenly think that doing a lot of hard selling and pushing the product is what's going to result in a sale. Nothing could be further from the truth. As we stated over and over again and attempt to help you become an effective affiliate marketer, providing value to your customers is what's going to close sales. Bombarding them with emails saying buy this or by that is just going to turn them off. If you take that type of approach you might find that basically, you end up losing subscribers.

Too Many Products

The first mistake that people make usually comes about because they're anxious to make money. New affiliate marketers see all the products that they could possibly earn money from and they start imagining lots of income streams coming into their bank account. It's pretty easy to rationalize. If you start promoting 20 products, you might start thinking to yourself - well if each one only sells one copy a day, look how much money I'm making.

Unfortunately, it doesn't really work that way. As mentioned earlier, one of the problems that you want to avoid is becoming overstretched. We hope that you pay close attention to our chapter which covered free traffic. If there was one thing that you would've noticed from the chapter, is that it entails putting a lot of effort into promoting a single product. Or at the very least, what you want to be doing is promoting one niche at the most. That doesn't mean that you always have to promote just one niche, but when you're starting out putting up a lot of blog posts for most people is going to be pretty limited.

You are simply not going to have the time required to be putting up with that kind of effort in three or four different areas at the same time.

Secondly, it can't be emphasized enough that you need to become an authority figure in your niche. It's not possible to become an authority figure if you're promoting multiple things at the same time. Don't get overconfident in your abilities and think that you can do it. Time and time again people have proven that taking on too many at once makes you unlikely to become successful.

It's understandable if you want to develop multiple income streams. And over time, that might be something that is possible. But your first task as a new affiliate marketer is to learn from scratch how to close sales. You shouldn't even be thinking about multiple products until you have a regular income from one product only. You can set a reasonable goal, maybe it's $500 a month, or better yet $1000 a month, and you will not add another product see your line until you have reached your goal. To be quite honest though, you can earn far more than that from most affiliate products. If you're doing affiliate marketing with click bank, that's doubly true. Of course, that's provided that you chose a good product, but there's no reason why you can't earn $10,000 dollars a month or more from a single affiliate product if you follow all the steps outlined in this book.

Not Enough Products

Yes, it sounds like we are contradicting the previous points. However, we're not going to be doing that. When we say not enough products, we are talking about for one niche only. So if we consider click bank as an example, you can find a product in some niche and sell it and make $30 from the customer. A lot of new affiliate marketers leave it at that. But that's a total mistake. You want to keep selling the customer. That doesn't mean continually pressuring them, but from time to time you want to offer them related products that you know they are going to be interested in. So if somebody's looking for weight loss products, new diet books, recipe books and so on. That way you can get more than one sale per customer and your $30 will turn into $100 or more.

Failing to Know Your Products

We have recommended that you get review copies of products you promote or even buy them using your affiliate link. That is something that you should see as an investment. It's an important investment because if you don't know the product that you're promoting, you're going to come across as shallow and unconvincing. You can't review a product that you haven't at least looked at. The more you know your product, the more authentic your reviews are going to be, and the more in-depth content that you can provide about the product. And this is one reason why promoting multiple products at once is not a strategy that is going to be effective. You simply can't know ten products as well as you can know a single product.

Falling Victim to Shiny Object Syndrome

One of the problems that come about when you're new to affiliate marketing is what we call shiny object syndrome.

This is actually related to our first mistake that we outlined above. What happens is new affiliate marketers are constantly intriguing buy new products that they come across. Whenever they find something that appears new or is at least new to them, that new product makes the old product that they're trying to market now not look so good anymore. So they dropped the efforts on the first product and started promoting the new one. This keeps happening over And over again. So what happens is that the people never get around to putting in the full effort that's needed in order To actually drive sales from one specific product. You can think of it as having a bunch of half done projects lying around the garage if you're in the home improvement. It's far better to have one and only one product that you are promoting and driving to make actual sales and then improving on your sales figures, then it is to have five or six things going at once.

Spending money when you don't have to

It's human nature to want to take the easy road to matter what you're doing. And one of the ways that the easy road appears when it comes to affiliate marketing is that you can simply pay your way to success. People have a vision of simply setting up a landing page and then driving traffic to it which automatically converts into sales. We hate to break it to you, but that's not really something that happens a lot often. More likely than not you are going to make very good customers out of that kind of scenario. In that case, people will feel like they're just getting sold to. It's a totally different feeling if you establish yourself as an expert in the niche.

But the important thing here is that people get anxious in lower looking for an easy way to start driving traffic. People can up spending thousands of dollars on advertising campaigns that may or may not convert. When the fact is, you don't need to spend any money at all if you are patient. Just think about it what have you been doing up until now? You haven't been affiliate marketing. So why is it so essential that you start getting sales tomorrow when you can just put some time and now to set up a system which is going to dry free traffic from months and years to come?

So especially when it comes to people who are inexperienced, they start driving pay traffic and waste a ton of money. This might work for experience marketers because they will have a perfect email sequence to convert customers into the sales. But as a new marketer, you probably aren't going to be nearly as skilled. This means that your advertising campaigns are more likely going to be a waste of money. That is until you get your entire system set up. So, in the beginning, we really would like our students to put their focus on building a blog and learning how to write and write good copy.

Not putting in any time

Earlier we mentioned that people often make the excuse that they don't have time. If you don't have time why are you reading this book? The fact is there is no magic Genie that is going to appear and create an Internet business for you. Generating quality content and even coming up with good, effective advertising campaigns that convert is not something that you can just expect to happen – it only works out when you devote regular time to your business.

Failing to track campaigns effectively

At some point, you're going to be running paid advertising campaigns. When you do so, one of the most important aspects of your marketing and advertising efforts is to collect and analyze all the data that you can possibly look at in order to assess whether or not a campaign is effective or not. It's important to know the cost per acquisition of each customer. That is one of the most fundamental things you need to know about any business. Then you need to know the lifetime value of the customer. It's going to take some time to collect this data, and hopefully, you're refining your advertising campaigns so that they become more effective with time. But at each stage, you should be computing these numbers. So run your first Facebook ad campaign for a week, and then at the end that week gather up how much money you spent to acquire each customer, and then calculate how much money was earned from each customer. You might not even make any money the first week. But of course, we hope that you do. In any case, you might find out that you are either not converting enough from the Facebook ad itself, that is not enough people are signing up to your email list, or you might find out that your email list isn't converting. In the latter case that would mean that you need to refine your emails and write better ones. Over time, this is going to be a process of constant refinement. Also on the backend, without overloading customers, you want to be able to sell them multiple products so that the lifetime value of each customer is increased.

Focusing only on price

Another mistake that happens with new affiliate marketers is they see dollar signs when they find products that pay high commissions. That can be a mistake. A product might pay a high commission, but it might take far too many leads to generate a single sale. Ask yourself what's better. We could have one product that pays $30 a sale and gets six sales out of the hundred leads. Or we could have a product that pays $100 dollars per sale, but you only get one sale out of 400 leads. So you need to be comparing products across multiple dimensions. Simply focusing on price alone is extremely naïve.

Being cheap

Ironically, we are going to look at the opposite problem when compared to people who have been looking for the easy way out. Some people are actually too cheap. So what we mean by this? When we talk about taking the easy way out we are talking about people that think that they can only spend their way to riches, and they don't have to worry about providing content. At the opposite extreme are people that don't want to spend any money at all. We certainly encourage people to take advantage of every opportunity to use free tools. However, you don't want to be cutting corners by being too cheap either. One example of this is in choosing your blog theme. We touched on this earlier. It might be tempting to try and make a business out of its free website on blogger.com, or create your own website and use a free template instead of paying for one. But impressions are everything, and you need to spend money when it's appropriate. Saying that you're going to go entirely free could work, but it's not the best strategy. You have to be smart about spending your money, that's for sure, but don't try to save pennies when you're trying to build a business.

Failing to adjust the copy

Any affiliate marketers start out with extreme enthusiasm only to find that their advertising campaigns fail. Then they give up saying it just didn't work. That's a mistake, one of the things that you need to do is constantly test your advertising copy. Sometimes simple changes on your websites including your landing page, or in your text that you're your including in your advertising can't cause dramatic changes in conversion rates. Many times people will have an expert look at their ads or their landing page, and the expert will spot one minor mistake that was inhibiting conversion rates. You may not have access to an expert, but what you do have the capability of doing is A/B testing of everything that you do. So if you start running advertising campaigns and they don't convert all don't get all depressed about it. Revise and repeat. You can also look at changing images and videos. Have friends take a look at them and maybe one of your friends can spot something that you're missing. Often when you're too close to something it's hard to see something that's obvious to everyone else. A simple change of an image in an advertisement could suddenly drive sales.

Sticking to a bad product too long

In the vast majority of cases, the Affiliate marketers give up too easily. But sometimes people get emotionally attached to a product that they started to promote. They've tried promoting it using free methods and running lots of advertising campaigns, but they just can't seem to get a sale. But they keep holding on hoping that sales are coming around the corner. If you have run a reasonable number of advertising campaigns and you just can't close the sale you might find out that it's time to give up on that particular product. So rather than holding on trying to continue pushing a product, try finding a product in the same niche and then promote that one instead and see what happens.

Paying too much attention to gravity

For people who choose to be click bank marketers, which is a common approach for affiliate beginners, one of the mistakes that they make is they only focus on gravity. Now, remember that gravity is an indicator that gives you an idea of how many affiliates closed sales over the past 12 weeks. But that doesn't tell the whole story as we indicated earlier. Beginning affiliates often make the mistake of picking the highest gravity possible. And so then you have these newbie marketers out there trying to compete with two or 300 more affiliates selling the product. And many of those other affiliates are extremely experienced. They may have a huge Internet presence and be running lots of advertising campaigns. Meanwhile, the naïve affiliate who is just starting out might be ignoring a lot of Products that have lower gravity but the very quality websites that convert well. Of course, the only thing to do is to actually test. But combine analytical research into the traffic going to the website, the quality of the website, and other factors along with the gravity rather than just focusing on gravity alone.

Chapter 11: Ten Tips for Success

Learn from others

A great deal of your research can be geared to studying what other affiliates and the vendors themselves are doing in their advertising. Start keeping an eye out for relevant advertising, and visit as many pages of the vendor's site that you can find. You might be in for learning some useful information that you can apply in your own campaigns. Focus on the way they have their website set up. Find the landing pages that the vendor themselves are using. Then sign up to get on their email list. The first thing that you are going to want to note is where does their website take you after you sign up for the email list? Second, study the emails they send you after you sign up.

You obviously don't want to copy anyone directly, but you can use what they are doing as a guide. They have thoroughly studied the target market and know how to get conversions. So why not learn from people that already know what to do?

Also track any advertisements you see in your niche, whether it's on a website, on a Google search, on Amazon, Facebook, or Pinterest. Study the copy that they are using and when you see a good copy, use it as a guide to improving your own copy.

You can also reach out directly to vendors. Be aware that some are more helpful than others. Some are even a little bit hostile, and others will just ignore you. But if you can find a vendor that will help you promote the product, then you should take advantage of that.

Remember the mobile space

These days many people spend much of their time online via mobile devices, whether it's their phone or a tablet. A lot of marketers are still focused on the desktop. Yes, the desktop is still important and will be for the foreseeable future, but ignoring mobile can cost you a lot of sales. The first thing that you'll want to be doing is making sure that your websites are mobile friendly. In fact, Google uses that as a metric when crawling sites, so you can get ahead of that by making sure your site is optimized to display on phones as well as on desktop computers. Also, make sure your landing pages look good on mobile. One of the things you might discover is a huge proportion of people use their phones to check Facebook, and so when you advertise on Facebook they might be going to the mobile version of your landing page. If you have 65% of your prospects clicking to the mobile version of the page, and it doesn't look very good, then you could be losing a lot of customers.

Focus on profitable products

Many affiliate marketers these days are using affiliate programs like Amazon. While they do have their advantages, they have huge amounts of competition, and low commission rates (relatively speaking). That can make it hard to compete. It's more important to find a profitable product than it is to focus on something that is well known. Not only are well-known products and websites overrun by competition, but they also suffer from a problem that arises from customers becoming numb to it. If a customer keeps seeing dozens of affiliates promoting the same book to them, they are unlikely to buy it when they see you joining in on showing them something they've already seen over and over again. Try showing them something new. There are many gems out there that don't have a high level of exposure that customers are eager to open their wallets for.

Focus on products you can believe in

It's easy to try and find products that have the promise of helping you make a quick buck, but if you don't really believe in the products that you are promoting, that isn't going to be a recipe for success. So you should try and pick products that you really believe in first. Then because of your heightened and more genuine commitment toward promoting them, you are more likely to succeed when getting conversions.

Do head to head comparisons

This is a good way to compete when promoting popular products. For example, Click funnels have a popular affiliate program that is pretty saturated. But there are competing products that also have affiliate programs, for example, LeadPages. One very effective technique you can use is to write an article with a head-to-head comparison review of two competing products, and you are an affiliate for both of them. It should be an honest review, so we recommend at least trying out a free trial of the products you are going to write about (but keep in mind to be an affiliate, they may require that you sign up). In the end, pick one product or another, but include a table of product features that shows the head to head comparison. Be sure to reference the names of the products in the review so that you come up on search engines, and use the word "review" and "comparison" in the article. Then recommend one or the other, but include buttons and affiliate links so that the people reading the article can visit the one that they like, and possibly sign up for one or the other so that you get an affiliate commission either way.

This can also work with more products, although we don't recommend using more than three. With three you can set up a product table with a list of features, including checkmarks for which one has what feature. This is not gaming the system, you are actually providing potential customers with useful information that can help them make a better buying decision. So think of it as providing a service, and you will write a good and more honest review, and that helps drive traffic and convert sales.

Pick a mid-range niche

It's always good to focus on the big evergreen markets. These include health and fitness, weight loss, romance and dating, and making money. But within each of these niches, there are several sub-niches that you can drill down in to reduce the negatives that could come from going with something that simply has way too much competition and overload.

For example, we can pick the making money niche. Everyone, well not everyone, is out there searching far and wide for ways to make money. At the top of this list are at home online business training websites, but those are oversold and saturated with affiliates. The problem with those is often that they offer high commissions and so everyone gravitates toward selling them.

But you can drill down to a more specialized niche, and then the competition starts easing. For example, we can stick to making money. You can narrow it down by saying making money with the stock market. That is still a pretty saturated niche, but its more narrowly focused and even here, there is probably less competition. Within the stock market, there are even more specialized niches that we can look at to further refine things down. For example, we could target people who want to learn about dividend investing, or people that want to learn how to trade options.

The same procedure works for health and wellness. Obviously, health is an evergreen niche. But what if instead of health, you focus on one specific concern? Products related to diabetes, for example, are targeting one specific group and they sell very well. You can think of others in the health and wellness niche that is specifically targeted at people who are suffering from one specific condition. Doing that will narrow your focus and not only ease the competition from other affiliates, but it will help you rank easier in the search engines. Using the example of making money, there are going to be fewer websites covering dividend investing than there are for the general term of making money, or for making money form the stock market in general. In any niche, there are many sub-niche products that can help you focus and stand out more.

Always add value

We hate to keep harping on this, but adding value to your customers is one of the most important tips for success. Many affiliate marketers are happy being a clickstream, driving traffic to the sales page without offering any value in between. Let's be honest, some people who are good at driving paid traffic are going to make a lot of money just pushing customers over to the sales page of the website. But if you add value, that is going to help you stand out in the marketplace. This will help you convert sales down the line when customers remember you as someone is an actual authority figure in the niche and as someone that added value and solved problems in their own life. This can also help you down the road, in the sense that you can keep your email list loyal. If you decide to launch your own product, then you are going to have a long list of customers that will be ready to buy it.

Add your own bonuses

You can create or have made bonuses to add for people that convert sales. So you could put together your own keto recipe book if you were promoting keto products from ClickBank, as an example. Then what you would do, is you give the recipe book to the customers that convert on sales to your affiliate products. This is going to help customers value you more and be willing to buy more from you in the future.

Use multiple traffic sources

Remember that the internet changes constantly and all the time. So you don't want to be relying on a single traffic source for your success. Companies like Facebook and Google constantly come up with new policies and algorithm changes that can leave you dry if you have been relying on one specific way to get people to view your website.

Give a thumbs down

Since affiliate marketers are trying to make money by convincing people to buy products, they often only have positive reviews on their websites. As a twist, try putting some negative reviews. Don't make a fake one, our suggestion is to actually review a product related to your niche that you don't like. By doing so, it can help increase the authenticity of your presentation. If a website is constantly pumping up one or two products but never says anything else, that can seem artificial and visitors might pick up on that. But a few well placed negative reviews could make you seem far more real, and therefore more trusted, and more likely to buy from.

Pay attention to call to action buttons

Don't leave the call to action to fate. First of all, it's important to have a call to action. You should not be shy about asking people to follow through with a purchase when you've recommended a product, and you should make it as easy as possible. The call to action button should be a bright color that stands out against the background and draws attention to itself. Don't use muted colors that won't serve this purpose. That includes not only sales buttons but also buttons to sign up on email forms. In your emails themselves, you should also have stand out calls to action. Try including HTML emails using colorful buttons instead just text links. People are more likely to click on buttons that stand out than they are to click on a link embedded in text that they might miss. Also, remember a fundamental principle of marketing, and that is that people sometimes need to be told to take action. They just need a little push to go over the top.

Use varied price ranges

Something else that often helps increase sales is giving customers options by price ranges. All companies (well except Apple) do this. You might have a customer base with some who are willing to spend a premium on a weight loss program that costs $100. Maybe it has a lot of added value like a personal coaching program or something. But maybe many of your customers wouldn't spend $100, but they would spend $50. Still, others would only spend $25. You should make sure that all price ranges (within reason) are covered, and then you might end up getting a lot of sales that you would have missed out on otherwise.

Use time limits

Scarcity is one of the oldest techniques in marketing. You can use time limits to your advantage, even if they aren't real, although sometimes you can make them real. For example, some ClickBank products offer discount links. You could put up a web page with the discount link, and offer it to your customers for 48 hours. Then take it down when the time runs out. It helps to be visual so add a countdown clock to it. ClickFunnels has one you can drag and drop onto your pages. You can even add these to your email signup forms, for example offering a free book in exchange for signing up on your email list. But put a countdown and say they only have 12 hours to sign up or you're taking down the offer. Many prospects look at a landing page and think well maybe they can come back later. But they never do. If you put a time limit on the page, then they might feel more compelled to take action on the offer.

The Rule of Seven

It's not clear that this has any scientific backing, but many marketers claim that you need to contact a customer seven times on average before they will buy a product. Whether or not this is true, it does bring to mind the idea that you need to contact your customers on the email list an adequate number of times. Sending three emails is probably not sufficient. Make sure to send at least seven, one per day. That way you are covered for a week, and maybe it would be fair to say that if people have not made a purchase by that time, they are pretty unlikely to make a purchase ever.

Don't use canned material

Some ClickBank vendors have a large collection of material for marketing purposes that they have provided to affiliates. It seems tempting to use them. They might look great, having been designed by professional graphic artists, and there might be emails and articles written by professional copywriters. That is fine as far as it goes, but the problem with that kind of material is that every affiliate that decides to try marketing the product is going to use them. So any prospects you come across may have already read the articles. Also, remember that Google penalizes sites that use duplicate content. Stay original. Another drawback is that emails are written for someone else's campaign sound fake when you send them. You want to sound as genuine as possible, so that could mean that you are better off sending your own emails even if they lack the flair of a marketing agency.

Banners rarely work

Another tool often offered by vendors are professionally designed banners. They are not going to work unless you have massive traffic. It also gives your website a spammy feel if you have a lot of banners on the site. Focus on using content instead and call to action buttons where appropriate.

Don't obsess on followers

The rise of Twitter and Instagram the world has become obsessed with getting a large number of followers. The fact that many accounts have been found to have fake followers doesn't seem to discourage anybody. Followers can be good to a certain extent, but the number of followers is not the real metric. The same holds true for the size of your email list. In other words, having 10,000 fans of your Facebook page doesn't do you any good if not they are not interested in purchasing any products. That's why the size of an email list by itself isn't necessarily a metric to how good the list is. Sometimes people can have a list that only has 3000 people on it, but if 30% of those people will buy a product, that can be better than a list twice as large that is only 1% responsive. So instead of worrying about how many fans your Facebook page gets an how many followers your Instagram page gets, focus instead on the quality of your prospects.

Make a business plan

You don't want to approach your business as a hobby. Just because you can run an affiliate marketing business out of your home, that doesn't mean that it should be treated as something like playing fantasy football. It's still a real business and so no matter how part-time you plan to make it, you need to treated as if it's a real business. Part of that is making a business plan.

A business plan helps you focus. It helps you set concrete goals and deadlines. This can only help a business to grow over the long-term. Of course, is no guarantee of success. But a business without a business plan is floundering and hoping for luck to help it grow. That isn't going to work. You should set targets, budgets, and whatever else you would do in any business plan so that you can help guide your business and then also use that as a metric to determine future success. You don't want to come away six months later and say well it seems like it's doing better. You need to have hard data to look at and see if you are meeting your goals or failing to meet them. Creating a business plan doesn't guarantee that you're going to have success but it sure helps get you more organized and on the right track as opposed to simply winging it. It will also help keep you disciplined so that you aren't wasting money.

Opt for Income Streams

At one point in our business, we were looking at different products for a certain niche. One of the products had a lot of appeals because it's sold for a one-time payment of $110. A competing product only gave an initial payment of $30. At first, we ended up going with the high-paying product. But we made a huge mistake which we later rectified. The mistake was that the payment of $30 was only on an initial payment used to sign up for service. It turned out that on average that product paid affiliates $193. So by selling the $30 product, and that is the upfront payment and not the total payments, you actually make more money. It's too easy to get greedy and I hope for fast cash coming right away. But you're actually a lot better off if you go with a product that brings continuous money. That way you start to build up an income stream from each customer. Those customers are still valuable anyway. So what you can do is lure them in, with a less expensive product such as the one that's only $30 dollars upfront. When people don't really know you well they are going to be a lot more willing to spend a smaller amount of money then they are to drop 100 bucks right away. But what you can do, is when you get them in with the $30 product, which is also producing that income stream for several months, is you can be pitching related products to them to earn money. In that case that we described, the product that was $110 was actually slightly different than the one that was $30. So even though they went for the $30 product, we were able to go ahead and continue marketing the more expensive product. And in many cases, you can convert prospects on both products. So that way we were able to take advantage of the subscription fees from the first product that was $30, and ends up getting an average of $190 in returns from them, and then over a certain proportion of the customers, we also got sales for the $110 dollar product.

Utilize PLR products

If you haven't heard about this before I encourage you to go on the Internet and search for PLR products. There are many websites that offer them. These are products that are the modest quality which is designed for niches in online marketing. So we've been talking a lot about the ketogenic diet, if you search PR websites there's no question that you will find Products for the ketogenic diet. The deal with these products is you are allowed to sell them or even give them away. The products are not, generally speaking, high enough quality to offer as a standalone product. However, it's a great resource to utilize when creating giveaways on your email list. Make sure that you evaluate a PLR product thoroughly before actually sending it out to your list. But it makes a great alternative to save you time when you're starting out to have something to offer for free in exchange for people signing up on your email list.

Chapter 12: Platforms to Use in Affiliate Marketing

An old Chinese proverb says may you live in interesting times, and one thing we can say for sure is that if you are an online marketer you are certainly able to do that. Changing technology means lots of different platforms and so there are different and changing ways to get at your target audience. The first thing that you always need to think about is who your ideal customer is.

Early on in the book, we did a little bit of research showing how different customer bases were for different niche interests. It goes beyond that, however, because different customers might be found via different platforms.

Take into account age

People of different ages use technology in different ways, so you need to know the age range of your customers. If they are 65+, to use an extreme example, they may be using Facebook on desktop computers, but they are unlikely to be using WhatsApp. On the other end of the spectrum, if your customers are 16 years old, they may not use desktop computers nearly as much as they use mobile phones. You need to know this information so that you understand how to effectively tap into your customer base.

Consider making apps

This is new to affiliate marketers – but something you should consider adding to the mix in order to target younger people (but not exclusively so) is to make apps to promote your products. There are two rules that you need to utilize if you decide to try this approach. The first is that your app should add genuine value. Don't try creating an app on the fly that is simply a clickstream. It might not even be approved to be on the app stores. But if you make a quality app that is useful to your customer base – it could be approved and for download on the app stores and bring you a new traffic source. Let's once again use a keto diet as an example niche. You could make an app that was a keto calculator, that people could use to enter their food items in and it would tell them the percentage of fat, protein, and carbohydrates they were getting in their meals and graph it for them. Even Apple would approve this app because it really does something for the user. But the app could have an additional feature, which is to have people sign in to use the app – and they would be signing up for your email marketing list. Then you can start pitching them keto diet-related products through emails outside the app.

Who the customer determines where to advertise

It seems like nearly everyone is on Facebook, but you need to research where your customers are spending the most time online to get the most bang for your buck when it comes to your advertising dollars. Let's go back and say that you are targeting women who are 65+. In that case, they may be on Facebook, but it's a solid bet they are not on Instagram. So doing Instagram promotion hoping to reach them would be a waste of time. Spending money by setting up advertising campaigns through the Facebook Ads Manager that also targeted Instagram users would be a waste of money. Knowing who your customers are, you can target advertising correctly.

Refine the target audience as much as possible

You need to know as much as possible about visitors to your website and who signs up for your email list. A lot of the information about people who click will be available from Facebook advertising, and that can be very useful to help you refine your campaigns. For instance, if you start a Facebook ad campaign targeting everyone over the age of 18, and after you have a reasonable number of clicks (500 or more to be statistically significant) then you need to take a look at your data. If it shows that you are getting 70% of your clicks from women age 35-44, then you can refine your campaign to target only that audience.

You can take it further. This would entail doing research on the target market to see what appeals to them. Use research into every aspect, like colors and color combinations and language, for example. Then you can start tailoring your landing page to meet the preferences of the target demographic.

Use surveys

One tool that many affiliate marketers fail to utilize is the ability to do surveys to learn more about their prospects. Surveys can be used to find out what their specific concerns are. This can be extremely important information, that can help you write very targeted emails. They will be amazed at how well you are communicating with them, and this will help heighten trust between you and the target market.

Chapter 13: Creating A Cohesive and Compassionate Presence

Affiliate marketing is a model that puts a single individual in the spotlight of many, and that can put a lot of pressure on you to behave in specific ways. Especially when significant events are going on in the world, you may feel confused about where to start and what you should be doing to improve the quality of your brand while also maintaining your earnings. At times, you may feel pressured to abandon your marketing and sales so that you can focus exclusively on social or global issues, especially when you are audience is particularly passionate about something. What can happen is affiliate marketers begin to feel confused and overwhelmed about how to respond, and may find themselves straying away from their integrity in favor of trying to please their audience. This can make for an incredibly weak business move, though, as it sets your brand up for failure.

One thing you must remember is that, as an affiliate marketer, you may be an individual at the face of your brand, but you are still a brand. This means that you are a company *and* an individual, not just an individual. A powerful tool you can use to maintain a cohesive and compassionate brand while continuing to earn exceptional profits is known as parasocial relationships. Whether you realize it or not, your brand is already in a parasocial relationship with every follower you have. The best thing you can do for your brand, and yourself, is to understand what a parasocial relationship is and use that to help you develop a cohesive and compassionate brand that remains profitable, even in times of adversity.

Understanding Parasocial Relationships

Parasocial relationships, when you get into them, are rather complex. Understanding parasocial relationships enough to add to the value of your brand, though, is not nearly as complex. In essence, a parasocial relationship is a relationship that naturally develops between a person in the media and their audience. You, as the person in the media, are then responsible for building a relationship with your audience.

A parasocial relationship defines the connection between a media persona and an audience by recognizing that the media persona has a relationship with their audience as a whole. In contrast, each member of their audience feels as though they have a personal relationship with that persona. Of course, the majority of your audience does not genuinely believe that you are best friends and that they could call you up out of the blue and request to hang out, but they do care about you and believe that you care about them, too. And, if you have a compassionate brand, you *do* care about them, partly because they are human, partly because they are a part of your audience, and partly because they are directly responsible for you being able to create the success you have created as a media persona.

To effectively leverage your parasocial relationship, you need to make it clear that you have compassion for your audience and care about them, their wellbeing, and their safety. While you do not have to take personal responsibility for the wellbeing and safety of your audience, it is helpful to encourage them to take personal responsibility for their welfare and safety, and for you to encourage them to be the best versions of themselves. By creating this positive association and offering this positive relationship back to your audience, you create a good give-and-take experience. Both you and your audience are giving back to each other.

It is essential to understand that the parasocial relationship is not always well-understood by your audience, though. They may believe that you are obligated to behave in specific ways, fulfill specific actions, or otherwise take on certain roles during specific worldly events to meet your obligation to them. Sometimes, they may express frustration, anger, or even hate toward you because they feel as though you are not committing to them in the same way that you ask for them to commit to you through brand loyalty. This can lead to you feeling obligated to take action or say things that are out of integrity with your brand, or that are entirely unreasonable for you to take on yourself. It is important that you first define the terms of the parasocial relationship in your mind. Then you decide how you can use your role to effect a positive impact on your audience while remaining authentic to yourself and your brand. For example, 2020 has brought a significant outcry for social justice among minority communities that are requesting equality. It may not be authentic to you or your brand for you to become an outspoken activist and attend protests in order to show your support, but that does not mean that you cannot show your support in other ways. You might educate yourself on ways to engage more compassionately with the members of your audience reflected by this minority, donate to a charity you believe in, or even bring awareness through using your voice and your platform.

Whichever method you choose, you must make sure it is in alignment with you first, and that it stands in integrity with your brand. Never allow yourself to be bullied into fulfilling imagined obligations to your audience. While it is valuable to give back to your audience, have compassion, hold them in high esteem, and help whenever you can, it is not your obligation to fulfill every request your audience has. You must hold strong, healthy boundaries so that you are able to continue focusing on developing your business without draining your own wellbeing.

The Power Of Your Voice

As an affiliate marketer, your voice is your strongest asset. It is what you are marketing, as you are asking people to listen to you, trust in you, and take action on your guidance. Your goal is to have people listen to your voice enough that when you recommend products, they go ahead and buy those products because they trust you to offer the best word-of-mouth reviews on the products they might be interested in.

The power of your voice is a double-edged sword in that it holds a lot of power, and it holds a lot of power. What I mean is, you have the power to build up your community and create a sense of compassion and connection within your community, and you have the ability to isolate members of your community or create shame and feelings of hurt within your community. Believe it or not, even if you use your voice to create hurt feelings or harm within your audience, many people will still cherish you and follow you. Some may even copy you and add to the creation of hurt feelings and harm for other members of the community. It has been seen when affiliate marketers develop a massive following and then, through their words or actions, create a sense of alienation or hurt toward a specific demographic who may or may not be a part of their audience.

While it is evident that you should never be intentionally causing shame, harm, or hurt to anyone, anywhere, regardless of whether they are a part of your audience, it is essential to note that it may not always be obvious. Often, affiliate marketers will say something without realizing how it can cause pain or troubles for anyone in their audience or in the general community. Even though it was not said with ill intentions, it can still cause those pains and troubles.

It is essential that you understand the power of your voice and that you use it to build up your community, encourage compassion and connection between members of your community, and create a safe and compassionate space for your community to exist. You should also be willing to embrace the words "I'm sorry" and accept that you might make mistakes from time to time. The best thing to do if you make a mistake is to address that mistake and educate yourself, and your followers, on why that was a poor choice for you. In doing so, you create the opportunity for your followers also to recognize the mistake and hopefully generate even more potent levels of compassion within their own lives with people they interact with daily, too.

When it comes to global issues or issues that may directly affect your industry or your brand, it is also important that you consider the power of your voice. Never speak without thinking, and always give yourself time to understand the words you are sharing thoroughly. Be clear in what you are saying, audit yourself to ensure it comes across correctly, educate yourself to ensure you have spoken in a way that is genuinely compassionate and considerate, and always deliver with intention and compassion. Through this, you develop the ability to create a more compassionate community through the power of your voice.

Compassionate Marketing

Compassionate marketing is achieved through one specific approach: inclusion. If you want to market your products in a compassionate manner, you need to be inclusive of everyone who may be a part of your audience, and even people who may not be. Your focus should always be on cultivating positive relationships between yourself, your audience, and the products you are using and the brands you are representing. Look for opportunities to include as many people as possible, build people up, and support them with feeling confident around the products you are advertising.

A great way to engage in compassionate marketing is to create campaigns that seek to answer people's questions, and that supports them with feeling confident when using new products or services. Many members of your audience are likely new to the products you are promoting or the brands you are sharing, and others may not be new but may find that they are not entirely educated on those products or services. Proactively answering questions and building up their knowledge in a way that promotes positivity and supports their desire to learn more without making them feel bad for not already knowing is a powerful way to create compassion through your marketing strategies.

If you want to take it a step further, don't just proactively answer questions but provide a side-by-side experience where you specifically show people how to get the most out of their products or services, while also educating them on those products or services. For example, if you are promoting a new kitchen device, do not just talk about the tool and show recipes you have made, invite them into your kitchen through an educational video. Bring your audience along with you by showing them how you unbox, set up, and use the tool, and by showing them all the different features. As you go, share interesting tips and guidance, educate them on the product, and let them know how they can feel more comfortable and confident with using that product. This is a great way to compassionately market to people who may be curious about the products you are marketing, but intimidated by them or worried about not knowing how to get the most out of them.

Supporting Your Audience

Supporting your audience can be done in a myriad of ways. Learning how to support your audience effectively is the ultimate form of leveraging parasocial relationships. It allows you to clearly define your role in the relationship and use it to nurture and maintain the connection between your brand and your audience. Even though you are marketing yourself as an individual, it is still essential to see the differentiation between the parasocial relationships you share with your audience, and the personal connections you share with people outside of your business.

The best way you can support your audience is through creating the illusion of face to face, which is the goal of virtually every brand there is. Every brand wants to make it feel like they are right there with you, helping you, supporting you, and engaging in the experience with you. While you may not have their presence, the presence of their products or services allows you to feel the value of that connection and feel supported. Whether you are going for a jog in your new sneakers or walking your dog around the blog with his new collar, you feel their support.

Creating the illusion of face to face can be done in five steps. Step one, speak directly to your audience. Always use terms like "you," "we," and "us." These terms create a sense of connection by making it sound like you are grouping yourself and your audience on the same level. Step two, use real stories. Your own personal stories, especially ones that may be less pretty to tell but that still fit your brand and represent you well, is a powerful approach. You can also share the real stories of your audience by talking about an experience one of your audience members shared with you, or an experience someone in your personal life had following one of your recommendations. This is a great way to move your content away from "me" to "we." Step three, mingle with your audience. Engage with them in the comments, ask them questions, encourage conversation, and be willing to meet them in person by hanging out in places they hang out. When you meet a member of your audience, don't be afraid to take pictures and upload them to your social media to spotlight your audience. This makes them feel included, cherished, and appreciated. Step four, create an idealized version of what your audience wants. While you might be appearing as an individual, your brand is empowered through the persona you develop and share. Your persona gives you a definite character to market to your audience, while allowing you to keep your personal life private. This way, you can separate your public life from your own reality in a healthy, essential way that every affiliate marketer should be taking advantage of. The persona you create should resemble something your audience wants and should play into that so that they can live vicariously through you. The more you allow your audience to live vicariously through you, the more they will pay attention. Step five, become a part of their everyday life. Create content on a day to day basis, especially content that encourages engagement, because it invites them to talk to you and check-in with you every single day. When someone feels inspired to check in with you on a daily basis, they are more likely to feel connected with you and to listen to you.

Maintaining A Consistent Approach

When it comes to branding, you must maintain a consistent approach. At first, it may seem unnatural to have to pause and audit your content before posting it, since *you* are what you are marketing. If it is something you would typically say, it may seem like a no-brainer that it is appropriate for you to post to your business page. This is not true, however.

As your affiliate marketing persona is just that, a persona, it is vital that you always stop and make sure that anything you post reflects the persona you are creating for your brand. If you do not pause, reflect, edit, and publish, you run the risk of having inconsistencies in your messaging and in your appearance, which can lead to people no longer trusting your brand. They may begin to believe that you are behaving in a fake manner, or that you are not who you say you are. This, of course, is not true. The persona you are presenting is an accurate image of who you are, except that it is a *piece* of the image of who you are. It does not represent the entirety of who you are, because you have maintained privacy in certain aspects of your personality, and your life. Which, again, is an essential part of developing an affiliate marketing business.

Before you post any content, it can be helpful to stop and define what your do's and don't's are for posting content. You should determine what your tone should sound like and what types of messages you want to send, and what your tone should not look like and what kinds of messages you do not wish to send. When you have this clearly defined, you can run every piece of content through this filter to ensure it comes across the way you want it to. This way, there is consistency across your entire brand, and people are not left wondering who the "real you" really is.

Building A Sense Of Community In Your Community

As you go about developing your affiliate marketing business, a community will inevitably develop around you. However, as the voice of the business, you get to decide what that community looks like and what you will and will not tolerate based on how you moderate your community and what you give to your community. It is important to understand that your community will copy you and will take your lead, so you set the tone for the entire community. You should be setting a tone that aligns with acceptance, compassion, respect, peace, and inclusion.

One of the most powerful ways to transform your audience into a community is to *talk to them*. The conversation is the most critical part of any community, and it allows you to truly connect with your audience and set the tone for what your community should be like. Ask questions, build your community up, empower them to feel smart, encourage their feedback, and pay attention to it, and talk *to* people, not *at* people. The more you can create this sense of equality between yourself and your audience, the more they will respect you and listen to what you have to say, while also assembling as a community around you.

Empathy is also one of the most vital energies to integrate into your community. Never speak to your audience like they are beneath you like you lack compassion for them, or like you are judging them for experiences they are having or issues they are facing. Even if your audience behaves poorly or does something that you deem unacceptable for your community, respond in a way that nurtures respect, compassion, and empathy. This is an excellent opportunity for you to lead by example and nourish this aspect of your community.

Lastly, engage in servant-based speaking. Normal speaking is very self-centered. It is focused on getting people to listen to you, having them be interested in what you are saying, laughing at your jokes, affirming your expertise, and knowing how good you are. It is primarily based on fulfilling your own ego, boosting yourself, and making yourself feel good. It has very little to do with your audience. Change that, and you will develop a community. Start asking yourself questions about how you can give them something valuable, tell them what they most need to hear, benefit their lives somehow, or feel as though they are a part of something important. When you speak from a place of wanting to serve your audience, they receive what you have to offer and return it with their loyalty and commitment to you and your brand. As a result, you end up earning far higher sales. You are already giving anyway, by providing content, reviews, honest opinions, and recommendations on what they should spend their money on. Why not take it a step farther and develop your content in a way that is meant *for them?*

Reviewing Your Vision For The Future

Now that you are clearly aware of everything it takes to become a powerful affiliate marketer and to turn your business into a massive success, it is time to revisit your vision for the future. When you first opened this book, your primary focus may have been on developing a passive income through affiliate marketing. Now, you may have a greater desire to expand that vision into something more impactful. Or, you may wish to maintain that vision but adjust how you will execute it to ensure it fully matches with what you aim to create.

I am not here to tell you what your vision should be or to encourage you to take on a grand mission just because it seems like the noble thing to do. Remember, no one can obligate you to develop a business that you truly do not want to create, not your audience, not me, not you. You have to create a vision that you truly want, that you are passionate about and that you can boldly stand behind. Now, with all of this knowledge about how to build your business, monetize it, grow your audience, develop a community, and use the power of your voice, you need to ensure your vision is still clear and aligned with the reality of what affiliate marketing truly is.

Routinely reviewing your vision and ensuring that it remains an accurate and honest image of what you want to create with your business ensures that you are always working toward something that is relevant. This way, your brand remains in integrity with who you are, you are able to show up in an authentic manner, and you are able to approach your brand from an organized, focused perspective. This clarity is invaluable when it comes to executing the day-to-day portions of your affiliate marketing business.

Chapter 14: Affiliate Marketing Trends of 2021

As we are now halfway through 2020, we have made plenty of headway into the year, and we have a clear idea of what types of trends exist in the affiliate marketing industry. If you are brand new to affiliate marketing, getting on board by starting with the latest trends is a powerful way to boost your credibility, get found a lot faster, and generate massive success in your business. If you have been engaged in affiliate marketing for some time but are looking to focus and expand your business and amplify your growth, these trends will help you with that, too.

No matter how new or advanced you are to any industry, you should always make focusing on trends essential tasks in your business activities. Trends represent what people are currently interested in and drive focus on different topics, issues, products, services, needs, or desires. Knowing what currently has people's attention means you can get on that by creating content that aligns with those trends so that you can capitalize on some of that attention. This way, your business works *with* the natural flow of your audience, rather than against it. Even if you plan on introducing something new or groundbreaking, you can follow a current marketing trend to get that new or innovative product or service to the market in a popular way. This way, people listen and care about what you are talking about, and you are far more likely to succeed.

Push Updates Are Still Useful

In 2020, push updates became the norm as affiliate marketers took advantage of this opportunity to get in front of their audience. Push notifications are activated through the browser and behave much like a text message, notifying your audience anytime there is new content on your website. It is somewhat like receiving a notification from Facebook, Instagram, Twitter, or YouTube, except it is linked directly to your website rather than a social media application. This exciting feature means that anyone who has a website has the capacity to position themselves in front of their audience in a way that garners as much respect and attention as high-level applications and websites do.

In 2021, push notifications will likely see a hit based on browser updates, and most significant platforms doing everything they can to eliminate fraudulent activity. However, they are still one of the top three most functional advertising methods when it comes to getting in front of your audience.

One thing you must be aware of is the fact that some browser changes that we should see in the next few months include browsers like Google Chrome blocking notification requests on sites where the "Block" option was chosen too many times. So, if you enable push notifications for your website and too many visitors click "Block," Google Chrome will disable your website from being able to request push notifications any further. This is being done in an effort to avoid annoying individuals who are uninterested in having push notifications, as Google and other browsers still need to maintain adequate standards to ensure their audiences are pleased with their browsing experience. Otherwise, they may begin to see a decline in their audiences, too.

An excellent way to avoid having your audience click "Block" is to refrain from enabling this feature until your audience is broad and active enough that you feel confident that they would click "Allow." As well, you may want to market the opportunity to your audience through other streams, first, to help get them on board with the idea before enabling it. If you have strong feedback, you can enable it and look forward to gaining all of the benefits of push notification features.

Run Compliant Campaigns

Every online platform that allows paid advertising has a list of standards that pages must comply with if they run paid campaigns to ensure that they are compliant with the platform. Until now, many pages have been able to get away with running non-compliant ads using loopholes, which are often referred to as "blackhat advertising." As algorithms and artificial intelligence increase in strength, running non-compliant or barely-compliant advertisements will become harder and harder. Although they may lead to higher sales for the companies that do them, they are also starting to lead to companies being completely banned from having a page or hosting advertising of any sort through that platform.

If you plan on using paid advertisements or running campaigns on online platforms in 2020 or beyond, and you should be since it massively increases your audience for much less of an investment, you need to be sure that your ads are compliant. Attempting to come back from a ban can be incredibly challenging and can ultimately destroy your business if you are not careful.

To those who are interested in attempting blackhat advertising or playing on the line of danger, it is essential to realize that while it may get you great results right now, it can lead to you destroying your business. Further, it can ruin your reputation, which means your ability to get a new business going can be much more challenging, too. Respect the platforms that are enabling you to run your online business and respect their compliance rules. There are plenty of ways that you can think and market outside of the box without sitting on the edge of non-compliancy.

If you want to generate massive success in your paid marketing strategies this year, work hard at finding new methods of advertising that have not been done yet, and that is entirely compliant. You can do this by getting creative yourself, researching what others' are doing, and paying close attention to trending advertising strategies. The first people to jump on board with the newest advertising methods will almost certainly be the most successful. If you can get yourself in that margin, you will see major growth in your business right away, and that growth will cultivate momentum that could lead to you being the next biggest affiliate marketer in the world.

Try Unusual Placements

Most advertisers, especially when they are within a similar industry, are vying for the same audience's attention. This means that platforms like Facebook, Twitter, YouTube, and Google are charging a premium to get your advertisements listed with these placements. Naturally, they are increasing their cost to capitalize on the fact that these placements have a massive demand.

As a marketer, especially if you are new to the business, this can seem daunting as it may seem like you are attempting to capitalize on an audience that you can barely afford to get in front of. Brands that are larger than you and that have more purchasing power than you do have the ability to essentially wash your ads out by buying a major share of those spaces. This makes the demand for them look even higher and effectively drives the cost up even higher, too. Ultimately this makes it even harder for you to get in there and turn any significant results for your business.

A better approach is to try unusual placements or placements that will still get you in front of your audience, but without being *so* in demand that you can barely afford to turn any results from your placements. The best way to use this approach is to pay close attention to keywords that are relevant to your audience and your business itself and to use keywords that are popular but not the most popular to place your advertisements. You can also start to market into specific geographical regions that have a high interest in what you are selling, but not the highest importance in what you are selling.

Although you may not be getting in front of the premium audience this way, you can also look forward to not paying premium prices. Further, these audiences are often still more than happy to buy what you are selling, which means that you will pay less for your results, and will see higher profits out of them.

The key to this strategic placement strategy is to ensure that you are not getting down into the bottom barrel areas of your audience. If there are too few interested in the keywords or in your industry in the area you are targeting; you will also be turning out poor results since there is simply not enough supply for your demand or demand for your supply. Look for those middle of the way ones and start there. You can always expand into the more premium locations once you have more money to place toward your advertising, allowing you to become a worthy competition to everyone else who is vying for the attention of that audience, too.

Quality Must Be Your Priority

Quality content is imperative if you are going to be successful at capturing the attention of your audience and keeping it. These days, the quality of your content is more important than ever before, because so much content is being pushed in front of your audience that they are becoming desensitized to anything that isn't spectacular.

Back in the day, the cost of getting into business was so high that very few people did it. This meant that, while there was competition, the market wasn't saturated, making it exceptionally challenging to get in front of your target audience and capture their attention. Companies could get away with low-quality images, generic wording, and fancy or bold colors as a way to capture people's attention and get them to invest in their products.

These days, its a much different world. The internet has made the cost of getting into business as cheap as $0, which means virtually anyone can do it. Further, many people *are* doing it because they, too, want the financial freedom that those who have struck it big have achieved, and everyone believes they have what it takes to make it happen. Unfortunately, this means there is a saturated market, and it is challenging for every single brand in every single industry to get ahead. At this point, it doesn't matter what industry you are in because the internet itself is loud with advertisements.

Quality, then, means that you have excellent content. Your images should be crystal clear and should feature something new and fresh while also being to-the-point, and striking an emotional nerve with your audience, in a good way. The wording you use should be authentic, thoughtful, relevant, concise, and should also strike a positive emotional nerve within your audience. It should largely focus on building a sense of unity and connecting you with your audience in a way that suggests you have become best friends in some way, shape, or form. If you are targeting new audience members, it should suggest that you *could* become best friends because the content you share is so relevant to your new audience that they feel personally connected to it right from the start.

Your entire presence should be made up of quality content. This means you need to be extremely thoughtful, concise, and careful in what you post. Whether it is on a social media channel or your self-hosted website, it must reflect quality. Further, if you do in-person engagements or meet up with fans in person in any way whatsoever, you must be ready to deliver on those same quality measures. Speak with the same authenticity, compassion, and generosity as you speak with online so that you maintain that consistent image.

You must be careful about whose advice you follow these days, too. Many affiliate marketers who started back when the internet was not quite so saturated started at a time when it was okay to have lower-quality content because there was not so much of it out there. Back then, people were excited about the internet period and did not care much about whether a blog had fuzzy pictures, typos, or lower quality written content. These affiliate marketers had a chance to learn alongside the development of the internet, which meant as they improved, the internet grew, and as the internet grew, they improved. For those of you who are starting now, you do not have that luxury. The internet has already advanced beyond "beginner/learner" stages and is now at a point where it demands high-quality everything, right from the start. It pays to invest in discovering how you can create that same great high-quality content so that you already stand out among the crowd.

I will repeat one more time: do not pay attention to what your favorite influencers did when they got started. Do not pay attention to influencers or aspiring influencers who suggest you can start with low-quality content and build up from there. Do not pay attention to these outdated rules of advertising. Look at what influencers are doing *now* and get started with the highest quality content you possibly can then improve from there. Look to create fresh, out of the box, unusual content with those high standards, and you will have everything you need to stand apart from the crowd and get noticed.

Whitehat SEO Matters

Blackhat and whitehat are two different strategies that online marketers use to get discovered. Blackhat marketers ride on the fringe, trying to find the loopholes in marketing so they can use those to maximize their results while also minimizing their investments. Until now, they have been wildly successful at running almost non-compliant or totally non-compliant campaigns and running almost non-compliant or non-compliant SEO strategies and other organic marketing strategies. These efforts lead to them being able to explode their businesses, so long as they remained uncaught and were able to hide their tactics. Those who failed had their businesses banned or were blacklisted and essentially lost their ability to make funds through their businesses. In worst-case scenarios, IP addresses were completely banned, meaning they could not even try to create a new account and start over because they were playing in the gray or black areas of marketing too much.

Whitehat marketing strategies, on the other hand, are 100% compliant. While they generally take longer to turn results, the results are sustainable, and they do not risk your business being run into the ground by bans and blacklisted websites. Further, they do not require you to use tacky or strange tactics, which means your website generally runs smoother and looks cleaner to your audience. The end result is far more sustainable and successful.

In 2020, whitehat SEO, in particular, has become the mandatory marketing strategy for anyone leveraging SEO. Which, by the way, if you are running an affiliate marketing business and hosting a blog, or even posting on an SEO driven platform like a social media platform, you should be using these strategies.

Whitehat SEO is achieved by offering high-quality content and services that are relevant to what people are looking for so that your content is likely to be looked for in the first place. You should also make sure your website's loading times are as fast as possible and that your website is optimized for mobile devices, which are where most people are tuning in from these days. Descriptive, keyword-rich meta tags and sites that are easy to navigate are also relevant, as they assist you with generating success with your business.

Never purchase links that reflect a popular search term to get attention, use deceptive cloaking techniques, or stuff keywords into a blog post, or into a website in general, in an effort to get your rankings higher. Search engines are becoming more intuitive than ever before, and as they spot these behaviors, they will rule you out and block you from being able to run your business any more. In some cases, you might even find yourself facing legal challenges, which means not only do you lose your income stream, but you are also faced with hefty fines.

Market For Transparent Brands

As an affiliate marketer, your money comes from marketing other brand's products and services. Your audience grows to rely on you to market products and services relevant to them, and as the game grows, what is considered relevant to them is changing. At one time, consumers were happy enough with a product that fulfilled a need they had. For example, if you were going to get into affiliate marketing to advertise makeup for beauty brands, you could get away with marketing any makeup product that seemed exciting or that would serve your niche audience. Way back in the day, you could market *any* makeup or beauty product, without even considering a specific niche audience, because of how new the audience was.

From 2020 onwards it will not work like that

Consumers want to shop through brands that are transparent, honest, that have clean and ethical products and production methods, and that are giving back to the world in one way or another. They want to know that the brands they are supporting are doing their part to make the world a better place. Brands can do this by contributing to more ethical and sustainable resources for their product development. They also will use some of their profits to give back to something relevant to their audience and their industry.

As an affiliate marketer, you are seen as an ally of your audience. Through the parasocial relationship you share, they see you as one of their friends, and so they hold you to the same standards they keep the people in their lives to. They want to see you marketing *only* for brands that are transparent, honest, ethical, sustainable, and that is giving back in some way. When they see you care about what they care about, their loyalty toward you increases even more because they realize that you share the same mission and same passion, and they see you working toward something that they deem positive. If they see you continuing to support dishonest or shady companies, they will assume that you are guilty by association. This will destroy the bond you have between your audience and yourself.

As an affiliate marketer, you have to be especially cautious about who you make deals with. You must do your research, find brands that are ethical and honest, and work with those transparent brands *only*. There is no room for you to work with a shady brand, as even one business dealing with a dishonest company can destroy your reputation or leave skepticism in the hearts of your followers.

The best way to ensure that the brands you work with are transparent and ethical is to have a system. Anytime a brand approaches you, you should be prepared to ask essential questions that validate whether or not they are transparent, honest, and ethical. If you contact a brand, you should also ask questions to ensure that there are no discrepancies between what you have researched and what they say.

After a brand approaches you, or before you approach a brand to propose a deal, ensure that you research that brand thoroughly. Look into how their business works, research their sustainability efforts and see how they give back to their communities and if those means of giving back overlap with the interests of your audience. Do not just rely on company websites for this information, but dig deeper than that and look for reviews or information being shared from third-party individuals. Of course, make sure you do your research on the sources, too, to ensure that you are relying on trustworthy sources for your information.

Once you have agreed to a deal with a transparent brand, make sure you make that a part of your marketing strategy. Discuss with your audience the fact that you like this company because they are open, honest, ethical, sustainable, and because they give back. Be sure to highlight that the reason why you care about this brand is the same reason why your audience would care about this brand, so they see you have that in common. This will lead to them feeling even more connected with you, which will lead to them trusting you and taking your guidance more frequently. As a result, you will get way more sales through your brand, and you will be able to land higher quality dealings with brands so you can sell better products and earn higher commissions.

Get On Facebook And Instagram

If you are not already on Facebook or Instagram, I'm not sure what business you are in, but you are probably not in affiliate marketing. You are certainly not on your way to becoming an influencer. In 2020, Facebook and Instagram are non-negotiable platforms. You *must* be on these platforms if you are going to remain relevant for your audience. Any brand not on these platforms will *immediately* be deemed a sketchy brand and will be ignored by anyone who may have otherwise considered doing business with you.

However, just because Facebook and Instagram are mandatory does not mean the rules are the same as they once were. These days, Facebook is more of a "proof" platform than anything else. Facebook now has a user base, which consists of 41% of individuals being over the age of 65, and that is not a popular age group for people who are engaged in affiliate marketing. However, that does not mean you can ignore this platform. 59% of people are under 65, which means a fair number of people will still be in your age range. Even with that to consider, Facebook is *still* not the same as it once was. Your Facebook platform matters, but it matters most for the widespread of social proof. Individuals will look you up to see if you are on Facebook, and they will follow you if they find you, but they are unlikely to interact with you as much on Facebook as they will on Instagram. That is because most younger users are on Instagram instead. Still, users must see you on Facebook as this proves that you are a legitimate and large-hitting brand, which means they are going to be more likely to trust you. The more significant platforms you show up on, the more people will trust you.

In order to leverage Facebook for that trust connection, it is important that you do not neglect it entirely. You cannot have a baren page, as this is also going to breed skepticism in your audience. Instead, you need to post frequently enough to get traction on your page. You will likely even run some campaigns, especially to reach your target audience, to get their attention on your page. However, your focus should not be to *keep* them on your page. It should be to get them over to a more active, younger platform, like Instagram.

Instagram is where the bulk of your action should be, especially as an influencer. Instagram offers an excellent visual-based platform that is beginning to nurture interaction and connection more than ever before, meaning it is an excellent platform for influencers. You can showcase products, share short videos of these products in use, and even upload longer videos to IGTV. You can also create other non-sales based content that adds value to your audience's life, such as by teaching them to use common tools or products or teaching them about techniques or concepts relevant to your industry. This content grows your audience by drawing attention to your brand and keeping you in their frame of concentration for longer.

On Instagram, you should be showing up every day. Pay close attention to stories, too, as the power of stories is still growing, and recent research shows that they are growing in their ability to generate loyalty and sales for brands. Consumers love a behind-the-scenes glimpse into their favorite brands, especially influencers, who are developing a parasocial relationship with their audience, and stories are the best way to do it.

Focus Largely On Single-Conversions

Not that long ago, sales funnels that were developed by generating escalating sales from your audience were all the rage. Having your audience first buy an "entry" product that was less than $15, then moving them up to a bigger product that was less than $50, then slowly gliding them up this escalation process until they reached your "target product" was a big hit. Beyond that, sales funnels included lengthy processes that ran audience members through free offers, videos, or long-form text webpages with tons of content to be watched or read and other lengthy steps that had to complete before they got to the offer. Webinars, free consults, and other such things were also famous for a while. When these worked, the idea was that you were providing plenty of free content while building rapport with your audience and earning their trust so that once you pitched an offer, they would buy it.

These days, audiences are bored with this approach. They are sick of spending hours upon hours watching content only to get to the sales page and realize the product is not that good, is out of their price range, or is somehow entirely irrelevant to what they wanted. Not to mention, then they end up getting tons of pressure from the brand to buy that product or buy their other products, depending on how far they made it through the funnel. It's an incredibly stressful sales system that does not work anymore.

Instead, you need to create a sales funnel that is as close to single-conversion as possible. The best way to do all of that is to host your content on social media and your website. Use places like Facebook, Instagram, or Pinterest, as well as your website or email list as an opportunity to provide free value, and to make your sales. When you do make sales, do not push people through a sales funnel. Instead, make your pitch right there and offer a sales link. Assuming you did everything right, the free value and day to day content you provided should have provided the opportunity for your audience to trust you and purchase from you. If not, they will continue to consume that content until they do, and then they will buy.

Currently, your audience appreciates your direct approach and will avoid being hassled into any lengthy sales process. Short of you trying to sell an incredibly high ticket item, they do not want to be bombarded with all the little bits of information you have to offer. Instead, they want to be given the specific details and then left to make up their own mind. If you provide enough generosity, value, and service on your platforms, they will virtually always make up their mind in your favor.

Chapter 15: The 2021 Affiliate Marketing Forecast

Now that we are halfway through 2020, it is easy to track what trends are likely to carry into 2021. While we cannot guarantee which new trends will arise, we are starting to see that many directions that laid their roots within the past few years are beginning to reach maturity, which is an exciting thing for marketers. This means that as you begin marketing your business, you will start finding many excellent new marketing opportunities that arise in 2021.

Affiliate Marketing Has Not Reached Its Peak Yet

One trend that marketers often watch for is the overall direction of a marketing opportunity. Their primary goal is to determine when and where that marketing opportunity peaks so that they can ditch that effort and move to the latest trending strategy. This is precisely why you see blog posts that say things like "____ marketing strategy is dead!" every year. Marketers attempt to predict the end of specific eras, while also using shocking titles to capture an audience.

Despite what rumors may speculate, affiliate marketing is far from dead. We have not seen it reach its peak yet, and we will likely not see it reach it's peak in 2021, either. Affiliate marketing is an excellent business strategy for anyone who wants to go into business for themselves. It is also a unique marketing strategy for anyone who runs a business and needs to invest in advertising.

If you are new to affiliate marketing, it is not too late for you to get involved. The key is to set yourself apart from everyone else so that you are able to make as much money as possible through your affiliate marketing venture.

Quality Marketers Will Earn, Low-Quality Will Not

One thing you do have to be aware of is the quality of your content. As affiliate marketing rages on, affiliate marketers are becoming a dime a dozen. It is not enough to start a brand with the bare basics, put yourself out there in a generic way, and expect to get results. Generic affiliate marketers are paid a generic value, and that's not much. If you want to earn the big bucks, you need to make incredible, high-quality content that has the earning potential.

As an affiliate marketer, you need to understand that what brands are paying you for is your marketing power. This means your number one focus should be about developing influence over people so you can influence them to purchase from the brands you choose to work with. You need to know how to create the best quality content, how to position your brand, so they see you as being high quality, and how to value your brand enough to turn down low-quality offers and deals, while also not producing low-quality content. Every single thing you put out should be of high quality, and you should always be researching how to do even better. No exceptions.

Your Website Strategy Needs To Change

Your website is still an essential element of your affiliate marketing business, but how it is used has drastically changed from previous years. In the past, all of your social media content was made solely for the purpose of driving people to your website. While web traffic still matters, and you still need to have your own website to run a successful affiliate marketing business, the way your website fits into your strategy is all different.

These days, your content should be equally divided between social media and your website. On social media, you should provide excellent, full content while offering the opportunity for people to read the rest of your content on your website. However, they should also feel as though they received something completely from your social media, too. This way, when they turn to your blog, its because they want more of what they already received.

A great example would be if you were a health and wellness blogger, and you wanted to market for a new fitness program you were doing. If your topic for posting was five workouts you could do from home, you would post those five workouts in list form on social media. Then, you would drive people to your website for descriptions or, better yet, videos about how the workouts work. This way, people feel like they received something completely from the social media post, but they also have the incentive to go to your blog post.

Push Traffic Will Change In Nature

Push traffic or traffic is driven from push notifications that are hosted directly through a web browser, and that point directly to your website, are still popular and will remain so in 2021. However, the nature of them will change as the outlook for push notifications changes in most browsers, too. You should be ready to embrace this change by continually looking out for updates in the primary browsers, including Google Chrome and Safari. The more informed you are, the easier it will be for you to generate a strategy that allows you to continue using push notifications in spite of any changes that will be made. And yes, changes are expected to be made by the end of 2020, and again in 2021.

New Affiliate Programs And Agencies Will Come Out

As an affiliate marketer, you are looking at ways you can develop an affiliate marketing business so you can make money advertising for other brands. Because there are so many people just like you that are eager to get into this line of business, and because brands have witnessed the immense power that affiliate marketers have when it comes to advertising, you can expect to see some impressive growth. In 2021, new affiliate programs with major companies, as well as new agencies to connect affiliate marketers and brands, are expected to come out. As you grow your business, it is important that you keep your eyes peeled to see what becomes available and that you constantly screen all new sources to see if there is a revenue potential for your own business.

Beware that just like there are low-quality affiliate marketers, there are also low-quality programs and agencies. Be ready to thoroughly research each one, and never take a deal or sign a contract without knowing exactly what you are getting into. Especially if you open an account with an agency or a program, be sure to read the fine print and never sign into something you don't agree with. Treat your contracts and agreements with great concern and consideration, as you are running a business, and you need to make smart business moves, not just jump on every opportunity you see. Not all will be great opportunities, but many will be. Pick wisely.

Conclusion

Thank you for taking the time to read *Affiliate Marketing*!

We sincerely hope this book has been inspiring and informative!

Affiliate marketing is an unprecedented opportunity. With the growth of social media platforms like Facebook, Instagram, Twitter, and others, there are more opportunities than ever to generate income using affiliate marketing. The opportunities are out there for anyone who is willing to put the upfront work in and build their business. You can do affiliate marketing for practically any niche, and the income opportunities are only limited by you, your passion, and your desires! Make sure you hop on those 2021 trends as soon as possible, so you can get an edge in on your strategy and smash all of your goals for 2020 and 2021!

We want to end this book where we started – we encourage you to take action. Far too many people in the affiliate marketing community fail simply because they did not take the steps outlined in this book. Take action, and you will find success.

We hope that you have found this book informative, educational, and, most of all inspirational!

Digital Marketing for Beginners 2021

Exceed 2020 Generating Passive Income with The Ultimate and Most Effective New Social Media Strategy, Using the New Proven Tips for Business and Personal branding.

Cristopher Clarke & Adam Preace

Introduction

Congratulations, and welcome to *Digital Marketing for Beginners 2021!*

It is safe to say that technology has rapidly evolved over the past decade. In fact, technology has rapidly evolved over the past *year*. Keeping up with the ever-evolving face of technology seems hard enough as it is, but what about when the entire world is changing just as rapidly as technology is? Over the past decade, the changes in digital marketing have always been made easier by one simple thing: the consistency in our audiences. So what happens when our audiences begin to rapidly evolve?

Emerging global crises has lead to many things changing rapidly. More things have gone digital, so there is a sudden influx of business that was once conducted in person now being conducted online. While everyone rushes to find more digitized solutions, our audiences are rapidly changing as they are faced with the growing challenges of having their needs and desires questioned, and their futures tossed up in a mess of fear and uncertainty. The result? Digital marketers have to figure out how to adapt to evolving technologies and evolving consumers, at the same time, so they can cultivate a brand that remains relevant and profitable through 2020 and beyond.

If you are brand new to your business, getting on board with digital marketing may seem hectic at this time. Even those who have been at it for a while are feeling overwhelmed and concerned by the changes they're seeing. Rest assured; there are plenty of excellent strategies you can implement that will allow you to master digital marketing so that you can conquer incredible profits throughout 2021, regardless of your experience with digital marketing or your time spent in business.

Firstly, you must recognize that the core of digital marketing has not changed. You are still using digital platforms to create campaigns that are intended to drive traffic to your brand and, ultimately, convert that traffic into paying customers. The steps you take to achieve this, on a technical and practical level, are still the same. The interfaces that digital marketers were using one year ago are still active and relevant today, and you must master those marketing interfaces if you are going to develop a successful marketing strategy.

The part that has changed is how those campaigns should be structured, and what sort of interaction they are looking for from your audience. Right now, your audience is looking for a sense of security, certainty, comfort, and something that seems familiar to the life they just had tugged out from under them in a matter of months. Your goal, as a brand, is to strengthen your community by adding to it and creating a sense of safety and belonging for your audience so that they feel drawn to your business. This way, they are more likely to seek you out and successfully flow through your marketing conversions.

Achieving the synchronicity between core digital marketing strategies and your evolving audience will allow you to create a strong marketing strategy that explodes your brand and maximizes your conversion ratios. It is important, however, that you do this from an authentic and servant-based place. In *Digital Marketing for Beginners 2021,* we are going to cover all of this in great detail using an effective step-by-step approach so that you know exactly what you need to be doing to maximize your profits in 2021.

As long as you follow the step-by-step procedure outlined in this book, you will feel confident in your ability to get in front of your audience and capture their attention, regardless of how noisy the world may be right now. Through that connection, you will plant the seeds for growth.

If you are brand new to business, as in you have not started any aspect of developing your business yet, I strongly advise you focus on developing your plan *first* and then focusing on digital marketing *second*. Digital marketing is a powerhouse for growth, but it will have zero effect if you do not have a clear business that is already developed and ready to be launched. You should know exactly what your business model is, what your income streams will be, and how you plan to grow that business before you start worrying about marketing.

Concise understanding around what you are launching will allow you to know exactly how to design, target, promote, and manage your digital marketing strategies. As soon as you have that plan in place, you can take advantage of digital marketing as your strategy for getting that plan in front of a paying audience so that you can turn it into a wildly successful venture.

If you are ready to get started with digital marketing, let's begin!

Chapter 1: What Is Digital Marketing?

In a very basic sense, digital marketing is any form of marketing that takes place online. If you are marketing on the internet in any way, shape, or form, then you are engaging in digital marketing practice. There are ten recognized forms of digital marketing: search engine optimization (SEO) content marketing, social media marketing, pay per click (PPC) marketing, affiliate marketing, native advertising, marketing automation, email marketing, online PR, and inbound marketing. We are going to touch on each of these marketing styles in this very book!

Before we dig into how you can start digital marketing, we should first cover the basics of understanding where digital marketing comes from, what it takes to get started, and who is most likely to earn the best income from digital marketing. Having a strong understanding of all of this information will help you determine if digital marketing is right for you. It will also start to give you an understanding of what strategies qualify as high quality modern digital marketing, and what strategies are outdated at this point in the digital marketing era.

How Did Digital Marketing Begin?

The first time the phrase "digital marketing" was used was back in 1990 when the first-ever search engine called

"Archie" was launched. At the time, developers proposed the possibility for people to one day use the internet for marketing their businesses by having their businesses show up on relevant search lists that would be displayed by Archie.

In 1993, developers created the first ever clickable ad banner, just like the ones you see on the internet today. These ad banners were displayed at the tops of websites just like they are today and were now able to be clicked so that people could instantly arrive on the website of the company selling said products. Just one year later, the first ever internet transaction was made in 1994 using an application that was known as "Newmarket." Two years later, more search engines were introduced, including Yahoo!, LookSmart, HotBot, and Alexa. Later, in 1997, the first-ever social media site known as "SixDegrees.com" was launched. Finally, in 1998, the infamous "Google" was launched.

Following the introduction of all of these websites, platforms like LinkedIn, WordPress, MySpace, Gmail, Facebook, YouTube, Twitter, and MSN were launched. Developers also began identifying new digital marketing strategies like split testing, which is used to help companies launch two separate campaigns at the same time to identify what reaches their target audience most effectively.

What Does Digital Marketing Require?

Digital marketing is one of the easiest marketing strategies to get involved in, primarily because it is inexpensive to start and because the information is available for virtually anyone to access. In other words, as long as you can read and apply the information that you are learning about, you can take advantage of digital marketing to earn an income in your business, or to develop a business to earn an income from in the first place.

Unlike traditional advertising, which could cost upwards of $250+ to start, digital marketing can cost as little as $100 or less to get started, and it can earn you a decent income in relatively minimal timing. That is why there are so many success stories out there of people replacing their traditional income and even replacing their traditional income ten times over in a matter of a few months to a year. The big key is using your startup budget effectively and set up the right tools so that you have something in place to make money from in the first place. That is exactly what you are going to discover right here in this very book, meaning that as long as you apply these techniques, have some time on your hand, and have a few bucks to start up, you have everything that you need!

Who Can Use Digital Marketing?

Digital marketing can be used by anyone, regardless of where you come from, how much money you have, or whether or not you already have a business in place to sell goods from. As long as you are willing to learn how to make it work and identify a product or service to sell, if you do not already have one, you can take advantage of digital marketing and make it work for you. In this day and age, there are plenty of alternatives to launching your own business or finding your own products or services to sell, which means that digital marketing is more accessible and successful than ever before. As long as you are able to connect with the right companies, you will have everything that you need to make an income with digital marketing.

How Will I Make Money with Digital Marketing?

When it comes to digital marketing, there are two key ways to make money: through selling your own products or services, or through selling someone else's. Below, we will discuss how each of these strategies can earn you an income with digital marketing.

If you want to sell products or services of your own, you are going to need to identify what you want to sell in order to earn an income. If you have a company in place with products or services already, then this is likely not something that you need to consider or worry about. If, however, you are just starting out with building a company that you are going to be selling from, you are going to need to identify something for you to sell. Online, virtually everything sells well as long as you are able to identify and market to your target audience. This means that you can find virtually any product, whether it is physical or digital, or any service and create a market for it. If you want to have greater ease with selling your products or services, it is ideal to do some basic research to identify what types of products or services are selling best at that time. Following the trends and offering trending products or services is the best opportunity that you have to easily access a buying market and offload your products or services quickly so that you can earn an income.

When it comes to offering your own products or services, you should know that this is a less passive form of digital marketing income than the alternative. This way, you may need to be involved in directly shipping or supplying the products, or fulfilling the service requests, which can take quite a bit of time. Of course, if you have the income, you can always hire someone else to do this part for you or outsource it to another company, but it will require more effort on your part.

The alternative is to market for someone else. This is often done either through affiliate marketing or dropship marketing, where someone else's company is responsible for receiving and fulfilling orders, and all you have to do is market for them so that they receive these orders. This way, you are paid a commission per each customer that you send through to make a purchase, which earns you an income. For people who want to create a truly passive income and who do not have the time, funds, or desire to hire anyone else to fulfill these services for them, affiliate marketing or dropship marketing is often the best way to go. Both of these marketing styles will be done with the same digital marketing tools, and both have the capacity to earn you an income. You will have to determine which one suits your needs best based on how much income you stand to earn, and how much time, effort, and resources it will take on your behalf.

Chapter 2: Identifying Income Channels

If you already have a company in place, then you already know your income channels: they are the products and services that you are already offering your customers. If, however, you do not already have a company in place, you are going to need to identify what your income channels are going to be so that you can discover where you are earning money from with your digital marketing business.

As you know, you can earn money by offering your own products or services, or by marketing for someone else. In this chapter, we are going to discuss four income channels you can explore, as well as what the pros and cons of each channel are so that you can identify exactly the income channel you want to use for your business. This way, you know exactly what you need to be marketing so that you can earn an income with digital marketing.

Selling Products

Designing a digital marketing business selling products tends to be the most labor-intensive digital marketing strategy because, on top of digital marketing efforts, you also need to consider the efforts it will take to manage your inventory. You will need to find a supplier for your products, purchase and receive your products, store your products, and handle and ship your products when they have been purchased. This can take quite a bit of effort on your behalf, so it may be a less passive income source than other digital marketing strategies.

One way that you can make your product-based retail business less labor-intensive is by outsourcing much of the work. For example, if you create a business through Amazon FBA, Amazon will manage everything to do with your inventory, aside from buying and shipping the products to the Amazon warehouse. All you will have to do is identify the products you want to sell, purchase them from a supplier and have them shipped to an Amazon warehouse, and then their employees will take care of the rest. In the meantime, you can use marketing efforts to increase your sales and offload your products quicker. Services like this, however, will cost more to be involved with since you are outsourcing a lot of your businesses work, so unless you want to include the added steps and costs, this may not be the best route.

If you do decide that this is the route for you, however, you can always go ahead and begin identifying products for you to sell online. This way, when you are digital marketing, you know that your focus will be on selling your products, and you can focus all of your efforts on getting people to purchase your businesses products. For some people, this rather traditional approach to retail and advertising is the easiest to comprehend and, therefore, makes the most sense for them to get involved in.

An alternative to this rather traditional form of marketing is to create digital products instead. Digital products include anything from downloadable eBooks to applications or even printable sheets for various purposes ranging from coloring to managing inventory in one's business. You can even make logos, digital graphics, or downloadable patterns, tutorials, or courses for helping people to learn a new skill. There are countless forms of digital products that you can create that can then be sold through digital marketing. If you choose to sell digital products, this becomes a lot easier as you will not have stock to manage in your business. Instead, you simply set up the digital product on a website like Etsy or Shopify and when people purchase if they receive an automatic download file while you receive payment. This can be an excellent way to design a retail shop and earn money from digital marketing, especially because once the products are created, they never need to be remade or reordered again.

Selling Services

Selling services can be another labor-intensive selling style with digital marketing, so understand that if you choose this route, you may not get the time freedom that you desire from your digital marketing business. If you are selling services, you are going to need to prepare to have time to actually fulfill those services after they have been purchased so that people are getting what they paid for. The alternative to fulfilling these services yourself is to hire people who can fulfill them for you, in which case you become somewhat of an agent who recruits people and then finds them work.

Using this income channel with digital marketing, especially if you become an agent, can be a great way to earn an income. There are many different types of services that can be sold online, ranging from consulting services to teaching people a new skill or offering the final product of a valuable skill like writing services or video editing services. As long as you have these skills or abilities yourself, or know of people who do, you can earn a fairly consistent income online through this strategy.

Affiliate Marketing

The most passive form of digital marketing is affiliate marketing. This particular marketing style also has the fewest number of steps to fulfill for you to be able to generate an income from it, as you are simply marketing products for another company.

In order to become an affiliate marketer, you will likely need to have some form of audience and engagement already cultivated online. This way, you can show companies that you are going to be successful in marketing their products because you already have people to market toward, which means you are going to be more likely to receive sales through your digital marketing efforts. For companies who are offering affiliate marketing deals, this is the best opportunity that you have to get in front of them and get a deal with them, allowing you to earn commissions from the sales that you earn for that company.

If you do not already have a healthy audience online, you can still get involved with affiliate marketing, but you will need to choose a different avenue. A common route for people who do not already have a strong online audience is to join an affiliate marketing company that they can earn money from. Affiliate marketing companies, also known as network marketing companies, offer people the opportunity to buy in and then begin marketing for that company. Choosing this method does have its pros and cons, as it can be incredibly lucrative and often comes with a much better compensation plan than standard affiliate marketing agreements. Typically, with a network marketing company, you are paid more if you perform better, so you can earn higher levels of compensation at higher levels within the company. However, it does generally restrict you in terms of what you can market for, as network marketing companies generally don't like it when you market for other companies at the same time.

One of the nicest things about affiliate marketing is that you can get involved with a company and then set up an automated marketing system so that you do not have to do much on a day to day basis to market their products. This way, the automated services run in the background and earn you money without you even having to be directly involved. This specific marketing strategy has earned many people thousands of dollars in passive income every single month, making it a wonderful strategy to use if you are willing to put in the work to set it up and make it successful.

Dropship Marketing

The final income channel you can consider online is dropship marketing. Dropship marketing is similar to affiliate marketing in that you are going to market products for another company, and they are going to oversee everything relating to stocking and fulfilling shipments relating to those products. However, it is completely different in how the business is set up. Unlike affiliate marketing, where you just use and endorse the product, dropshipping generally requires you to set up a business, brand, and a website where you can sell products from. Then, you will upload someone else's products to your website for sale so that people can land on your website and shop the products that you are marketing. When they do, you will get paid a commission, and then the drop shipping company will fulfill the orders of the people who have purchased through your website.

This strategy does require more effort and more funds to get started with than affiliate marketing, but it is also easier to do than selling products or services because you do not have to oversee inventory management and order fulfillment. You will, however, need to get a proper website set up and put effort into establishing and promoting business and brand to people so that they can purchase from you. Once you do establish, however, you can stand to make quite a bit of money as people who are purchasing will be more likely to purchase more products at once, meaning that you can earn a higher commission per sale than you might through affiliate marketing.

Choosing the Right Income Channel for You

Deciding what income channel you want to use is really going to depend on how much effort you want to put into earning sales and making money through digital marketing. Remember that all of the aforementioned income channels will require digital marketing efforts on top of any additional efforts that said the channel would require in order to be fulfilled. For example, selling products will require you to put effort into digital marketing as well as effort into identifying, sourcing, managing, and fulfilling inventory requests.

The best way to decide what strategy is going to be the most effective for you is to determine how much money, time, and effort you want to put into your digital marketing strategy. If you want to be as minimally involved as possible and do not want to invest too much money into your startup, choosing affiliate marketing or network marketing is likely the best income channel for you. If you are interested in putting in more effort, money, and time into your business, you might choose something more intensive, like selling products or services.

After you have identified the best income channel for you, you need to begin educating yourself on how that particular channel works and who you can work with to set it up for you. So, if you choose to be an affiliate marketer, you need to start growing your audience and finding companies that you want to market for so that you have companies that you can earn an income with. Or, if you want to sell products, you need to start researching what products you want to sell and then identifying sources for where you can purchase those products from and places that you can sell those products on. You want to make sure that you identify every person or company that will be involved in making your chosen income channel work so that you have the right people and resources to get started, as well as the right information around what it will take to do so.

Chapter 3: Tapping into a Global Audience

Once you have identified what income channel you are going to be using, you also want to identify who your audience is going to be and how you are going to tap into them. The nice thing about digital marketing is that you are going to be marketing to an entire global audience, meaning that you can customize your audience in a very specific way, ensuring that you reach exactly the right people for your income channel.

Why You Need a Clearly Defined Audience

Online, billions of people are engaging with various online platforms every single day. Ranging from social media platforms to search engine platforms, there is a massive number of people engaging with the internet on a day to day basis. For this reason, you need to have a clearly defined audience that outlines who you are talking to, and why. If you do not take the time to define your audience online clearly, you are going to have a hard time marketing to anyone because the global market that you are tapping into is simply way too large. Unless you have multiple millions of dollars to invest in marketing, you are not going to be able to tap into a large and undefined audience reasonably.

Clearly defining your audience ensures that you do not waste any of your time, or your budget, on marketing toward people who are not likely to purchase from you. This way, you are spending your time and money on the people who *are* likely to purchase from you, making each click you get on your advertisements more valuable. Think of it this way: if you spend $100 on an advertisement and 1,000 people click it, but only 3 people buy that may not be a valuable advertisement for you since you are not earning much of a return on it. If, however, if you spend $100 on an advertisement and only 500 people click it but 8 people buy from you, you have made a much better earning from that advertisement. This way, you have invested your digital marketing budget in a way that is earning you a better income, making it more worthy of your time and effort. You can make that happen by targeting a very specific audience and spending your entire marketing budget on that audience.

How to Identify Your Custom Audience

Identifying your target audience requires some logic and some research. You will identify your custom audience by first picking the broad audience that you are marketing toward, and then refining that audience so that you have a specific niche that you are catering to.

First and foremost, you want to start identifying your audience by using the logical part of your identification practice. Start by considering what income channel you are using, and who is logically going to be the most likely person to purchase from you. For example, if you chose the income channel of network marketing for a health and wellness company that targets female wellness, logically, your target audience would be women who are interested in personal wellness. This is a broad audience that clearly identifies who you are marketing toward and what your marketing efforts need to look like. This is also a fairly obvious direction to go with your marketing, so there is no need to research whether or not this part of your audience is actually going to purchase from you or not.

The next part of identifying your custom audience is narrowing your audience down to find which niche is going to be most likely to purchase from you. At this point, you want to consider two things: who you are going to be most interested in marketing to, and who is going to be most likely to purchase from you. You need to know who you are going to have the most fun marketing to, because this is going to help you determine who you will have the most knowledge about marketing toward. Generally, the markets you find interesting are also the ones that you understand more intricately, meaning that you will have a clearer understanding of what they need in order to purchase something. In other words, you will know what wording, colors, and placements to use to have success in marketing to them. Ideally, you should identify 3-5 niche markets in your industry that you would have the most fun marketing to. For example, if you were doing the female wellness network marketing company, you might consider targeting working moms, women who live a luxurious lifestyle, women who have a demanding and time consuming career, women who like working out with friends, and women who like attending yoga classes. These types of niches give you the opportunity to clearly identify who you are talking to, and how you can reach them.

Once you have identified 3-5 niche audiences that you could market to, you want to begin researching these audiences so that you can verify that they are going to be profitable audiences. You should pay attention to how large that audience is, how active that audience is, and how likely that audience is to purchase products like the ones that you have available. You also need to determine how easy it would be to market to that audience in terms of how easy it would be to come up with content or sales strategies that would reach and impress that audience enough to encourage them to purchase from you. Ultimately, you want to choose your exact custom audience based on who will be the most likely to purchase from you so that your time, energy, and resources are well invested. This way, not only will you have fun marketing to this audience, but you will also receive great returns on the time that you have invested in marketing to this audience.

Discovering Where Your Audience Is

With your custom target audience fresh in mind, you can begin to discover where your audience is hanging out online so that you can effectively market to them. This means that you need to identify what social media platforms they are using, what e-commerce platforms they spend time on, and where else they are spending time online such as on blogs or forums. Accessing this information is going to ensure that you know exactly where you need to place your digital marketing strategies in order to be seen by the audience that is going to purchase from you.

Because the global audience is so massive and there are countless niches available for people to market in, we cannot reasonably give you every single piece of information regarding the audience that you have chosen for your digital marketing efforts. However, we can give you some basic information about where people are spending most of their time online so that you can get a head start. Then, all you need to do is begin researching your specific audience so that you can really get clear on where they are spending their time.

At this time, consumers are spending their time in three primary areas online: social media and communications platforms, mobile games, and entertainment apps. If you want to get in front of your audience, you are going to need to look in these three areas to see where they are spending most of their time. Pay attention to which specific platforms or apps they are using and downloading so that when you target them, you are placing your ads not only in the right categories but also in the exact places where your audience is likely to see them.

Avoid placing advertisements on apps related to news or website-specific apps, as they are actually decreasing in popularity due to the rising number of "fake news" and click-bait type posts being made by many news and gossip platforms. Placing advertisements on platforms like this will likely result in you not being seen because you are going to be advertising in areas where not as many people are spending their time. Remember, just because 1,000 people see it does not mean that 1,000 people are buying it. You want to be accessing the right audiences where you are going to get more purchases per view, meaning that your budget is being well spent.

Once you know where your audience is spending most of their time, do what you can to test these markets. Do not be afraid to use split testing, or even to spend a small amount of time engaging on your own to see just how engaged these particular audiences are. The more that you can feel confident that you're chosen market is going to be present and visiting your advertisement, the easier it will be to create the right advertisements that are going to earn you sales in your digital marketing business.

Chapter 4: Interacting with Your Audience

Getting into digital marketing is not just about locating your audience but also about interacting with them. Regardless of what income channel you have chosen, there is going to be some level of trust and credibility required in order for people to actually purchase anything that you are marketing. The rapid growth of e-commerce sales and success in recent years has also lead to the rise of many scammers and low-quality companies wasting people's time and money, which means that your target audience already has built-in skepticism. They are not going to buy a product because they saw an advertisement for it, they are going to buy a product because they saw an advertisement from it *through a company or individual whom they trust.*

Fortunately, you do not have to know your audience face-to-face in order to cultivate trust with them, nor do you have to spend many years building up trust with them in order to really generate a large number of sales in your business. All you need to do is prove from Day 1 that you are not selling a scam or low-quality products in exchange for a quick buck so that people trust when they buy from you. This means that if you can establish yourself as being relatable, you can earn your first few sales, which will earn you positive reviews and a positive reputation. From there, you can build on these positive reviews, and the momentum will carry you forward into quick success with your digital marketing business.

In this chapter, we are going to discuss how you can establish this trust and credibility early on so that you can begin building momentum and earning a massive income through digital marketing in minimal timing. Understand that early on, it may take more time, effort, and investment to establish credibility and trust with your audience. However, once you have all you need to do is maintain that credibility and trust, meaning that your own efforts in your marketing strategies will be minimized. This way, you can really begin engaging in digital marketing as a passive income opportunity.

Hanging Out with Your Audience Online

When it comes to establishing credibility and trust with your audience, the first thing you need to do is start hanging out with them online. This is a basic, and perhaps rather an obvious strategy that is going to help you get in front of your audience and begin establishing recognition and a reputation for yourself and your company. Think of it this way: if it was your first day at a new job and you walked into the office and talked to no one, how would people respond? They would probably be curious about you, but concerned about why you were not making an effort to engage with anyone or build any relationships with the people around you. After a few hours, they may grow skeptical about who you are and begin to make up stories in their minds about how you are not trustworthy because you are not making an effort to establish a connection with anyone around you. Others might not even know you were there because you never identified yourself and began connecting with anyone.

If, however, you walked in and immediately introduced yourself and began behaving in a friendly manner, people would recognize that you were nice and would begin to trust in you. Over time, that trust would grow as you continued to establish yourself and prove that you were a trustworthy, hardworking, and relatable employee.

The same goes for establishing your presence online. If you show up and cultivate a presence but never actually use that presence to leverage connections with anyone online, you are going to find yourself being ignored or even judged as an untrustworthy person online. People might begin to believe that you are not safe for them to do business with because they cannot reasonably determine whether or not you are trustworthy or credible, and so they will skip over you and go somewhere else to shop.

You need to get online and actually hang out with your audience in the same areas that they are hanging out. You need to be posting, sharing, and updating your content so that they can see you and get to know you, while also developing a sense of a relationship with you. This way, they know you exist, they can see what you are all about, and they experience positive and memorable first impressions with you and your business. Then, all you have to do is continue to create that relationship so that it grows and your business grows, too. Believe it or not: this does not have to be an incredibly labor-intensive practice, either, as long as it is done right.

Creating a Relationship with Your Audience

The first step to really creating a relationship with your audience is to engage with your audience so that you are not playing the role of the quiet new employee. Engaging with your audience gives them the opportunity to recognize that you even exist, and helps them begin to have a reason to engage back with you. When it comes to marketing, you always have to be the first person to establish a connection with your audience. Otherwise, no one is going to connect with you. Remember, there are thousands of people trying to reach your audience too, no matter how niche you are, so you need to be the one going out of your way to make positive and lasting connections with your own audience.

You can engage with your audience easily by having a social media presence or by establishing yourself on an entertainment platform such as YouTube. This way, your audience has the opportunity not only to discover that you exist but also to see your personality and actually engage with you in a way that contains personalized connection. This is truly one of the key elements in establishing a relationship with your audience so that you can continue to have success in marketing to them.
If you look at any other successful and established a brand, you will discover that they have become masters at creating strong relationships with their audience. They

are constantly sharing updates that make their customers feel like they are a part of the "behind the scenes experience," asking questions and creating content that encourages conversation, or engagement, to happen. The more that you can create and post content like this on your platforms, the more success you are going to have in growing your business and building relationships with people online.

The process of creating and sharing content is one of the more time-consuming steps in digital marketing, but it also is a step that is going to offer the highest payoff. Without creating these relationships, it is going to be hard for you to establish yourself and encourage people to purchase from you and your business. Building momentum will be slow, which means that you may never reach the level of success that you desire to reach in your business.

To date, digital marketing has revolved largely around automated marketing. Companies use post schedulers to schedule content for their platforms and use bots to engage with their audience by posting pre-created comments or sending automated messages to new followers or subscribers on their platforms. Automation is still incredibly powerful, and it is necessary if you are going to create a passive income using digital marketing. That being said, going into 2021, you are going to need to adjust how you approach automation to avoid causing your audience to think that you are just another generic, bot-using, spam company selling a low-quality product. Yes, this is a very real reputation that many companies earn by using automation ineffectively, and you are at risk of receiving that reputation if you are not careful in how you automate your business.

Going into 2021, the key to automating your business is to make sure that everything you create is still personable and impressionable. Do not create posts just to create them and schedule them, as this is going to dilute the quality of your posts and, therefore, dilute your reputation in your business. Instead, you need to write content that is meaningful, purposeful, and effective in serving that particular purpose. For example, if you are writing content for the upcoming week, think about what is going to be relevant to your company and what is going to be relevant to your audience. Then, you need to write posts that fill the bridge between what you want to say and what your audience wants to hear.

For example, say you are having a sale on one of your new products in the coming week, and you want to tell your audience about it. For you, you would want to talk about how great the deal is and how much money your audience would be saving because for you, the entire sale is exclusively about earning more money in your business. For your audience, however, the sale is more about getting a great deal on something they want or need in their lives. For that reason, you need to focus on talking about the value of what you are offering and add the sale in as being an excellent way to get their hands on it faster and cheaper. This way, you are marketing for your business in a way that says what your audience actually wants to hear. In other words, you are marketing for your audience, rather than for yourself and your business, which is exactly what it takes to earn more sales online.

In fact, that is exactly what it takes to earn more in your *relationships* online. You need to center your entire approach on serving your audience with what they want and need to hear, but without making it sound like you are just saying these things to make a sale. By now, people have already heard every line out of the book, and for most people, the marketing messages they are reading sound more like a generic pickup line than a strong and authentic marketing message. Understand that people don't mind being marketed to, they just don't like to receive *generic* marketing materials because this is what leads them to believe that your business lacks any personality, authenticity, or uniqueness. Going into 2021, people are more committed than ever to buying products that have a deeper meaning than just serving some form of want or need in their lives. They want to buy products that are serving *them* while also investing in companies that are serving *real* people who own them. They don't want to be investing in some generic company that comes across as being just another soulless corporation. They want to be investing in a person who is passionate about what they are doing and what they are sharing with other people.

Of course, this does not mean that you need to spend every minute of your day engaged deep in passion and obsessing over the products or services that you are offering to other people. However, when you do create and upload content, send out marketing materials, or engage with your audience, it should be clear that you care and that you are a real person. This way, they have someone specifically that they can connect with and establish a relationship with, helping them to have a deeper sense of trust and respect for you and your business.

With this in mind, whenever you automate anything in your business, always write every piece of content with the intention of establishing a real and meaningful connection with your audience, even if it is not *you* responsible for hitting "post" every single day. People can still sense that it is truly you writing your content, or someone who cares, and not just a generic post copied from a marketing blog that the company leverages for money. This way, when people read your content, they connect with it and take time out of their day to engage with it and develop a deeper connection with your company. Then, all you have to do is take a few minutes out of your day or an hour or two out of your week to engage back with everyone who has been engaging with you so that you can establish the two-way connection with your audience. This way, your relationships online will flourish, even if you do not have multiple hours per week to invest in them.

Building Trust and Credibility

As you build your relationships with your audience, you need to use every opportunity that you have to build trust and credibility with your audience. A large part of what is going to establish trust and credibility with your audience is word of mouth, so you are going to need to get people to purchase from or through you and leave positive feedback in order for people to really begin trusting in you. However, you can encourage and grow that trust through how you behave, as well, allowing you to really build on that momentum and grow even further in your business.

The primary keys for establishing trust and credibility between your audience and your brand are the same ones that are going to help you build trust and credibility with other people in your life. These things include honesty, transparency, consistency, devotion, kindness, and considerateness. If you can leverage all of these characteristics in your brand and showcase them in your marketing efforts, you are going to have great success in growing your digital marketing business and earning money online.

Honesty and transparency go hand-in-hand with digital advertising, and they come through how you share with your audience. Businesses that are thought to be honest and transparent are ones who are clear about where their products come from, what values they represent, and what they are offering to their audience. They also tend to showcase the people behind the brand so that their audience can see exactly who is responsible for the company they are shopping with, giving them the opportunity to feel clearer on who they are buying from. You can be honest by letting your customers know why you are selling in the first place, by being honest about where you source your products from, and by being honest about what keeps you committed to offering high-quality service. If you make a mistake or do something wrong in your company in any way, you should also be honest about that as this ensures that your customers know that you are not trying to hide anything. For example, if someone leaves a comment about a negative experience they had on one of your posts, rather than denying responsibility or passing the blame, you should be honest about why that person may have had a negative experience and how you can help them. This way, the customer who had the negative experience feels as though you are being honest and taking responsibility, anyone who reads it feels that you are being honest and taking responsibility, and you are transparent in the experience, too.

Establishing consistency comes from keeping the same image, the same values, and the same approach in your business no matter how long you have been in business for. Consistency shows people that you mean what you say and that you are committed to offering exactly what you said you were going to offer from day one. It also helps establish a clear and consistent reputation for your company, making it easier for people to trust you. This way, people do not begin to question who you are and what you are offering because they see you offering the same things in the same way time and time again. When you are consistent, it also shows that your company is constantly being showcased with the same level of high-quality service and attention to detail that your audience has come to know and expect.

Part of being consistent is being devoted, and showing your devotion to your business, and your audience is also an important part of building trust and credibility with your business in digital marketing. Your audience wants to see that you are devoted to more than just your bottom line by having you show that you care about things like the quality of the products you are marketing and the quality of your customer's experience with your business. If you are not devoted to these things, your customers will believe that the only thing you care about is making a sale, which could translate to you not being overly concerned with the quality of products or services coming along with that sale. In fact, they may even fear that you are willing to cut corners on quality and service in order to earn more money, which is something that no one wants to do business with. Proving your devotion through your content and through how you handle every single customer experience or customer concern establishes credibility and trust within your business, helping you to earn a better relationship with your audience and greater profits.

Although this comes without saying, being kind and considerate in terms of how you market and share with your audience is important. To put it simply: no one wants to do business with a company that is rude, inconsiderate, or impolite. Not only does this mean they are going to have an unpleasant experience with your business, but it could also mean that they are going to experience low-quality products and services. Being kind and considerate in your marketing and in any engagements that you share with your audience will help everyone have a more positive experience. It will also help spread the word about the fact that you are a positive company to do business with, meaning that people will be more likely to do business with you in the first place.

If you are planning on becoming an influencer in 2021, you might be wondering just how you can apply these techniques to your own digital marketing business so that you can earn sales in 2021, too. The key here is simple: you need to make sure that you yourself foster as much of this as you can, and that every business you are affiliated with represents these qualities, too. Showing your audience that every product you recommend comes from a high-quality company and features high-quality manufacturing proves that you are not just going to promote any product that will earn you money. This way, you can establish your own reputation as being the kind of person who promotes products that are actually *good*. As a result, people are going to start trusting in you and seeing you as being a credible resource for helping them to find out what they should buy and who they should buy it from. One of the best benefits of being an influencer this way is that if you only choose to work with highly rated companies, you do not have to work as hard to justify that they are highly rated companies. While you will certainly want to point this out in your marketing content, people will be able to research the companies for themselves and all of the positive reviews they find online will prove that the company is high quality. As a result, they will be far more likely to trust you and invest in the products that you are endorsing.

Gaining and Maintaining Positive Momentum

As you begin to establish momentum by cultivating relationships with your audience and building on your trustworthiness and credibility, you are going to want to keep it going. One of the best tools that you can take advantage of in your digital marketing business is the power of momentum, which is why you need to be willing to stay on top of this momentum to keep your business growing.

Keeping your momentum going is actually easier than establishing it, as all you need to do is continue to create the same level of high-quality content for your audience that you have all along. The key here is remaining consistent and making sure that you are offering the same reputation and image that got you the momentum that you began to build in the first place. If you begin to skimp on your consistency or adapt your image to your growing success in a way that does not seem congruent with the reputation you have already begun to build, you might find yourself losing momentum just as rapidly.

In 2021, the easiest way for you to establish and maintain momentum is to create your business in a way that is sustainable long term. For example, say you are going to establish yourself as an influencer and use digital marketing to earn money by promoting other company's products. In order to successfully do so, you are going to want to start by uploading content and talking about products as often as you plan to in the future. In other words, begin your business by committing in the same way that you anticipate that you will be committing to your business in the future when you achieve the level of success that you desire to achieve. This way, you do not appear to have a sudden change in your approach or reputation the moment you have success in your business, which can lead to suspicious followers and a possible wrench thrown in your reputation, and in your momentum.

Creating your momentum really comes with maintaining your consistency by continually focusing on the same core values, the same purpose behind your work, and the same personality that you launched your business with. In other words, you want to keep doing what you have been doing that launched your success in the first place so that you can continue to be successful.

That being said, every business needs to adapt as they grow, so you are going to want to leave room for change and evolution. As you make a change in your business, make sure that you are doing it in a way that continues to remain consistent with the image and personality that you have built for your business in the first place. This way, people see your changes as being a positive new way for you to serve them, rather than being something that is done with the only purpose of earning more money. Remember, the more that you can make your marketing and business about your client, especially going forward into 2021, the more success you are going to have with your business. This type of approach sets you apart from every other business that is saying "look at me!" because instead, you are saying, "look at you! Here's how I can help you!" This simple switch is mandatory if you are going to stand apart from other businesses in 2021 and really cultivate a deep and meaningful relationship with your audience which, as you know, will ultimately determine the quality of your profits going forward.

Chapter 5: Digital Marketing Delivery Channels

Digital marketing can be done in several ways. However, there are 10 primary ways that people engage in digital marketing in the modern era. Some of these ways have been around for more than two decades now, whereas others are just starting to become more popular in recent years. Regardless of how long they have been around for, virtually every method is receiving a new approach as business owners continue to turn the attention onto their audience instead of themselves. If you want to have success in your business in 2021, the key is to avoid attempting to reinvent the wheel, but instead, spin it at a different angle to achieve your success. In other words, use what is tried and true but build it with the approach of being of service to your audience, rather than being of service to yourself.

In this chapter, we are going to briefly discuss the 10 most popular delivery channels for digital marketing going into 2021, and how you can put a modern spin on these delivery channels. This way, you are using tried and true marketing methods in a way that will serve your business better using the newer, more modern perspective of marketing. If you begin to apply these techniques right away even in 2020, you will find that you are ahead of the curve and that you are able to stand apart from the rest of businesses rapidly, giving you a greater competitive advantage for the 2021 marketing year.

Search Engine Optimization (SEO)

When search engines were invented all the way back in 1990, they needed to have an algorithm that would help them retrieve the proper sites or information for people who were using them. This way, if you searched "cat" you actually received information about cats, and not something random like information about animals in general, or catalytic converters. Without these algorithms, the search results on search engine platforms would likely be low quality, and people would be less likely to use them.

For years now, people have been using SEO to their advantage by seeking to understand how the algorithm for a search engine works and then inputting certain pieces of information into their websites and platforms to improve their search results. This way, they could ensure that they were more likely to show up on the first page, or even as the first search result than anyone else. As a result, they were also more likely to receive the traffic from that particular search, improving their own business results, and helping them generate success through digital marketing.

These days, SEO is certainly not a new term or concept, and it has been described in virtually every digital marketing book out there. However, as algorithms continue to evolve to accommodate growing numbers of searches and search results, the methods required to achieve effective SEO ratings are evolving, too. Going into 2021, you are going to need to improve your organic rankings if you are going to be discovered on search engines like Google, YouTube, Yahoo!, or Bing.

Content Marketing

Content marketing refers to any form of marketing that comes from creating and uploading content to communication or social media platforms. Status updates, blog posts, forum shares, and even link and photo or video sharing on various platforms all count as a variety of content marketing. As you may have gathered from what we talked about in Chapter 4, content marketing is one of the primary methods for establishing a presence and creating a connection and relationship with your audience. Virtually every business that is going to succeed in 2021 is going to need to be using content marketing in one way or another, as we have watched this marketing strategy steadily grow in importance over the past few years.

Creating content to share for your audience can seem intimidating, but as you will learn about in chapter 6, the content that you need to create is actually not too complex, nor time-consuming. You will quickly discover that the key is to produce consistently high-quality content that can be shared on a regular basis, allowing you to get discovered by and connect with your audience. Rather than the "feed the machine" mentality that took shape over the past five or so years where businesses and digital marketers were being instructed to post 3-5 times on each platform every single day, we now realize that this is not necessary. While you do need to have a rather high amount of content being output, there is no need to produce so much content, especially if you do not have that much to say. Instead, producing incredibly high content a few times per week is plenty, which we will discuss more in the next chapter.

Social Media Marketing

Social media marketing and content marketing are closely connected, but understand that social media marketing does have its own purpose aside from content marketing, just like content marketing has its own purpose aside from social media marketing. If you want to establish any level of presence in 2021, you are going to need to be leveraging social media in one way or another. As we have seen in previous years, people turn to social media to learn about the businesses they are considering buying from, and if you do not have a well-established presence there, you are not going to succeed in earning many sales. Social media offers you the benefit of word of mouth, as well as perceived value and credibility, plus it gives you a clear place to establish your presence and leave an impression on a possible customer.

Creating a social media marketing strategy that is passive is not as hard as it may seem, especially because we are moving into an era where the quality of content is far more important than the quantity of the content. This means that rather than trying to upload 3-5 times per day or upload enough content for 3-5 posts per day into an automated poster, you can cut back and produce higher quality content and share it less frequently. The key to really leveraging social media, as you will learn, is to have a strong well-developed profile that immediately showcases who you are and what you have to offer. In the online world, people have a very short attention span, and if you do not capture their interest and set yourself apart from the rest of the world in a matter of seconds, you are unlikely to earn a follower or a sale.

Pay Per Click (PPC)

Pay per click (PPC) advertising is a form of advertising where you produce an advertisement and then pay a larger company like Amazon or Google to display your ad in the ad space that they own around the internet. These types of advertisements, as you may expect from the name, are charged per click, which means that if no one clicks on your advertisement, you are not going to be charged. Similar to native advertising. However, they do come alongside a budget, which means that you determine how much you want to spend, and then launch your ad. The ad will then run until you have received enough clicks to have spent your entire budget.

PPC advertising is an incredibly popular form of advertising that, at one time, was able to exclusively earn thousands of people a high income. In fact, it still has a powerful capacity to help you earn a higher income through digital marketing because the companies that you are advertising through typically have a well-known reputation, which immediately gives you credibility. For example, say you choose to run an Amazon store, and you use Amazon FBA, you could run an advertisement through Amazon, which would then carry the reputation and credibility of Amazon itself. In this way, you do not have to establish credibility for yourself as Amazon has already done that for you, allowing you to put a little less effort into proving yourself. When it comes to marketing, this can have a huge impact and can help you earn an incredible amount of money, especially if you have the right budget and the right demographic being targeted by your advertisements.

Affiliate Marketing

Affiliate marketing was explained in chapter 2 as an income channel, but it also identifies as a specific form of digital marketing. Affiliate marketing is arguably the most "pure" form of digital marketing in that it leverages the power of digital marketing without individuals ever having to touch a product or launch a business. If you become an affiliate marketer, all you are doing is identifying high-quality products and marketing them to your audience. Plenty of affiliate marketers maximize their income by using various other channels of digital marketing ranging from social media marketing and content marketing to PPC and SEO. For many, affiliate marketing is the core structure of their digital advertising business, or it is an added method they use to improve their sales and earn a higher income.

The alternative to becoming an affiliate marketer is recruiting affiliates for your business. If you chose the income channel of selling products or services, recruiting affiliates could help you advertise your products to a broader audience that is already proven, allowing you to save some funds on your advertising fees. For example, if you want to market a new product, putting it in the hands of 3 well-known influencers who are known to produce high sales results can be more effective than spending the equivalent of those products' value on advertising. This is even truer if you are a younger company or one that does not yet have a high level of recognition, as this bypasses the fact that you have yet to build a strong level of trust and credibility within your market.

Native Advertising

Native advertising is similar to PPC, except that instead of being displayed around the internet, it is displayed exclusively on specific platforms. For example, if you run a Facebook page and you launch a Facebook-based advertisement that shows up on people's newsfeeds, you are running a native advertisement on Facebook. Native advertisements are different from PPC advertisements in a sense that they are only displayed within the newsfeed of the social site you chose to advertise on, meaning that it shows up in line with organic posts. For many, this improves results because people see it as being just another post, rather than an actual advertisement displayed in traditional ad space, such as on the side of the screen.

One of the greatest benefits of native advertising is that if you already have an established audience and demographics on your social media sites, you can use these as the audiences that you are going to advertise to. Since they have already begun to pay attention to and engage with your business, these are also people who are far more likely to actually spend money on your business. Advertising to these individuals can pay off big time in the long run, making native advertising one of the most popular paid advertisement strategies of 2021.

Marketing Automation

We have discussed marketing automation a few times in this book, but it is worth pointing out that this strategy is a form of marketing all on its own. People who choose to use marketing automation are engaging in a strategy that enables them to run their businesses in minimal timing, allowing them the maximum amount of time freedom. This is because all of their posts, emails, and advertisements have all been scheduled in advance, meaning they just need to check in from time to time to make sure that everything is running as planned.

Marketing automation is an incredibly powerful tool that can help you really turn your digital marketing business into a passive income stream, so long as you are using it properly. If you want to use this method, you should seek to automate no more than 1-2 weeks in advance, especially going into 2021, as this will allow you to ensure that everything you are posting is relevant and recent. Attempting to automate too far in advance can lead to you talking about things that are completely irrelevant at any period in your business, which can kill your momentum and really make your business suffer?

Another tip with marketing automation is ensuring that you still put the level of consideration and authenticity into each post that you would if you were posting it spontaneously. A big mistake that people have made in the years of 2018-2020 is that they have attempted to create more content in a single day than they can reasonably create, resulting in the content coming out as low quality. For example, in an effort to reduce the amount of time they spend online they may attempt to write all of their posts in just one day, resulting in the quality being lower because at some point they become uninspired, and so they dilute the quality of their content. Furthermore, they have no idea what will be going on in their lives or businesses at that point, making it harder for them to really create posts in advance that still capture attention and share in an authentic manner effectively. Again, choose quality over quantity every single time, and you will already be well ahead of the crowds in 2021.

Email Marketing

Email marketing continues to be a popular marketing resource for people, although it is becoming increasingly apparent that this marketing style is optional. In the past, if you did not have an email list, you were irrelevant and probably not running a successful business. These days, people can successfully run a business without an email list and often do. That being said, an email list is still crucial, as it provides you with a level of security that no other marketing strategy can provide you with.

If you want to be successful with email marketing in 2021, the key is to use this strategy *sparingly*. Many people are receiving 1+ email per day from a single company, causing them to ignore most email marketing campaigns. If you attempt to market through email too consistently, recent studies show that you may actually train your audience to delete your emails rather than look at them because they are tired of having them show up. The simple fact is: virtually no one in your audience wants to hear from you in their email inbox every day. Some don't even want to hear from you more than once a week. Keeping your email newsletters more modest ensures that when your emails show up, people get curious about what you have shared and so they actually open them.

Many businesses aren't even doing that, though.

Many businesses are building email lists and emailing their list just 1-2 times per month, or even less. The reason why they are even bothering to build their lists in the first place is simple: it offers security. In the summer of 2019, we have already seen Facebook and Instagram crash twice, with pictures, status updates, comments, and messenger features not working or only working here and there for many users. While these crashes only lasted one day, they proved to be extremely detrimental to business owners. Think about it: if Facebook or Instagram were to go down for a week, could you make any money? Probably not, because you would not have a way to reach your audience *unless* you had invested time in building an email list. An email list cannot be taken away from you, nor can it "crash." So, if your primary platforms go down, having that email list you built will still give you an opportunity to connect with your audience. Even if you do not plan on emailing your audience frequently, build a list. You will be grateful that you did.

Online PR

PR means that you are gaining coverage on your business from other people. For example, if you launch your business, and a popular blog writes about it, you are gaining PR. Online PR is an important opportunity for you to market your business and establish credibility and authority, while also reaching the eyes of new possible consumers. You want to take advantage of this marketing style so that you can increase your reach and become more recognizable to the people in your audience.

Hiring affiliates to help you market your business is one great way to market using online PR, but there are other strategies, too. One way is to reach out to reporters and journalists and let them know about your business as a way to encourage them to do an interview with your company. However, remember that many other people are doing this too, so you need to do it in the right way if you are going to spark their interest, receive an interview, and maintain the credibility while also boosting the reputation of your company. Attempting to contact them in a pushy or impolite manner can result in you being seen as unprofessional or rude, which can possibly tarnish your business. Remember: they have a large pull in the community!

Other ways that you can engage in online PR include engaging with reviews of your company and engaging with comments made on your website. You can also personally comment or respond back to any comments or emails that come into your business, allowing you to establish yourself and add a personal touch. Any way that you can personally engage with your audience, especially if it is going to be spotlighted in some way for others' to see, is a great opportunity for you to take advantage of online PR.

Inbound Marketing

Inbound marketing is more frequently known as "attraction marketing" in the modern era, and it is an incredibly powerful marketing strategy that you can use to help you get more people coming to you for the products or services that you offer. The biggest benefit of attraction marketing is that you are not pushing customers to buy from you; you are encouraging them to come to the decision of buying from you on their own. In other words, you are attracting them to your business without having to use any form of "used car salesman" tactics.

Inbound marketing is actually a strategy that uses a series of tools to encourage people to do business with you.

When you are using this strategy, rather than asking for the sale, you are offering multiple opportunities for the customer to ask you for the sale. For example, using a blog to build interest in your business, creating videos that show off how awesome your products or services are, and using email as a point of contact rather than a constant source of marketing with newsletters are all ways to use inbound marketing. As long as you use tools like this, you will be sure to spark an interest in your audience and encourage them to want to buy from you, rather than pushing for them to buy from you. The difference is that your sales are a lot easier to make, and your reputation improves tenfold because you are seen as someone that people want to buy from, rather than someone that people feel pressured to buy from. In 2021, this particular marketing strategy is expected to grow even more popular than it already has in recent years, so expect to take advantage of it in your own marketing strategy if you actually want to succeed!

Chapter 6: Using Social Media for Marketing

Social media marketing is possibly one of the most well-known forms of digital marketing in recent years. It may also be one of the most powerful strategies to add to your digital marketing efforts, depending on how strong your plan is and how well you execute it. Regardless of what form of company you are running for your digital marketing platform, social media is a tool that you need to be using if you are going to generate any level of success going forward into 2021. In this chapter, we are going to discuss why social media marketing is an essential tool in 2021 and how you can leverage it, as well as how it can be combined with other marketing tools to create a complete digital marketing strategy.

Why Social Media Marketing Works

You may have noticed that we have been stressing one of the most important elements of digital marketing in 2021: *personal connection.* These days, people are tired of service that is automated to the point that it is no longer personal or customizable. They want to receive service that is personal, suited to exactly their needs, and capable of helping them to feel like they are part of something bigger, and something more important. They want to see the "face" behind the business that they are dealing with, and they want to feel like they have some form of connection with the person they are doing business with. That is unless, of course, you have billions of dollars to pour into advertising and state of the art automation services like Amazon, Walmart, or other mega giants do for their online services.

As a beginner, however, you are going to need to create a face for your company that people can identify, get to know, and feel comfortable doing business with. This is where social media comes into play. Social media is a tool that was designed to help people keep in touch. Originally, it was a great opportunity for family members and long lost friends to reconnect and keep up with each other's lives through social sharing. However, it has become an incredibly powerful marketing tool that people can take advantage of, too, especially in that it lets smaller businesses create a name, profile, and personality for themselves online.

When you incorporate social media into your digital marketing strategy, you give yourself the opportunity to create business pages for your company, which allow you to share updates with your audience. In a sense, you give yourself the opportunity to really engage with your audience in a way that feels like you are friends, rather than in a way that feels like you are just another business trying to earn their money. For this reason, social media is one of the most powerful tools for building and maintaining relationships with your followers and customers.

Beyond helping you create a presence that establishes a social connection with your followers, social media has become one of the most popular places for consumers to find new businesses to shop through. These days, platforms like Facebook, Instagram, Twitter, YouTube, Pinterest, and even LinkedIn are all platforms where people are searching for new businesses to shop through. Getting on these platforms and establishing a presence for yourself means that when people begin to look for someone to shop through on these social sharing sites, they come across your profile. If you did not have a profile, they would be less likely to find you.

The reason why social media platforms are becoming a more and more popular platform for people to search for new businesses is that social media sites also come with word of mouth built right in. When a consumer lands on a new profile, they can see just by scrolling whether or not the company is relevant, as well as the quality of services that they offer. Companies that have great engagement with their followers and who seem to have positive relationships with their customers are ones that people will automatically begin to trust, regardless of whether or not they have heard of the company before. Just having a strong social media presence can set the tone for inbound marketing to take place which, as you will learn about, is one great strategy for really leveraging social media marketing.

Who Should Be Using Social Media Marketing

Given the popularity and power of social media marketing, everyone who intends to make any level of money online should be engaging with this marketing strategy. If you want to earn money online, creating a social media presence to make money is a great opportunity. Even if you plan on doing most of your marketing through paid advertisements, establishing a presence and putting up a few organic (non-paid) posts to nurture that presence is a great opportunity to build your business. For most platforms, if you do not have an account, you cannot engage in native marketing, which is one of the most powerful paid marketing strategies that digital marketers can use going into 2021. So, in short, if you are running a business online or plan on making any level of money online, you need to establish some form of presence on social media to help leverage you into higher levels of success with your business.

Creating Your Social Media Presence

The first step in generating a social media marketing strategy is to create your social media presence. For many people, creating a basic presence is all that they will ever need to do, and they use this to leverage their growth elsewhere on the internet. In essence, the social media presence is exclusively designed to help identify new target clients and lead them elsewhere so that they can engage with the business either in person or on their website. For others, their social media presence is their primary source for finding new clients, as well as nurturing those relationships and creating sales. Which method you choose will depend on where your primary sales are being made, and how. If your primary strategy is going to be selling products online on a platform like Amazon, Etsy, Shopify, or Big Cartel, you might favor paid advertisements over organic marketing, and so your presence may be more basic. If, however, your primary strategy is going to be affiliate marketing or running your own business on your own website, you are likely going to need a stronger social media presence to help funnel more people through your sales process.

Creating any level of presence on social media all works in the same way; the only difference is how much you will be posting on your platform. If you only need a basic presence, a few posts per month will be plenty to help you succeed with your business strategy on social media. If you need a bigger presence, you are going to want to post a few times per week, or even a couple times per day, depending on what type of presence you need to establish for success in your digital marketing strategy.

You can start creating your presence by identifying what platforms your audience hangs out on the most and then create a profile on these platforms. When you are creating your profiles, make sure that you are creating them for your business and not for yourself. This means that you need to use your business name, a username that is relevant to your business, and images that are all relevant to your business so that it represents your brand rather than yourself. If you are your brand, pick certain aspects of yourself to highlight on your feed and leave the rest behind. For example, if you are going to become a fashion influencer and leverage digital marketing to earn an income, center your profile around fashion and your passion for design, and leave your love for mechanics out of it. This way, you are creating a profile that is relevant to what your audience wants to be seeing. Later on, when you are more established, it may make sense to begin incorporating smaller amounts of other areas of your life into your presence if you are an influencer, as this gives you a more personal "real" element to you. By sharing small segments of other parts of your life, you show that you are a dynamic person who is interested in many things, not just the one that you market for, which can actually improve your relationship with your followers by increasing your relatability. If you are a specific brand and not an influencer, though, always keep your posting entirely focused on exactly what your brand represents, and nothing more.

These days, there are countless blogs, articles, and books out there telling you about how you can design a branded profile for your social media platforms. That being said, many of them still have a cold, corporate marketing strategy involved that results in you creating a presence that is very isolated from your audience. If you follow many of the strategies that worked in recent years, you may end up building a profile that has an invisible "wall" between you and your audience, making it more challenging for them to connect and resonate with you. You need to make sure that you are cultivating your presence in a way that is open and encourages engagement right from the start so that people feel comfortable connecting with you and doing business with you.

The best way to create this personalized, friendly experience through your platforms is to look at every single element as an opportunity to create a *personal* connection with your audience. Whenever you can, use images that involve faces and language that connects you with your audience. For example, instead of saying, "I am an artist looking to share my art," you could say, "I am an artist looking to share my passions with you." This form of connection-based language helps people instantly feel that the ice has been broken the minute they land on your profile, making it easier for them to engage with the content that you have made available for them to see. When you create this type of personal connection through your language and images, people instantly feel like they are your friend and are more likely to trust in you and all that you have to share with them.

When you first create your presence on social media, in addition to creating a profile, you should also upload at least 3-6 posts right away, or within the first hour or two of creating your profile. This way, whenever someone finds your page, they instantly find some content for them to look at as well, making your profile more worthy of staying on for a while than a bare page. This will also help your early page visitors decide if they want to follow you or not, which will begin to build the momentum of new followers finding and engaging with your page online.

Engaging with Your Audience on Social Media

After you have established your basic presence, you need to start determining how you are going to engage with your audience on social media. This is where you can switch between being someone with a basic presence or someone with a more advanced and engaging presence. The way that you engage with your audience will be the same either way; the only difference will be the frequency of posts you are sharing on that platform. Even if you have a basic presence, you are still going to need to upload at least a couple times per month so that new visitors know that you are still active and not an abandoned profile of a business that may no longer be operating.

When you are engaging with your social media audience, there are three things you need to do: create content, engage with people who engage with your content, and engage with other people's content. All three of these strategies are going to help you grow your presence on social media and build your engagement up more so that you are able to have more loyal followers and more consistent sales through your digital marketing business.

Creating content for your social media will largely be done using content marketing strategies, which we will talk more about in chapter 7. For social media, creating content is going to be the primary foundation of how you connect with other people, so learning how to create proper content for each platform and audience is crucial. Content is what people are going to see and engage with on your profile, and it will give you the opportunity to keep your audience up to date on what you are doing in your business.

Engaging with the people who engage in your posts is important. Especially as a newer business with lower levels of engagement, engaging back with your followers is your opportunity to essentially "reward" their engagement and encourage even more. People like to engage with people who engage back, so the more that you engage with your audience, the more they are going to engage with you, too. They will come to recognize that you are going to engage back and so they will leave their opinions on your posts more regularly, offering you the opportunity to continue engaging back. Not only will this nurture that particular relationship with your business, but it will also show other followers that you engage back and boost your posts through the algorithm of the platform you are sharing on. As your profile grows more popular, it may not be reasonable to try and keep up with every single comment that is made on your posts, so at least taking the time to acknowledge several and comment back to as many as seems reasonable for your help. This way, people see that you are still engaging and that you are still friendly, despite the fact that your profile has grown so massively.

It is also important to go to other people's posts and engage. Especially as a small business, getting your business name out there by engaging with other people's content is going to help you grow faster. You can do this by finding your audience online and then engaging with their content by liking it and, better yet, commenting on it so that they see your profile pop up on their notifications and posts. This way, they may click through and come check out your profile, possibly earning you a new follower for you to engage with on your profile.

Another way that you can engage with other people as you grow your platform is by sharing other people's content. User-generated content, as it is called in digital marketing, is content that other people generate that pertains to your business in one way or another. For example, if someone Tweets about your business or shares a picture of them using your products, this is called "user-generated content." You can then share their images to your own profile and credit them for taking those images, while also sharing a word or two thanking them or acknowledging them for the picture they took. This is a great opportunity for you to acknowledge people who are sharing pictures or updates about your business, while also creating more credibility and awareness for your own profile.

Combining Social Media Marketing and Other Marketing Strategies

Social media marketing can be combined with many other digital marketing strategies. As you have noticed, social media marketing and content marketing tend to go hand-in-hand to help people generate an organic outreach that supports their clients in finding them and engaging with them. Other styles of marketing that combine well with social media marketing include native advertising, affiliate marketing, online PR, automated marketing, and inbound marketing. You can use all of these strategies together with social media marketing to create a well-rounded digital marketing strategy that funnels more sales into your business, allowing you to generate a greater amount of profit from your social media presence.

Which combinations you will use with social media depend on what type of business you are running online? If you are an influencer, for example, you might seek to combine all of these marketing strategies in one way or another to create a complete marketing strategy for your business. If you are a retail store, you might combine social media marketing with native advertising, online PR, and inbound marketing to help you generate more sales in your business. Identify what channels are going to be most effective for you and seek to structure them into a sales funnel, using social media as your primary platform for bringing new followers into your business. These followers can then become leads, and eventually, customers in your business. In other words, social media should always be seen as your first line of contact when reaching new possible clients for your business, no matter what type of digital marketing strategy you plan on using.

Chapter 7: Creating Organic Content

Content marketing has become a more popular topic in recent years, and for good reason. Through content marketing, you have a much greater capacity to create meaningful and memorable relationships with your audience, improving your odds of growing your business through digital marketing. If you are on social media, using a blog, or taking advantage of email marketing, you are going to want to know how to use content marketing effectively to help you succeed. In fact, more recently, content marketing has even been combined with targeted paid advertisements to create an even more powerful impact through these paid pieces of content. Knowing how to create content properly in a way that is going to reach your audience is powerful, and it can be the difference between success and failure in your business.

In this chapter, we are going to explore what organic content is, why it is important, who should be using it, and how you can put it to work in your own business. Understand that virtually every business, no matter what the industry, can benefit from having some knowledge around how content marketing works, so do not overlook this chapter. Furthermore, content marketing has changed drastically in recent months, so understand that anything you may already understand for content marketing may no longer be relevant in this marketing style.

What Counts as Organic Content?

Organic content is any form of content that is shared with your audience without using paid features to improve its odds of being seen. Unpaid social media posts, email newsletters, blogs, and videos all count as organic content. Some people also consider product descriptions and other content uploaded to websites as a form of content creation that falls under the organic content category. Anything that can be consumed either through reading, viewing, or watching, can be considered a form of content, meaning that there are a lot of ways that you can leverage this marketing style to grow your business.

Who Should Be Using Organic Content Creation?

Regardless of what industry you are in, you are going to need to use content in one way or another. Whether you are writing the content for your launch email, updating about a new product in your blog, or sharing something to social media, you are going to be engaging in content marketing. For that reason, everyone needs to be aware of how content marketing works and how it is evolving so that they can take advantage of it and grow their businesses with greater success going into 2021.

Creating Social Media Content

Social media is one of the most well-known places for content marketing to work, as most people are producing content for their social media platforms multiple times per day. Or, if they are combining content marketing with automated marketing, they may be spending an entire day or two creating content and then having that content released on a schedule multiple times per day. Regardless, on social media, virtually everything you post and share to your profile counts as a form of content marketing.

When you are in business, content marketing on social media is important. Due to the volume of marketing that is being done, you need to be mindful of how each piece contributes to your marketing experience, as well as how each piece ties together with other pieces to create an overall image. Unlike emails or blogs, where the content within one email or article stands alone, your social media pages come together to display all of your content in one linear experience, meaning that you need to upload your content strategically. You need to make sure that when people scroll your feed, they have an overall experience where all of the content flows together to create an overall message, rather than all of the content being repetitive experiences of each other. So, where you may be able to send 3 emails in one week about your upcoming launch without having to talk about anything else in between, you will need to be more diversified on your social media posts.

You can diversify your social media posts in many ways, ranging from changing up what exactly you are talking about to how you are delivering that information. For example, say you are going into a launch where you will be releasing a new piece of technology for your customers to purchase. You may do this by uploading a picture of this new device with a caption relating to the device, by uploading a video of someone using your device, and by creating a small write up about why your new device is superior to other devices. In this example, the content has diversified in terms of exactly what is being said or shared, and what medium is being used to share it. Still, the overarching theme remains the conversation around the new piece of technology.

This is exactly how your strategy should be, too. The overarching theme should be relevant to your business and what is presently going on in your business and should continue to remain present in every single post that you make, in a tasteful way. This way, when people land on your page see what you are talking about they can immediately get a feel for what your brand is and what you offer, but they do not feel that your page is spammy or repetitive.

To give you a deeper understanding of how each piece of content can be made in a way that will support its success going into 2021, below we are going to discuss three primary forms of content that are made on social media: written content, graphic content, and video content.

Written Content

One big mistake that people have made in the past when it comes to social media is writing incredibly long posts that do not feature any images or anything else relating to the post. In fact, for the most part, long pieces of written content do not do well on social media in general because it provides way more content than people are typically willing to consume when they are scrolling their newsfeeds.

When you do write content for social media, you want to base its length on two things: who is reading it, and what platform you are using. On a platform like Twitter, for example, the entire point is provided smaller pieces of written content updates on your profile for people to see. For this reason, attempting to put too much-written content is going to get your post ignored, unless you already have a consistent following, in which case you can get away with doing the occasional thread on your feed. On a platform like Facebook, the general consensus is to keep your content smaller. However, you can certainly get away with writing longer texts for your audience, depending on who they are and what type of business you run. On Facebook, texts should range from one sentence to three small paragraphs of content, as anything longer is likely going to lose people's interest. The one exception to this rule is with businesses that are based on your personal story, such as coaching businesses or affiliate marketing businesses where you are sharing your story for marketing. In these circumstances, longer posts with 5-8 paragraphs have been proven to be very effective in helping your content reach and resonate with the right people, improving your odds of being able to market and sell to these individuals. On Facebook specifically, another benefit of writing shorter pieces of content is that the words will be larger than other status updates, which help them stand out from the rest of the posts. Alternatively, you can use a colored background to help your post stand out or stay on-brand, too.

Ideally, most of your content should be shorter if it is exclusively in writing. This ensures that it is short and easy for people to consume, making it more likely that people will actually read it and engage with it. If they agree with what you have shared, they may even share it to their own feeds because it reflects their opinions or feelings, too.

When you are updating social media with something that is exclusively in writing, it is important that you share content that is interesting and complete. Never share an incomplete thought or experience, or something that seems completely irrelevant or pointless, as this is going to dilute the quality of your presence. Remember, you always want your content to make an impact and leave an impression, so use everything from small sentences to longer pieces of content to really get your message across. This way, people will always have respect for you and your business, and they will always see your profile as being worthy of following and paying attention to.

Graphic Content

Graphic content is an incredibly popular form of content marketing on social media, and for most companies, it should be the primary form of marketing that you are using. Graphic content marketing on social media is simple: all you need to do is find a graphic that is relevant to your business and share that graphic with your followers. Many brands will combine graphics content with written content so that they can capture people's attention with the images and then offer their stories or experiences through the written text. In most cases, longer forms of written content will perform much better with a graphic because the graphic encourages people to stop and pay attention to the content in the first place, and it also offers more context to the written word that you are sharing.

When you are sharing graphic content, make sure that everything you share is relevant to your audience. In the modern internet days, it can be easy to get caught up in sharing memes and graphics with your audience to the point where you begin to sway away from what your actual image and purpose is. The simple way to overcome this is to save all non-branded stuff for your personal profile or to ditch it altogether. Even if you think your audience would like a certain image, sharing something that is too off-brand for your business can result in you creating a confusing appearance on social media. Remember, everything needs to remain uniform and consistent if you are going to have success in reaching your audience. Otherwise, even if your audience relates to what you are posting, they may not follow you because they do not know exactly what your purpose is or why they should follow you.

Video Content

Video content works similarly to graphic content, except that instead of images you are going to be posting videos. For many brands, video content works as a great primary form of content on their social media platforms because they build their entire brand around sharing video content for people to watch. For example, if you are an affiliate marketer, you might find yourself using video content to show people the products that you have been using so that they can visually see why those particular products are worth their investment.

With social media, video content can be incredibly powerful in helping people feel more connected with you. You can use video content for everything from showing off new products to live-streaming events that are going on in your business to sharing short video clips of exciting experiences that your company is having. Video content is being leveraged as a way to help bring customers into an exclusive experience with the company that makes it feel like they are right there with the company in whatever the experience may be. For example, if you are having a brand new product launch within your company, you might film the experience of the launch so that people who follow you online can see all of the excitement and build their own excitement, which will likely lead to them purchasing your new product. The more that you can share through video content, the more you are going to help your audience feel close and connected with you and the more they are going to want to purchase from you. Video content is the single form of content that offers your audience the chance to feel face to face with you or your company, so never underestimate the power of a good video.

The key to leveraging video content in 2021 is to make sure that you are sharing content that is high quality, and that breaks the screen barrier with your audience. Even if you have recorded your video privately and not through live stream, can still talk to your audience and ask for their opinion, as they will go ahead and leave their opinions and comments on your video later when it has been uploaded to social media. As much as you can, really play with the fact that video content is meant to make your audience feel like they are right there with you and use that to create a custom, enjoyable experience for your audience.

Creating Email Content

Emails are another form of content marketing that many companies are still using to date. Despite how many people seem to get annoyed by this particular marketing strategy, it continues to be incredibly successful with many companies receiving large volumes of sales through their email campaigns. The key to successfully using email content marketing in 2021 is to create emails that are catchy, interesting, and not overwhelming. In other words, lower volumes of emails with a higher quality of content can go a long way in helping you take advantage of this marketing strategy and reaching your audience through their inboxes.

An alternative to creating email content which has become more popular in 2020, and that will continue to grow in 2021 is using Facebook messenger to create "emails." With Facebook, anyone who messages your business can be messaged in a mass message where you offer updates about your shop and any sales that you may have going on. Using this approach sparingly can be a wonderful opportunity to reach your audience to help let them know what is going on in your business and any other important information that they may need to know about.

When you are creating email content or Facebook messenger content, it is important that you do so effectively. You need to make sure that your emails or messages come across in a way that is polite, informative, and enjoyable to read so that when people open it, they feel compelled to read it all the way through. If your email is too flashy or filled with tacky marketing strategies like clickbait or an excessive amount of sentences that say things like "I'm about to reveal a big secret to you, but first..." you are going to lose people's interest because they will become overwhelmed with or annoyed by the hype in your email. In email marketing, this is the equivalent of walking past a store that has every type of bright flashing light and signs trying to lure people unimaginable, to the point where no one wants to even look at the store, let alone walk in because it is too overwhelming. You also need to make sure, however, that your emails are not too boring. Not offering enough to really draw people through the email can result in them ignoring it because what they are looking at is boring and failing to capture their interest.

The key to email marketing is to keep your email short and value-packed. Your emails should offer three tiers of value, in succeeding order, starting with free content, then full price deals then discounted deals. This way, when people open your email, they see that you are not immediately trying to sell to them in the first sentence of the email. Then, once they have read the free value content, they will see the full priced items as they scroll down to the discounted items, offering them the opportunity to see everything. If you lay your email out in any other way, people may not pay attention because they will assume that your email is just one big advertisement. Although it is, it does not need to look like a flashy, tacky advertisement.

When you are writing the content for your e-mails, keep it friendly and charismatic. Talk to your audience as if you are having a conversation with them, as this will help break the barrier between what you are saying and what they are reading. In a sense, they will feel like they are reading an e-mail from a friend rather than another marketing email in their inbox. This strategy really helps to create that connection experience with your audience, improving the likelihood of them actually reading your emails, and engaging with any of the sales content that you put in it.

In addition to writing content for your emails, make sure that you create strong graphics for your emails, too. These days, basic white-page emails are not going to get nearly as much interaction as ones that are actually designed to match your brand. Using a platform like Mail Chimp or Constant Contact gives you the opportunity to create branded templates that you can then use for your email content marketing. You should make 3-5 branded templates and alternate between them, while also adding additional images into your emails each time you send them out. This way, there is plenty of visual content for people to look at to keep them interested in your emails. If you do not want to have to take so many of your own images for your emails, you can always use a high-quality stock image platform like Unsplash or Pixabay. Remember. However, people do want to have a more personalized experience so you should also include a high-quality image of yourself or someone representing your company in your emails so that your audience gets that face-to-face connection. This will also help them remember who you are since they likely receive many emails from smaller business owners, so this way they remember who they are receiving the email from, why they signed up in the first place, and what drew them to you.

Finally, when you send out emails, you are also going to need a subject line for your email. When it comes to creating email content, your subject line should always be the last thing you write so that it clearly summarizes everything that is going to be inside of the email. This way, you can create a short, quick summary of what is inside in a way that is also inviting and interesting, improving peoples' likelihood of opening the email. For example, if you are announcing your summer sales and you find that your theme has been focused on the wide selection of pineapple decor you have, ranging from pineapple pool floaties to pineapple drink cups, you can use this to create your subject line. In this case, you might make your subject line something like "You + Us = Pineapple" followed by pineapple, sun, and sunglasses emojis. Remember: emojis became popular in email subject lines in late 2018, and they continue to be popular now and going into 2021, so do not be afraid to use a few of them in your subject lines when you are writing emails!

Creating Blog Content

Blog content is similar to emails in that you are going to be creating long handed written content that needs to keep people engaged enough to have them reading everything that you have to share. For the most part, creating blog content has not changed very much in the past few years, as many of the strategies that have already been in action are still incredibly valuable in creating and growing blogs. There are, however, some changes that need to be considered from previous marketing styles that can help you make your blog have even more success online.

To create your blog content, you want to start by picking a topic and then writing about it. Every single blog post should be created with SEO in mind, which means that you need to use specific tools that are going to help search engines recognize your page as being relevant in certain searches, improving your odds of becoming discovered. The four primary things to pay attention to here include keywords, title, paragraph lengths, and images.

When you are writing a blog post, your keyword should be included in your title, and your title should be around 30-50 characters long. Too short of a title can lead to search engines believing that your content is too vague, meaning it may not be as valuable for their audience to read. Instead, they will retrieve an article that seems more relevant, and yours will be left behind.

The keyword that you use in your title needs to be used in your content, too, but it should account for no more than 3% of your entire post. Using it too frequently can result in search engines thinking you are creating spammy content, causing them to lower you in their search results. In addition to using it 3% of the time, you also need to make sure that you are using *exactly* the same keyword that you used in your title. So, if your keyword is "Branding," you need to say the word "branding" in your title and in around 3% of your content that is uploaded into your post. "Brand," "brands," "branded," and any other alternatives to the word "branding" will not qualify toward your keyword percentage, which could result in you not using the keyword enough to be deemed relevant.

Even though blog posts are predominantly written, search engine algorithms know that people do not like to read long pieces of written content without a break in them. When it comes to blogs, a long white page filled with tons of paragraphs is less likely to be looked at than one that has the exact same information but broken up with headlines and photographs. If you want to appeal to the algorithms, you need to refrain from having more than 300-350 words between headlines. This way, you can offer your content in a way that is easier to digest because it draws people's attention through it and offers those breaks in between paragraphs in a complete manner.

Finally, images are a necessary element in your blog posts as they also provide your audience with a visual break in between reading. Ideally, a standard 1,500-word blog post should have 3-4 images in it to help break up the content and offer a more enjoyable viewing experience, in addition to an enjoyable reading experience. When you do upload your graphics, make sure that they are high quality and that they are relevant to your blog so that when people see your page, they see that your content is valuable. You should also make sure that the Meta tags and Meta descriptions of these photographs are relevant by going into the information of the image on your blog and adding a description of what the image is. Since search engines cannot read images, this helps them see that even the graphics are relevant to what people are searching for.

Creating Video Content

Video content is another powerful form of content that can be shared with your audience, but it needs to be done in a tasteful and proper manner. When you are creating videos for your audience, you want to keep your videos 1-10 minutes long, unless you are uploading them on a platform like YouTube where longer videos that are 30-60+ minutes long tend to perform well as well.

When you are creating video content for your audience, make sure that each video has a very specific topic that is relevant to your audience. Then, create a video surrounding that topic that features information around what that topic is, why it is important, and a lesson or two that your audience can learn about the topic itself. This way, when people are watching your video, they have a clear reason behind why they are watching it. The exception to creating videos with lessons is to create videos that are entertaining. However, they should still have a purpose for why people are watching them. This way, people know why they have clicked onto your video, and they feel compelled to continue watching the video until it is done.

In 2021, there is absolutely no room for low-quality videos, so make sure that you are using some basic high-quality filming practices to keep your video worth watching. You can do this by using a camera that shoots in 1080p, or better yet one that shoots in 4k, using natural lighting, and having a visual experience that is enjoyable. This means that you should be well dressed and presentable and that your background should be neat and easy on the eyes. If you are going to be showcasing a product or a certain event, make sure that is clearly visible and that people can easily identify what they are looking at so that they will continue watching. If your video is too hard to watch because it is cluttered or shot in low quality, people are not going to watch it.

Combining Organic Content with Other Digital Marketing Strategies

Organic content marketing can be combined with virtually every other digital marketing strategy. These days, people are using it in everything from native advertising marketing strategies to social media marketing strategies and online PR marketing strategies. Because virtually everything requires some form of content or another, knowing how to create consistently high-quality content that clearly showcases your brand and offers an enjoyable viewing experience is important. Whether you are writing something or sharing a picture or a video, you should always make sure that the message being shared is relevant and that it makes sense to the overall message that your brand stands for. As well, if you will be producing graphics or videos for your content, make sure that the visual experience is relevant, too, by keeping the colors and content of the image or video relevant to your brand. This way, your entire online presence, regardless of where it is being consumed, all fits a similar image.

Chapter 8: Targeted Paid Advertisements

Targeted paid advertisements are well-known in the digital marketing industry, and we have all come across them in our online browsing experiences. In fact, you likely come across them multiple times per day, as they are now placed just about everywhere online! These days, they are placed everywhere from on our social media feeds to our browsing pages, and even on apps and games that we download and play on our phones and computers.

When targeted paid advertisements were originally introduced, the way they were used was significantly different from how we use them today. Back then, companies and website owners would create private deals and then create their own graphics of their advertisements. The company would then pay a website owner a set amount of money for ad space on their website, and the website owner would display the company's ad for a specific period of time. At that time, the deals were virtually always private.

Digital marketers soon caught on to an ideal market niche and began to create advertising agencies. This way, companies and website owners could all go to one agency to be connected with people who were willing to engage in a deal with them. This made it easier for companies to find websites that were relevant to their niche that we ready to create a marketing deal, and it made it easier for website owners to find companies who needed to purchase ad space.

Nowadays, digital marketing is done through mega marketing giants like Amazon, Google, Facebook, Pinterest, and Twitter. All of these platforms are known for offering state of the art technology complete with incredible algorithms that automatically target certain segments of their built-in audience, allowing businesses to market to their ideal audience with ease. This way, anyone who browses online is able to be targeted and have advertisements placed on their feed. As a digital marketer looking to make money through advertisements, this is an incredible advancement that gives you the best opportunity to earn money through your digital marketing efforts.

Why Targeted Paid Advertisements Work

The first step in understanding why targeted paid advertisements work is understanding how they work. These days, every person who browses on the internet has a profile on something or another. These profiles are generally linked to Facebook or Google, or whichever other email service provider the individual may be using during their online browsing experience. When those individual browsers on these platforms, their browsing habits are stored in their "data," which feeds an algorithm that serves a myriad of purposes, including the algorithm that feeds and directs targeted paid advertisements. This means that their specific interests, including products they are curious about and topics they enjoy researching, are fed into the same algorithm that helps targeted paid advertisements, be displayed to the right people.

Once this algorithm is fitted to a person's specific browsing habits, the advertisement company can show these individual advertisements that are more likely to be of interest to them. For example, a person who enjoys cooking and purchasing new small appliances may be identified based on their browsing habits of looking for recipes and researching small appliances. This information would then be uploaded into the algorithm, and they would begin to see targeted advertisements from companies selling small appliances online, especially if they are selling the same type or model that the individual was already looking at.

The system does not rely entirely on the algorithm, though. Businesses are expected to have some basic idea of who they are advertising to so that they can upload these parameters into the technical backend of their targeted paid advertisements so that these algorithms have a general idea of who to advertise to. These two elements combined create the perfect opportunity for your products or services to be displayed to the people who are most likely to purchase your products or services.

The fact that your advertisements are only being seen by the people who are most likely to buy what you have to offer is exactly what leads to this particular marketing strategy being so effective. Now, rather than paying to have a large portion of your audience be individuals who are unlikely to purchase your products, you can feel confident that a large portion of your audience are individuals who are in fact interested in buying what you have to offer. This way, you have a higher conversion ratio, and you are far more likely to earn an income through your targeted paid advertisements.

Who Should Use Targeted Paid Advertisements

Unlike some of the previous marketing strategies we have talked about, targeted paid advertisements are not for everyone. While many businesses will benefit from using targeted paid advertisements, there are people who are going to find that their funds would be better spent elsewhere, at least early on in their marketing experience. The people who are least likely to benefit from targeted paid advertisements are brand new companies who have no credit established in the industry and who are advertising in a way that emphasizes sales rather than recognition.

If you launch a brand new business and from day one your sole focus is on selling products, you are probably going to make sales. However, it will take a long time for you to establish trust and credibility, which means that you may not make as many sales as you could if you chose a different approach. Instead of putting such a massive emphasis on sales, you should be focusing on simply growing brand recognition by using paid targeted advertising that is designed to get more people to land on your profile. Alternatively, you can choose the cheaper route of using organic content marketing to get your business out there and then use paid targeted advertisements after you have established some trust and credibility in your industry.

Another reason why you might not want to begin using targeted paid advertisements right away if you are brand new in business is that you may not know exactly who you are marketing to just yet. Remember, you are tapping into a global audience, which means that you have to know exactly who you are talking to if you are going to be effectively received by an audience unless you have millions of dollars to invest in targeted paid advertising. Investing some time on organic content marketing first is a great opportunity for you to get a clear idea of who is paying attention to your business and who is engaging with you and shopping with you first. This way, when you create your targeted paid advertisements, you know exactly what audience you need to define in your demographic section of the technical backend of your advertisement to have the biggest impact on reaching your audience.

Where You Can Use Targeted Paid Advertisements

There are two types of targeted paid advertisements: pay per click (PPC) advertisements and native advertisements. As you have already learned, PPC advertisements are advertisements that can be displayed anywhere online and that are typically used for one very specific purpose. With PPC advertisements, you are either trying to drive traffic to your website or trying to drive traffic to a specific product or category of products in your business. With native advertisements, you are using a paid feature to ensure that your posts are seen by the right people in your audience, helping to grow more awareness through your social media platforms. Native advertisements can be used to gain more followers, get more traffic to your website, or sell specific products or services through your advertisement.

Targeted Paid Advertisements That Are Right for Your Business

Choosing the right type of paid advertisement for your business is important, as each type of advertisement is going to be displayed in a different location. If you do not get the right location for your advertisement, you are going to struggle to get your advertisement seen in the first place, which means that you could be wasting your entire marketing budget on a misplaced advertisement.

The first and possibly easiest way for a new business to determine what type of advertisement is right for your business is to think about your budget. Generally, PPC advertisements are more expensive and require larger budgets in order to be run anywhere online. Alternatively, social media budgets can be significantly smaller and can still turn a wonderful profit for you as long as you create them properly.

Aside from the budget, there are a few other things that you can consider when it comes to picking the right placement for your advertisement. For example, local businesses generally do better on social media or Google, as they can leverage the structure of each advertising platform to target a local audience. This way, you are not reaching a global audience that you may not yet be ready to serve with your business. Global businesses can generally use any advertising platform as they all also have the capacity to tap into global audiences and be seen by the right people.

You can also consider what specifically you are working on marketing. If you want to increase recognition or engagement, focusing exclusively on social media, advertising is likely going to be your best opportunity to reach the market that you are trying to reach. If, however, you want to advertise a specific product or sale to get more people buying it, Amazon or Google PPC advertisements may be a better option. Social media native advertising can still be effective in helping you sell specific products or market-specific sales, too.

Finally, you need to think about where you want your advertisements to be seen. If you are trying to target an audience on social media, getting on your chosen social media platform and creating a native advertisement is ideal. If, however, you want your advertisements seen on blogs, websites, YouTube channels, and elsewhere on the net beyond social media, you are going to need to design a PPC advertisement with a company like Google or Amazon.

Creating Pay Per Click Advertisements

PPC advertisements are not too challenging to create, although it does take some practice to design an advertisement that is actually going to work. Fortunately, most PPC advertisement backend platforms look fairly similar, and they will walk you through the process of creating an advertisement through their platform

Regardless of what platform you are using for your PPC advertisements, there are five things you need to consider to make sure that you are creating a high-quality advertisement. You need to know: what you are advertising, who you are advertising it to, how much money you have to advertise it with, what you want it to look like, and what you want it to say. These five elements will help you create a well-rounded advertisement that reaches the right audience every single time.

When it comes to what you are advertising and who you are advertising it to, this should be fairly simple. You should have a goal going into every single advertisement, and that goal should help you determine whether you are going to use PPC advertising, native advertising, or both. You want to make sure that you get very clear on what demographic you are advertising to as well, as you need to have a very specific audience that you are targeting your advertisements toward in the backend. You are going to be asked questions about the demographic you are targeting based on what age they are, where they are from, what their interests are, and even how much money they make or what cultural background they have. All of this information helps PPC platforms determine the right audience to show your products to, so you need to have this information so that you can input it into the system. The algorithm will then narrow down the global audience to a specific demographic, and then narrow down your specific demographic into people who are most likely going to buy products from you.

Every single advertising platform requires you to know what your budget is, too. You need to know how much money you are willing to spend over how many days so that the platform knows how much it can spend per click, and when it needs to stop showing your advertisement. If there was no budget and timeline feature, you could risk being charged an enormous amount of money on your advertisements as the platform would not know when to stop showing your advertisement. It is crucial that you pay close attention to the wording around your budget and how long you want to display your ads for, as this part can be confusing. Some platforms will say, "how much do you want to spend *per day?*" and others will say, "how much spending do you want *overall?*" Be very certain that you have read it correctly, as you do not want to put your overall budget as your daily spending limit as this could get expensive, quickly. You also do not want to accidentally put your daily budget as your overall budget as this would result in your advertising not performing well due to not having enough money to really get your advertisement seen by enough people.

When it comes to considering the graphics of your advertisement, you need to think about a graphic that is going to be relevant to what you are advertising, while also being on-brand *and* on-trend. Having all of these elements involved in your graphics will ensure that they are more likely to capture the attention of the person that you are attempting to advertise toward, improving your odds of having them engage with your advertisement. If you are not a graphic designer, it may be worth your while to hire someone who can custom design a graphic that is going to be useful for your advertisement. In general, PPC-style advertisements are usually very simple as they do not want to overwhelm their viewers. Creating a graphic that has too many design elements to it can result in your graphics looking overwhelming, causing people to scroll on by rather than pay attention to it and develop an interest in it.

The alternative to creating a single graphic is creating a video, which can be done for Google-based PPC advertisements. These videos are often shown between other videos that people would be watching online, such as on YouTube. They also occasionally show up on blog posts where the blogger has chosen to add a video-based advertisement to their website. These videos require high-quality video content that is easy to see, clear to understand, and worthy of their time to watch it. Ideally, your video should be filmed with the same level of high-quality attention as commercials on TV would be filmed with, as this is the level of quality that people expect to see when they are watching video advertisements. You also need to make sure that the content of your video is relevant in that it captures the attention of your audience and tells them about what you have to offer them within seconds. If you do not capture their attention within the first 5 seconds of the video, studies have shown that you will likely not capture their attention at all.

After you have created your graphic content, you need to think about the wording related to your PPC advertisement. For some advertisements, the ad will be exclusively wording, so the wording is extremely important. Even for advertisements that feature graphics, however, you need to have catchy phrasing that is going to encourage people to pay attention and actually want to purchase from your business. To create the proper type of written content for your PPC ad, you need to think about where it has been placed. If your ad is being placed somewhere like the top of a Google search, you need to have a clear title and a catchy caption that is going to encourage people to click your link. For example, if you are selling beads online, your ad's title could say "Phoenix Bead Store," and your caption could say, "The largest selection of wholesale beads on the internet!" This type of content clearly displays who you are and what you offer, and gives people the option to click through on your ad and begin to shop for your products.

If you are sharing an advertisement elsewhere, such as blogs, you are also going to need to keep your written content short. On some forms of advertisements, they continue to offer a header and a caption that you can use for your written content. In this case, you would use the same direct, to-the-point, and captivating strategy as we used for "Phoenix Bead Store" above. If, however, you only get one space to write some information in, you want to make sure that you take advantage of it and put the right information in. For advertisements with just one section, you want to be even more direct in your approach. Ideally, you should share no more than 8-12 words about your product so that people do not have to read quite as much in order to get to the point. Something like "Phoenix Beads – Largest Whole Sale Bead Supplier!" is excellent as it captures interest and sells your brand in just a few short words.

Creating Native Advertisements

Native advertisements are actually designed in almost the exact same way that PPC advertisements are made, except that there are some other customizable features that you can take advantage of with native advertisements. If you want to make a native advertisement, you should follow all of the steps outlined in creating PPC advertisements above. However, you can also factor in the following subtle differences that can be taken advantage of to help you make a better advertisement that will likely perform better on social media.

When you are creating a native advertisement, you still need to consider your audience and your specific goal with your advertisement. In these advertisements, the platform you are using will actually let you define a rather specific goal that you want to reach with your advertisement. It is important that you select the right goal for your advertisement as this will go a long way in helping the platform you are using to identify the exact audience for your advertisement to be shown to.

As you create your advertisement, there are generally four styles of advertisements that you can use: you can promote your profile, you can sponsor a post that is already performing well, you can create an advertisement to sell a specific product or service, or you can create a video. All of these advertisement styles are going to be designed exactly according to the PPC standards, except for the following adaptations that you should consider:

Promoting Your Profile

Promoting your profile on social media is like promoting your brand or your website in a PPC advertisement. This is a very basic promotional experience where you are not trying to sell any one specific product, but rather you are looking to boost attention toward your brand and improve brand recognition. On social media, aside from increased followers, one of the biggest benefits of this is faster brand recognition because people are more likely to see and read about your brand several times over in a relatively short period of time. This works much faster than organic content advertising, meaning that it will take less time for you to establish credibility and recognition, as well as grow your following, as long as you are advertising to the right audience.

You can promote your profile on virtually any platform by first ensuring that you are working with a business account. Then, all you have to do is open up the advertisement dashboard of your chosen social media platform and select the goal of "Increasing Brand Awareness" or "Getting New Followers." Both of these goals will help the platform know that you want to get more people landing on your profile. Then, you will follow the same steps of outlining your budget and your audience, choosing your graphic, and creating the written content for your post.

Sponsoring a Post

Sponsoring a post is a style that is unique to native advertising, and it can be an incredibly powerful tool to take advantage of in your business. When you create a post online that performs well, social media platforms allow you to boost that post so that it gets seen by even more people. Boosting posts is a great opportunity to improve brand recognition, while also helping promote whatever the content of your post was. For example, if you were talking about an upcoming launch, and many people liked your post, you could sponsor that post so that even more people would see the content that you were sharing. Plus, because you already have so much engagement on the post, you can identify what demographic (or two demographics) you reached the best with the organic post and target that particular demographic when you sponsor the post. This way, you are getting seen by the right audience, too.

Selling A Product or Service

When it comes to using native advertising for selling a product or a service, the structure of your advertisement will be largely similar to a traditional PPC advertising. You will want to have your product or service highlighted in the graphic of your advertisement, coupled with a few words about what your product or service is and how people can buy or book through you. The two differences of a product or service advertisement being done in this way are that you can add a "buy" or "book" button to most social media advertising platforms. This way, people can click on that button, and it instantly takes them to the page where they can buy or book through you. The second difference is that you can display multiple pictures in a "carousel" advertisement on certain platforms, allowing you to promote and sell multiple products or services in one advertisement.

There is an exception to the written content rule for native advertising when selling products or services, too. When it comes to selling products or services through native advertising, you can use long-form text content depending on who your audience is. In recent years, many people have had a lot of success in writing out a "story" of sorts to help them sell their product or service. This long form text can be used to help create a deeper connection and purpose behind your products, helping people to not only buy into your product or service but to also buy into your brand. This type of promotional post can be extremely beneficial in helping you gain sales and brand recognition and loyalty all at once.

Creating a Video Advertisement

When you are creating a video advertisement for native advertising, the way that you create your video advertisement for PPC advertisements. There truly is no difference between PPC advertising or native advertising with videos, other than the fact that you can add a "buy" or "book" button to your video on the native advertising format.

Combining Targeted Paid Advertisements with Other Digital Marketing Strategies

Targeted paid advertisements can be used in conjunction with virtually every other digital marketing strategy out there. However, you can also use targeted paid advertising as a stand-alone digital marketing strategy that you can take advantage of to sell your products. For example, if you are running an Amazon FBA business as your income channel, you can easily get away with only using Amazon's targeted paid advertising features to promote your products without ever having to create any other digital marketing channel. This way, you keep your income as passive as possible, and you are not required to do anything beyond create, update, manage, and pay for your advertisements, in addition to managing your income channel itself.

Chapter 9: Online Marketing Events

Online marketing events have been rising in popularity since 2005, and have continued to rise through the years. More recently, the way that online marketing events are hosted and how they are leveraged as a marketing tool has changed. These days, it is not enough to simply use your webcam to launch a basic webinar and throw it up on a website and make thousands of dollars through it. Although these methods worked in the past, they are no longer strong enough to really generate enough income for anyone who is using them. If you were to spend your time making things like this, you would find yourself making content that virtually no one was paying attention to because they did not have a strong enough reason to. Elsewhere online, other people would be making higher quality modern content for your audience, and they would likely go to that person instead of you because the content is more enjoyable to consume.

These days, online marketing events are still powerful, but they require a much more personalized approach. You need to be willing to approach them in a way that offers high-quality value, and enough so that it is worthy of people actually investing in it. In other words, you need to refrain from rephrasing something that has already been shared countless times online, you need to deliver your content in a personable and enjoyable manner, and you need to know how to monetize your online marketing event properly. Without these pieces in place, your online marketing event might fall flat and result in you not making a significant impact with your audience.

In this chapter, we are going to discover how you can modernize the outdated webcam webinar so that you can create online events that are going to captivate your audience and have them wanting to do business with you. This way, you can take the strategy that was perfected by previous generations to create a new strategy that is going to be functional in this generation. Going forward in 2021, it is all about quality, personalization, and the fun-factor.

Why Online Marketing Events Work

Online marketing events work for the same reason why any event works: they are fun, and they are easy to build energy and momentum around. Using online marketing events as an opportunity to market to your audience gives you the opportunity to connect with your audience over an enjoyable event while building relationships and encouraging sales to take place in your business. When it comes to online marketing events, you gain all of the same values as you would from an in-person social networking event. You have a mutual interest that has you meeting with other people, you have the opportunity to meet and get to know your audience, and you are given an opportunity to turn the event into a funnel of sorts. Generally, the funnel of an online marketing event looks like this: people have an interest in what you are offering, and they join the event with the intention of learning more. These people may or may not already know about your brand. They sign up to join the event, and then come event day they join in on the event and pay attention to whatever video content is being shared with them. Typically, they also comment and interact through the platform being used, allowing them to have a proper back-and-forth connection with the host. Through this, they get to know the host and whatever the host is talking about, whether it is information, a skill, a product, or anything else that is relevant to the host's business. Once the bulk of the event is done, the host moves into offering a way for them to keep in touch and work together, allowing the attendees to continue to "network" with, or do business with the host. By the end, the people who came and were highly interested in what you have to offer are walking away as new or future clients who are going to bring money into your business.

Who Should Be Using Online Marketing Events

Online marketing events are another form of digital marketing that is not necessarily for everyone. Plenty of product and service-based brands have an easy enough time marketing their products online without ever hosting any form of marketing event, allowing them to thrive without these strategies. That being said, nearly every industry can benefit from using an online marketing event in their business, whether they are selling products or services, or growing their business as an influencer or drop shipper. The key is to choose a creative way to identify how you can connect and share with your audience in a way that helps them feel connected with you so that they can shop through you.

Types of Online Marketing Events to Consider

When it comes to online marketing events, there are four types of events that you can host to help drive more awareness and money to your business. These four event types include webinars, product demonstrations, courses, and online PR. Each of these styles is going to help you generate the level of interest in your business that you need in order to be successful with your sales.

Webinars are an excellent opportunity for any business to communicate with their audience for any number of reasons. Webinars have been hosted to introduce a new business, to introduce a new product, or to talk about why people would be a good fit with a certain business. A popular industry that has used webinars for years is the network marketing industry, where webinars are used to help inform new or prospective marketers on what the business is about and why it would be beneficial for them to join.

Product demonstrations offer businesses the unique opportunity to give their audience a "hands-on" experience with their products through the internet. In the past, salespeople were taught that one of the key ways that sales personnel could encourage people to buy was through getting the product directly into their hands. Test driving cars, trying out a new video game console, or trying on a new outfit were all ways that people could develop a "connection" with the product, making it easier for them to purchase it. Of course, online it is not nearly as easy to create this experience, but it can still be done through product demonstrations. By showing your audience what you are selling and giving them a demonstration of how it works, you can help people determine that your products are worthy of buying and encourage them to make the purchase. This way, you are more likely to make sales online.

Courses are a way that many people have been making money online in recent years. Courses can be used to educate people on certain knowledge or skills which they can then use in their own lives to achieve certain results. Courses can be made on virtually everything from sales strategies and tips to how to do a certain DIY project, depending on what your industry and niche are. There is almost always something that can be taught in any industry, regardless of what you are selling or offering in your business. Creating courses online can be done in two ways: live or evergreen. We will discuss both of these ways in this chapter.

Finally, online PR is a strategy that you can use with online marketing events to help get more eyes on your business. Online PR includes being hosted by popular interviewers on platforms like Facebook or YouTube, or even being hosted by popular interviewers on podcasts. Any opportunity that you have to talk about your business can help you increase awareness around your business while also driving sales into your business. Plus, these PR events help you get in front of a new audience, which will help you get even more eyes on your business.

Hosting a Webinar

If you have decided that hosting a webinar is ideal for your business, you need to begin by choosing what platform you are going to host your webinar on. These days, platforms like Vimeo, Facebook, and Zoom are all great platforms that you can use that allow webinar hosting services to take place. There are four things you need to look for when you are choosing the platform that you are going to host your webinar on: the length of video you are allowed to have, the number of attendees you can have, whether or not people can engage with your videos, and if you can download the video after. You need to have a platform that is going to allow for you to have a video that is long enough to cover your entire webinar, as well as a large enough amount of viewers to make it worth your while. You also need a platform that allows viewers to engage so that you can break the screen barrier and have a positive experience with your viewers. Finally, you need to be able to download the video after so that you can use it in future marketing engagements.

Once you have found the right platform, you need to outline the details of your webinar. First, you need to identify what you want to talk about with your audience. You need to pick a topic that is relevant to your brand, and to your audience, as well as one that is going to provide you with enough content to talk about. Once you have picked your topic, you need to outline about 3-5 main points that you are going to cover in your webinar, depending on how long your webinar is going to be. If you only plan on hosting one for 20-30 minutes, 3 topics should be plenty. If you plan on hosting one for a full hour, you will need about 5 topics to cover so that you have plenty to discuss in that hour.

After you have your topic picked out, you just need to determine what date you are going to host the event on, and at what time. Then, you are going to begin marketing the event. To market your event, you want to get e-mail signups which will allow you to send everyone a reminder through their emails for when the event has started. It will also give you the opportunity to send them the replay, or encourage them to catch a future event if they have missed your webinar. You can encourage people to sign up for the email to get the link to your webinar through social media marketing, targeted paid advertising, and organic content marketing.

In the past, slides were used to offer a slideshow that discussed the topics that the individual was talking about. These days, this is considered impersonal, so avoid doing this on your webinars that you are hosting. Instead, allow the image to be of your face so that people can get a look at you and the screen barrier is broken. This can be more uncomfortable at first, but as you grow used to offering live video-based content, it becomes easier.

Turning your webinars into a monetized feature can be done in two ways. One way is to charge a fee for people to join your webinar, which is only going to work if you plan on offering enough value that they can walk away, having completely learned something from you. The other way is to offer your webinar for free, and then offer something for sale at the end of the webinar. This way, the people who watch it are lead into a sales pitch. You can also combine the free webinar with a paid course and leverage this as a marketing feature by calling your webinar a "freebie" that is added to your paid course, encouraging people to join.

Hosting Product Demonstrations

Product demonstrations, as I mentioned, are the online version of getting your products into the hands of people so that they can feel them and begin to imagine themselves having them in their own day to day life. Using this strategy helps you show people why your products are amazing and why they are worth buying in the first place. When you show people how they work and what they do, you give people the opportunity to imagine what it would be like to use that product in their own lives, too. This marketing strategy is so powerful that even children are watching videos of other children playing with toys, only to then go and ask their parents if they, too, can have that particular toy. Many people are using product demonstrations as a way to market their products, and you can, too.

There are a couple of different ways that you can use product demonstrations in your marketing strategy. Some people use them from time to time on their social media platforms, such as doing a spontaneous live stream demonstration on Facebook. Other people have a YouTube channel or social media presence exclusively dedicated to product demonstrations that they leverage to show off the products that they are selling or marketing. These particular strategies work great for companies selling products or services, or influencers who are marketing for another company.

You can create a demonstration video easily by simply getting in front of a camera and showing a product in use. It can be as simple as a quick 30-60 second demonstration, or a longer 5-10 minute demonstration. The key to making it work in 2021 is to use it in a real-world situation and to be genuine about how you are sharing about the product. Avoid using that overly excited, fake-sounding infomercial voice that everyone has grown immune to, as this will cause people to ignore you. Instead, use an excited but realistic voice and be authentic in how you are sharing, as this will help people feel like it really is exciting, and not like you have to fake excitement around the product.

Hosting Courses

Courses can be created in many different ways, including as a text-based course that is hosted on a site and sold as a digital product. For this section, we are talking about a specific style of offering online courses which consist of hosting a live course first and then, if you want to, turning it into an evergreen course, or a course that is offered without a live element.

Hosting courses starts with identifying what you have knowledge about that you could educate someone else on. Then, you want to do all of the same preparation as you would for a webinar by choosing your topic, outlining your teaching points, and planning the date and time. The difference with courses and webinars is that your courses are generally going to happen over 2-3+ sessions, and they do not always offer a sales pitch at the end of the video. That being said, they certainly can offer a sales pitch to encourage people to buy something from you if you desire to leverage the course even further.

You will market your course in the same way that you market a webinar, too, using features like social media marketing, organic content marketing, targeted paid advertisements, and automated marketing features. To get people to sign up, they should be added to an email list where they will then be given information about the course as well as provided with the necessary links to join the live videos.

As you host the course, make an effort to treat each live session, just like a teacher would treat a classroom. Have the goal of introducing information and educating people on this information, and having them leave each "class" feeling as though they have learned something valuable. By the end of the course, they should be able to put everything together as one big lesson that they have learned, with plenty of smaller pieces of information to apply, too.

Once you are done hosting each class, you can download that day's video. Then, in the future, you can put those videos together to make an evergreen course. This simply means that you choose a hosting platform such as Squarespace, Teachable, or Udemy, and you put the content together in the form of a course. You may choose to include workbooks or written content in the course so that there is even more value offered for people who want to join. Then, all you have to do is market that course and people can buy it and take it without you ever having to talk about the content on a video again. Many people have made hundreds of thousands and even millions of dollars this way, making it a wonderful opportunity for you to earn money while actively designing the product that will continue to earn you money.

Online Marketing with Online PR

Online PR with online marketing events is a great combination to market your events with. With online PR, you are not actually hosting the event, but instead, you are being hosted as a guest speaker or guest visitor by someone else who is hosting the event. You can get engaged with online PR by identifying major online interviewers in your industry on platforms like podcasts, YouTube, Facebook, Instagram, and anywhere else where these individuals may be located in your industry. Once you have found those individuals, you can look at their websites and discover what the requirements are to be interviewed by them. Make sure that you always look first and that you approach these individuals in their desired manner, as this shows your own professionalism and makes them more likely to actually want to interview you. If you are rude or if you approach them in any other way, they may ignore you or even respond with something negative, while also possibly disrupting the reputation that you have worked so hard to make. In this case, it is your fault too for not having respected the individual that you were approaching.

Once you have approached an individual, you will work together with them to arrange the online PR event that you will be doing together to help get the word about your business out there. After this, all you have to do is prepare by looking proper if you need to present yourself visually, and by having the right filming or sound equipment available. Then, you simply show up and talk to the individual and complete the interview or the PR event.

Most times, the individual hosting you will want you to do to some level of marketing to your own audience, too. Be prepared to make social media updates, send out emails, and otherwise communicate with your audience to let them know about the interview that you are doing. This not only helps fulfill your own requirements to be a part of the event but also helps get even more eyes on your event. The more that people see it, the more likely even more people will see it, increasing your chances of having success with your online PR marketing event.

Combining Online Marketing Events with Other Digital Marketing Strategies

Online marketing events can easily be combined with social media marketing, organic content marketing, and targeted paid advertising marketing to help you get the word out there about your business. The key to marketing your online event is to choose every avenue that may be possible for you and use it. Most people will start with using social media marketing and content marketing to advertise their events and may use native advertising as a way to get it out there, too. Then, once the event has been done, they will offer a replay of the event and market that, too. At this point, they often use native advertising and PPC advertising as a way to increase the reach even further, making it even easier for you to get in front of a larger audience and grow your business even more.

Chapter 10: Tips to Help You Succeed

Although we can give you a lot of valuable and strategic advice to get you started and thriving in digital marketing, there is one thing that we cannot give you in this book. That is the value of hands-on experience in your marketing strategy. No matter what new strategy or skill you are trying to pick up, there is a certain level of subtle knowledge and intuitive understanding that comes from having actual hands-on experience with what you are doing.

While we cannot give you that specifically, we can give you some information to help you begin to understand these subtle pieces of information, allowing you to step even closer to digital marketing mastery right here, right now. This way, you can bypass a large amount of the learning curve and step right into the art of practicing and refining your skill. The tips given to you in this chapter are ones that master marketers know and have been suggesting are going to be even more valuable going into 2021. By applying this information right away, you give yourself a jump start and help yourself have greater success going forward.

Keep Your Website Up to Date

First things first, if you want to be successful in digital marketing, you need to keep your website up to date.

Your website is the page where people will end up going to either learn more about you, consume content by you, or even purchase from your business depending on how you have set your business up. If you want to have success in digital marketing, you need to make sure that you are keeping your website up to date, as this will provide a myriad of benefits for you and your online business.

The first benefit that you are going to gain from keeping your website up to date is that it will keep your page updated for SEO. This way, when people look for businesses like yours, they will be more likely to come across yours in the searches. SEO can be kept up to date on your website by updating information as needed, as well as by running a blog on your website. Even a basic blog with weekly or monthly updates can do wonders in keeping your website up to date, helping you to get located on SEO better.

The second major benefit that you gain from keeping your website up to date is the benefit of your customers being able to have updated information. This way, they are not coming to your website and finding outdated information, which can lead to many issues. This could cause your customers to try and get you to hold up an outdated sale, or it could cause them to believe that your business is no longer operating because the information is outdated. Keeping information up to date ensures that what they are receiving is relevant and recent.

Design and Evolve Your Customer Experience

Every single business, no matter how basic or intricate, needs a customer experience. Your customer experience accounts for the experience that your customers have when they interact with anything that has to do with your business. This includes marketing materials, the sales process, and the experience of getting anything from your business, such as products or services.

The more that you focus on your customer experience, the more you are going to be able to design an experience that is enjoyable and memorable for your audience. This way, when they think about your business, they do not just think about the great products that they gained from your business, but they also think about the great *experience* that they had. Furthermore, the experience can cause them to feel like they are a part of something special, which can actually increase their customer loyalty.

Whenever you are creating something for your business, think about how it is going to contribute to your customer experience. Think about how it will be for your customer to come across that piece of marketing material and to discover more about your business, and try to make this experience as enjoyable and easy as possible. Make it so that when your customer goes through this experience, it is personal, makes sense, and is easy for your customers to move forward with. This way, you can feel confident that you are cultivating an experience that is worth enjoying.

Get Your Business on Google

One step that many new businesses overlook, especially in 2020 and 2021, is getting your business on Google. Google is a search engine that has an archive of virtually every website and the company that is online, and if you want to be relevant online, you need to have your business on Google, too. This goes for more than just having a website that Google retrieves. You also need to have a business that Google retrieves, especially if your business has a physical address.

You can get your business on Google by creating a Google business account and then uploading information about your business into it. Once you have, you will be prompted to verify some information about your business, allowing you to confirm with Google that it is, in fact, your business. After your business has been verified, Google will be able to showcase it to other people who are looking to find a business just like yours.

Master Your Call to Action

Back in the day, businesses were told to master their "elevator pitch," which would help people propose their business and encourage people to buy from them. These days, you need to master your call to action in your business in order to succeed, as this helps you become clear and confident in pitching your call to action. You can master your call to action by picking the one thing that you want people to do with your business, such as purchasing or ordering through you and then master pitching that calls to action. This means that you master the art of asking for the sale in posts, advertisements, and videos that you share online. You can do this by identifying how you want to create this call to action, and then by practicing it and using it as often as possible. Eventually, it will become easy and comfortable for you to share your call to action, helping other people feel more confident in you, too. This level of confidence and comfort will drastically increase your sales through your call to action because it will come across smooth and effortless, making it easier for people to trust in you and act on it.

Track Your Performance with Analytics

Finally, you need to track your performance with analytics. Many new business owners find this part to be particularly challenging because it can be hard to know what analytics you need to pay attention to and how you can use them to help you grow your business. When you are tracking your analytics, the primary thing you want to pay attention to is your level of engagement. If you have offered a link or a call to action, you also want to track the number of people who actually click the link or follow through on your call to action, too. These are the most basic analytics that will help you get started with tracking your performance in an easy manner.

Paying attention to these numbers is going to help you determine what you're best performing content is so that you can recreate more of that. You will also be able to determine which posts could be boosted or turned into paid marketing campaigns, helping you get even more content in front of your audience.

Chapter 11: Mistakes to Avoid

To help you even further advance your own knowledge and understanding of the subtleties of marketing, we can also explore mistakes that you need to avoid. In this chapter, we are going to cover five mistakes that you need to avoid when you are marketing your business to ensure that you do not make a fatal mistake from day one. Unfortunately, many marketers who are getting involved in digital marketing are known for coming across outdated or low-quality advice and putting it to work, only to find themselves completely destroying the reputation of themselves and their businesses. This can destroy your success far before you ever get a chance to begin, so you need to avoid these things if you are going to succeed with digital marketing.

Avoid Outdated Marketing Tactics

The first thing that you really need to avoid is outdated marketing tactics. Due to the nature of search engines, the advice shown to you is going to be the advice that is considered the most relevant to what you have gone in search of. This means that if you type in "digital marketing strategies that work," you might just find yourself coming across posts from the mid-to-late 2000s, which will be full of outdated advice. If you follow these strategies, you are going to find yourself marketing in the wrong era, which will result in you struggling to get in front of your audience and make a success with your business.

When you are looking for marketing strategies online, look to find ones that are still relevant. To do this, check the date of the post or article that you are reading to make sure that it was made within the last month or two. Never pay attention to anything created more than 6 months ago, as most of these strategies will have evolved in the past six months to become even more effective. Yes, marketing strategies evolve that quickly.

Avoid the "Abandoned Profile" Effect

One big mistake that people make with their businesses is creating a profile on a platform and then never updating it. Even if you do not intend on using a platform as a primary part of your strategy, you need to keep it up to date to avoid creating the "abandoned profile effect." If you create a profile and abandon it, even if you are active elsewhere online, you might lose possible customers. People who find you on that platform may think that you are no longer in business and not pursue you any further. Instead, you could upload that profile a couple of times per month with information to guide them back to your profiles where you are more active. This way, rather than missing out on the opportunity to connect with these individuals, you are funneling them over to one of your more active profiles.

Avoid Going into Digital Marketing Without a Plan

No matter how basic you think, your digital marketing business is if you go into it without a plan, you are going to find yourself struggling to make any form of success. In this book, we have given you tons of strategies and plans that you can use to make your business a success. The best way to take advantage of this information is to sit with it and make a specific plan for how you are going to put it to work in your business. This way, when it comes time for you to actually put it into action, you know what you are doing, and you can do it consistently. Remember, in digital marketing, consistency is key, and if you do not adhere to this rule, you are going to find yourself failing, fast.

Creating a plan is simple: you need to decide what your goal is and then choose a step-by-step approach for how you are going to reach that goal. For example, if your goal is to make passive income off of selling a course online, you could start by hosting the course as a live event and marketing it through social media and content marketing. Then, when it launches, you could sustain sales and your passive income using targeted paid advertising. Having your plan clearly defined means that you know what you need to be doing at all times, which will keep you moving toward total success in your business every single day. It will also prevent you from wasting time on activities that are not contributing to your bottom line.

Avoid Underestimating the Importance of All Devices

It is expected that by 2020, 4.78 *billion* people are going to own mobile devices. This means that close to 4.78 billion people are going to have access to the internet through their phones, making the mobile market a massive one. Even right now, we are already seeing many companies finding themselves struggling to stay afloat if they are not creating a presence that caters to both desktop and mobile. The simple truth is: people love using mobile devices and find them to be convenient and easy. If you are not optimized for mobile, people are going to look beyond you and to someone else instead, because it is not worth their time to try and fuss with your platform.

Trust that going into 2021; there are several competitors ready to take your place if you are not stepping up to the plate. When it comes to designing your online platforms, *always* think about both mobile and desktop. Make sure that your pictures are high enough quality and cropped right for both, make sure that your website is easy to navigate on both, and make sure that your buttons and links are all accessible on both. This way, more people have the capacity to do business with you, and you are more likely to earn more sales.

Avoid Not Diversifying Your Approach for Greater Reach

In the past, throwing something up and relying solely on PPC advertising was a great way to make an income online. People made hundreds of thousands of dollars doing this and had great success with it. In fact, these are the people who exposed just how easy making money online could be and are responsible for why so many people turned to the internet to try and make an income. That being said, these days, it does not pay to have such a simple approach to making money online.

This does not mean that you cannot still be just as passive in making your income, but it does mean that you need to make better use of a diversity of platforms and approaches if you are going to have success. If you still want your business to be highly passive, you simply need to take advantage of automated marketing or hire someone to manage your marketing for your passive income opportunity. Otherwise, you need to put effort into diversifying your approach and getting your business and marketing materials in front of as many people as possible. This is how you are going to not only create some success online but thrive online.

Chapter 12: The Power of Staying Relevant Through Conflict and Disaster

When chaos ensues, what are some actions a business can take to stay relevant? 2020 has shown us that when disaster strikes, the media can rapidly be taken over with a large focus on the current disaster, and nearly zero focus on anything else. This is not only relevant to 2020, though. Many businesses have faced the question of how to stay relevant when chaos ensues, whether it be because of a disaster going on in their industry, or a disaster going on in their geographical region. For example, a realtor selling houses amid a housing crisis may be worried about staying relevant and getting their job done, while a business that managed to survive in the wake of a tornado may be wondering if it is ethical to keep doing business.

The reality is, even when disaster strikes, regardless of what that disaster looks like, there needs to be a plan in place to help you stay relevant and continue doing business through that disaster. A failure to maintain your business and keep yourself relevant can lead to you being forced to shut your doors, which is not helpful to anyone. With that being said, staying relevant during normal times and staying relevant during peculiar times are two entirely different scenarios. Since we will not always be living among peculiar times, I want to enrich your business by offering you guidance on how to stay relevant during both sets of circumstances.

Staying Relevant During Regular Times Vs. Peculiar Times

Staying relevant during regular times and staying relevant during peculiar times are two different scenarios based on a little thing called ethics. When it comes to the individuals behind businesses, it may feel overwhelming to keep your brand relevant during peculiar times, because it may seem inappropriate to do "business as usual" when your community is suffering. That's because, in a way, it is inappropriate. However, there are shifts you can make to make your effort to stay relevant entirely appropriate. One starts with realizing that without your business, you are not making any money. Businesses cannot shut down or stop existing just because there is something major going on at that moment. In fact, businesses *must* keep running because they keep money flowing through the economy, and that money keeps the people being affected by disaster afloat during peculiar times.

If you are attempting to stay relevant during regular times, your primary focus is on keeping your brand fresh and updated so that you continue to be liked by your audience. All of the standard practices of leveraging trends, developing a sense of community within your audience, engaging with your community, and keeping up with the changing times are perfect when it comes to staying relevant during regular times. Your largest focus is to continue offering the latest and greatest so that when people are looking for an excellent experience, especially one that is specific to your niche, they look for that experience with you rather than with anyone else.

During peculiar times, that shifts. While you still need to keep up with all of the aforementioned elements of staying relevant, you also need to find a way to acknowledge and accommodate for the disaster that has struck your community. Whether that is your industry, your local community, or the global community, you need to know how to address it in a way that clearly acknowledges what is going on, positions you in a spot where you can help your audience, and makes it clear that you have compassion and empathy for what everyone is going through. Your audience wants to see the faces behind your brand that proves that you are right there with them, enduring the disaster together.

Deepening your sense of community, standing beside your audience, and becoming engaged with the people you are serving through your business is a powerful way to position yourself during a disaster. Firstly, it helps you stay relevant in a way that has compassion and consideration for the people who have been loyal to your brand in the past. Secondly, it allows you to play an integral role in helping your audience through that challenge. What ends up happening is they realize that you supported them when they needed it most, so they experience gratitude toward your brand, and they want to support you, too.

Sales, promotions, and other big events are still relevant and important, if not more important, during challenging times. Sales and promotions make it easier for your audience to get their hands on what you are selling, while celebrations or large events give them something positive to look forward to and enjoy. The key is to manage expectations and perceptions by marketing appropriately. For example, if you are doing a big launch and a disaster strikes, the solution is not necessarily to postpone the launch. It is also not to ignore the disaster and carry on with the launch as if to say you "do not care." Instead, it is to acknowledge the disaster and make it clear that you will carry on with the launch anyway to give your loyal followers something fun and exciting to look forward to after all of the tragedy they have faced recently. You might even plan something extra special to coincide with the event to take even better care of your audience throughout the process, such as a charitable donation, a giveaway or additional promotion, or something else to help give back to your customers.

When you are able to acknowledge and work mindfully around disasters, business can carry on as usual, and all of your standard practices for staying relevant continue to be true. The entire success of your ability to stay relevant starts and ends with your capacity to acknowledge disaster, express compassion for your audience, solidify your unity with your community, and give back in some way that genuinely supports your customers. If you manage these four steps effectively, you can carry on with "business as usual" despite anything going on in the world, which means you can confidently maintain and grow your business, even through tragedies.

Leveraging Trends to Stay Relevant

No matter what is going on in the world, one of the most powerful things you can do is leverage trends to stay relevant. Active trends show you what people care about, and allow you to directly serve people by engaging in what they are focused on. They provide an excellent opportunity for you to recognize where people's attention is going and allow you to use that attention to find ways to effectively remain at the center of people's attention.

The difference between trends during regular times, as opposed to during peculiar times, often lies within what types of things people are focusing on. During regular times, when the average population is relaxed and going about life as normal, trends are often fun and lighthearted. These trends are easy to get on board with because, as a brand, you can have fun and be lighthearted alongside your audience. You gain the opportunity to enjoy easygoing connection, effortless interactions, and your only focus is on how to incorporate these into your business in a more fun and enjoyable manner.

When disaster strikes, trends change. Often, people start focusing on heavier topics and things that may feel more challenging for you to address, especially from the perspective of your brand. The key is to acknowledge these trends and partake in both lighthearted and negative trends in a tasteful way. This shows your audience that you stand by them and that you care about what they care about, while also working toward bringing something fun and lighthearted in the mix for them to care about.

It is vitally important that, especially when particularly sensitive trends arise, you are considerate, compassionate, and direct in your approach. You should never attempt to avoid a topic that your audience cares about just because it is a sensitive topic because, in doing so, you show a disconnect between your passion and theirs. Brands who entirely ignore important topics are often seen as being superficial and insensitive, and may rapidly lose members of their audience, which can be devastating, especially if you have a small or medium-sized business. Essentially, you become irrelevant because you show your audience that you do not stand with them on *all* issues, only the ones that serve your growth.

While addressing something your audience cares about, especially when it is a heavy or sensitive topic, you must be extremely careful in your approach. Before you say anything, you must think about how your brand serves your audience and how your audience has come to expect being supported by your brand. You also need to consider what position you can take that will allow you to support your audience in a realistic manner, while still keeping your brand afloat. Then, you need to consider how you are going to convey this position through your messaging and wording and ensure that whatever you say is said in a way that remains compassionate and sensitive to the subject and everyone affected by it. It is a good idea to get someone else to read through your copy to ensure that you are marketing your brand in a way that truly emanates sensitivity and compassion.

Lastly, *never* try to connect your brand's campaign of addressing an important issue to a sale, promotion, or other offerings. Attempting to use a sensitive issue to sell more of your own products will come across as self-serving, insensitive, and will rapidly make your business irrelevant. You must make this a marketing campaign that is focused exclusively on your audience and benefit them, not your brand. In the long run, this will have a far greater impact on your bottom line than attempting to leverage a disaster to make more sales in your business.

Avoiding Tacky or Insensitive Campaigns

This should go without saying, but as you run any digital marketing campaigns, it is imperative that you avoid using tacky or insensitive campaigns. During the rise of 2020's disasters, some brands made the terrible choice of attempting to leverage this tragic trend as an opportunity to earn more sales in their businesses. It may seem like a no-brainer not to do this, but unfortunately, it happened. A good example of a campaign that failed included a sandwich company offering free facemasks to any customer that purchased two sandwiches. While something like this may not seem obviously insensitive, at the time, it was challenging for professionals to acquire masks, which meant this company was hoarding them and using them as a way to increase their sales during a pandemic. Tacky.

During any trend, regardless of whether there is a tragedy going on or not, you should always take time to audit how your marketing campaigns will look and sound to your audience. They may seem brilliant to you, but you need to ensure that they are going to be received in an intended way by your audience first. If there is a chance your audience will not get what you meant or may take it the wrong way, you need to adjust your campaign, so there is no room for accidental misinterpretation.

Another thing you need to be aware of is the importance of running service-based campaigns. In fact, one way that the aforementioned sandwich company could have increased their sales, without looking tacky, through a service-based campaign would have been to offer free masks to anyone who dropped in, regardless of purchase. Or, they could have donated all of their excess masks to the local health unit and run a campaign that said something like, "Thanks to your loyalty, we were able to donate 15,000 masks to local hospitals!" These campaigns would have been entirely focused on them giving back and would have developed a positive association around their brand in a way that recognized the current trends in a compassionate and sensitive manner. As a result, they likely would have seen a major influx in sales due to the fact that people would have wanted to offer them greater support so that they could do even more to give back.

Always be extremely mindful of what your campaigns look like, and always adjust them if you are ever doubtful about how your audience will receive a campaign. While being edgy and pushing boundaries can be a great marketing strategy, being insensitive is not.

Deepening the Sense of Community Within Your Brand

If you want to make a power move in your ability to gain and maintain relevancy within your brand, you need to deepen the sense of community within your brand's audience. Brands who are not tapping into the power of the community are doing themselves a disservice by creating a situation where they have to repeatedly gain the attention, trust, and respect of their audience over and over again. If you manage to remain relevant enough to continue earning sales, you will be sinking insane amounts of money, time, and effort into getting those sales because as soon as you earn sales, you will lose the attention and interest of your audience. Then, you will be back at ground zero, and you will have to do it all over again.

Building a sense of community around your brand means that your brand becomes an entity that people care about. Now, rather than coming, buying, and disappearing until you lure them back with great marketing, you are encouraging them to join you and stay with you, whether you have active sales going on or not. In a sense, you leverage the parasocial relationship or the one-sided relationship your audience shares with your brand, to create a sort of lasting friendship. This keeps your audience investing more emotional energy and time into your brand because now they feel a sense of connection, and they want to keep your brand in their circuit.

There are two adjustments you can make to the digital marketing strategy that will allow you to deepen your sense of community and grow your brand to greater heights. The first is in your targeted campaigns, and the second is in the way that you engage with your community.

In your targeted campaigns, always make an effort to clarify how everything is about community. Are you selling a new pair of sneakers? Great, which friends should your audience show those sneakers to first? Or, should they take a special photograph of their sneakers and upload it with your community hashtag, so they feel like a part of your community? Do this with any product or service you might be selling. Always look for a way to get your audience to share it with their community, with your community, or both, as this increases the idea of community being an integral part of your brand. The result? They feel more connected to you, and they stay more loyal to you.

In your everyday engagement, create personal posts that resemble something someone would share on their personal page. Ask questions, share pictures of your brand's team, or of something going on behind the scenes with your company, share funny pictures your audience might enjoy, and otherwise share content you believe they would like. Creating a brand page that resembles a personal timeline means that your brand's entity is being personified, making it even easier for people to relate to it. The outcome is that your audience will develop a sense of loyalty and will personally seek you out and invest in your brand, the same way you are investing in your community.

Engaging in the Way Your Audience Is Engaging

One of your primary digital marketing research tasks should be to spend time observing your audience so that you can better understand how they engage with each other, with brands, and with your brand, specifically. Observing your audience allows you to more clearly understand what their behaviors are like, what their preferences are, what dislikes they have, and other important pieces of information about them. The more you understand what your audience likes and dislikes, and what their natural engagement sounds like, the easier it is for you to identify opportunities to engage with your audience in a way that they will understand.

Your goal as a brand is to talk the same talk and walk the same walk as your audience. You want them to feel a sense of connection with your brand by being able to relate with it, understand it, and feel as though they can develop a personal connection with it. This is how you get into their "inner circle." It is easy to understand this by taking a quick look at basic human psychology. Think about yourself for a moment. Chances are, there are people you absolutely don't like, people you don't know, people you don't mind, people you like, and people you love. The people you love are the only ones you invest consistent, significant energy into, while the people you like may get some of that energy, too. Everyone else is either ignored or receives negative attention from you.

Likewise, other people have this same circle around them. They, too, will invest the majority of their energy into the people they love, and then they will invest a small amount of energy into the people they like.

You want to turn your brand into an entity that they can personally relate with, and get it into the inner circle of being an entity they love. If you are in the circle of "don't mind" or beyond, you will either receive no attention or negative attention from these individuals. If you are in the circle of "like," you may seem some attention, but you will have to push hard to continue to receive that attention, and it may be inconsistent at best. But if you are in the circle of "love," your brand will receive attention from your audience in a way that completely transforms the face of your company, while also maximizing your sales potential.

How do you get to be in the "love" circle? You share mutual interests, concerns, passions, mannerisms, behaviors, vocabularies, and other key aspects of a personality makeup. Even though your brand may not be based around a single person, you can create an entity for your brand that can easily be personified by your audience through developing these human-like characteristics as a part of your brand identity and profile. As a result, you find yourself relating with your audience far more effectively, and receiving far more love and attention from your audience, which leads to significantly greater sales, too.

Keeping Up with the Changing Times

Lastly, you need to keep up with the changing times. Part of staying relevant is advancing into new technology and leveraging new tools as they become available to you. Whether it is new techniques you can use to improve your customer service, new software you can use to improve your online user experience, or new tools you can use to improve different aspects of your business processes, you need to keep up with the changing times.

Companies that allow themselves to grow outdated become irrelevant in the eyes of customers because they are using technology and techniques that actually reduce the customer experience. The purpose of evolution and advancement is improvement, which is why companies are always staying at the front of these improvements. They are always looking for ways to use these new and advanced technologies to boost their improvement and increase their ability to provide a better customer experience.

Certain companies, specifically those which intend to have a traditional feel to them, may be reluctant to add new technology for fear of losing their ability to offer a traditional experience. In these cases, the best opportunity is to use improved technology but implement it in a manner that provides an exceptional traditional-like experience. As well, remember that the traditional "energy" of a brand is often created through the interactions of customers and customer service representatives, so you can easily maximize that energy through effective customer service training that maximizes traditional service.

Anytime you implement a new technology or technique into your business, regardless of whether you have a traditional brand or not, you should always look at how that resource fits into your overall brand and how it can be best used to improve customer experience. While you do need to keep up with evolution, you should not rush the advancements as this can lead to detrimental side effects, which ultimately destroy the customer experience and could put a serious damper on your brand's reputation. Instead of rushing the process, think it through, consider how a resource could be best used, and phase it in with careful consideration and monitoring.

Then, use it as a clear marketing point. Anytime you create an advancement that directly benefits the consumer, which all advancements should, you want to talk about it and let your audience know. This shows them that you are constantly doing everything you can to improve their customer experience with your brand.

One last thing I must point out when it comes to keeping up with the times is digital marketing technology specifically. Technology advances and fast. You must always be paying attention to changes that are occurring in the advertising platforms you are already using, as well as watching for new platforms or marketing opportunities that become available. Constant, on-going research allows you to spot changes immediately and leverage them right away, which means you end up with far more effective campaigns.

You should be researching existing platforms, campaign rules on different platforms, algorithms, marketing trends, organic and paid marketing strategies, and new platforms that may be emerging. You should also be researching your target audience so you can pay close attention to what their preferences are and how they might shift over time so you can accommodate for that in your marketing strategies. The more receptive and responsive you are with your campaigns, the more success you will have with them.

Chapter 13: The Latest Trends in Digital Marketing

You will hear it constantly: digital marketing is always changing, and if you want to be successful with it, you must be prepared to ride the waves of change. What worked two years ago, one year ago, or even six months ago, will no longer be the most effective marketing strategy. These days, you must be paying attention to the day to day shifts if you will be successful in keeping your brand ahead of the competition and driving your way to the top.

At the beginning of 2020, it was predicted that platforms other than Facebook would emerge as being stronger and more useful to digital marketers, and that has remained mostly true. It was also predicted that new platforms would rise, automation would takeover, and yet personalization and individual attention would maintain importance and be required if a brand were going to be successful with their marketing campaigns and strategies. So far, all of these predictions have come true.

As we are now halfway into 2020, I wanted to update this book with plenty of excellent content that would help you understand how these predictions are coming true, and how you can use them to help you launch your business into even greater levels of success. We will address each of these claims, discuss what they mean, and understand how you can implement these changes to your digital marketing approach. In doing so, your brand will be far more likely to stay relevant while also being able to leverage that relevancy in a way that increases your sales potential.

Facebook Is Losing Grounds with the Younger Demographic

People have been predicting Facebook's decline for a few years now, and while this may not be the case yet, we are definitely starting to see Facebook reach its peak. These days, 41% of Facebook users are over the age of 65, which is a highly niche audience that is not exactly popular to target among online business owners. When marketers start to see terms like "losing grounds" or "decline," it can be easy to automatically assume that a certain marketing strategy is becoming irrelevant. However, that is not necessarily the case. In some situations, it may be a good idea to hop off board. When it comes to an icon like Facebook, though, it is often a better idea to take it slow and play your cards right.

Despite the fact that Facebook is losing grounds with the younger demographic, there are still 51% of users who are under the age of 65, and a good chunk of those are going t be a part of your target audience. This means that Facebook needs to be a part of your marketing strategy. However, the way it fits into your marketing strategy should not be the same as it would have been in years gone by. Disregard marketing strategies that suggest Facebook should be your primary platform, because this is unlikely to be a sustainable platform long term, and it could result in you minimizing your growth potential or setting yourself up for trouble in the future.

As a part of your strategy, you *should* have a Facebook page. You should also post on it and drive traffic there, as this turns it into an active spot that will effectively attract more audience members your way. What should change is not whether or not you use Facebook, but what you do with the traffic you gain on Facebook. In 2020 and beyond, you should be driving that traffic to another platform, like Instagram, where you can post in a way that is more interactive for younger demographics. Through that, you will find the ability to connect and engage with your audience better, and they will be more likely to convert better.

One other reason why you should not leave Facebook behind is because Facebook is a necessary component of Instagram advertising. You must have a Facebook business page linked to your Instagram page if you are going to do any paid advertising since all paid advertisements are run through Facebook's ad center.

Instagram Is the Most Popular Platform for Younger Kids

Instagram is an incredibly popular platform, and it is actually gaining traction around the youngest demographics, too, such as children and teenagers. Because of the visual content and the ability to see new products and games that people are playing, younger crowds love being a part of this platform. That breaks down to two things for your advertising strategy.

Firstly, if you are targeting any generation under 65 years old, you need to be on Instagram. If you are targeting even younger generations, like those under the age of 25, Instagram will likely be one of the most successful platforms for you to use. Here, you will find that exact audience, and you will be able to create content that caters to their preferences for content consumption, too.

The second thing you need to consider is subject matter and targeting. Because so many younger children are on Instagram, it is important that you are especially careful about the types of content you are posting. If you are specifically targeting young adults over the age of 20, you can get away with more swearing and edgy content. If, however, you are targeting anyone who is in any way a part of a family unit with younger children, such as parents or the younger children themselves, you must keep your content PG. This means no swearing, adequate coverage on models, and portraying content that is acceptable for younger children. Another important thing to consider is what messages you are sending, as parents will be unlikely to let their children or teenagers follow you if you are sending messages that are likely to make them feel inadequate or develop unhealthy world views. Always be considerate of your audience, and of other people who may accidentally find their way into your audience.

Properly Designed Chatbots Are Excellent for Customer Service

Chatbots are becoming more widely acceptable, and many businesses, no matter what their size may be, are starting to rely on them as a business strategy. These days, people's attention spans are incredibly short, and most people have very little desire to sit around and wait for a response. If you are a smaller business, prompt replies may be challenging, especially as you start gaining traction and receiving more inquiries from your customers. Chatbots can help.

It is important that if you use chatbots, you are upfront about it, and that you do not attempt to hide the fact that you are using an automated service. Some brands even name their chatbots so that when their customers message in, they know they are receiving a message from an automated bot, but the message feels more personal because the bot has a name and speaks in a conversational tone. You can program yours as you see fit.

The benefit of chatbots comes in two fold. First, your chatbot improves your response time, lets your customers know you have received their inquiries, and creates a sense of instant gratification for anyone that is looking to get a response from your business. Second, chatbots can be programmed to answer basic questions or provide basic support to people. On Facebook, for example, you can program common questions and answers into your chatbot so that when people message your page, they can receive answers to some common questions they may have. You can use these questions to answer anything from shipping-related questions to how your customers can get prompt service or anything else that seems relevant to your business model. Make sure the questions are actually commonly asked questions; however, as this ensures the bot will truly be helpful to your customers.

It is also vital to ensure that someone is monitoring the inbox so that prompt replies can be given even after the chatbot has done its part. Even though they have received some form of communication, customers will still not want to be kept waiting on responses.

Messaging Apps Are Excellent Tools for Marketing Through

Chatbots are excellent when it comes to customer service, but they are not the only way you can spruce up your marketing strategy. So far, in 2020, we see messaging apps as being excellent marketing tools that can be used to inform audiences of new promotions or offers, as well as upcoming launches or events that a business may be having.

Most messaging apps work by having people automatically subscribed anytime they message your business page for any reason. They can easily opt out by unchecking the box in the top right corner of their messenger app, which will allow them to stop receiving automated messages from you.

For those who want to receive messages from you, though, this is a unique way of sending them. Messaging apps provide the opportunity for it to make it feel like you are directly addressing your audience and sending them a private, personal update about what is going on in your business. Because the messaging approach already has a personalized feel, it is important that you capitalize on that by writing messages in a way that sounds personalized, too. By combining automation with personalization, you will be capitalizing on the two major trends moving into 2021, before 2021 even hits.

Video Content Must Be Used for Your Brand to Stay Relevant

As of 2020, video content is no longer strongly recommended or recognized as a trending content style. It is now recognized as *the* content style to be creating, and if you are not creating video for your brand, you are seriously hurting your growth. Studies have shown that failure to produce video not only stunts your growth but can actually have people ditching your page in favor of people in the same industry who are producing video content.

What type of video content you create depends on what industry you are in, what you are marketing, and where you are posting that content. On advertisements to new audience members, for example, your videos are likely to be short and based on building awareness around who you are and what you have to offer. With advertisements to existing audience members, however, you may create video content that is designed to teach people how to use the products they have already purchased, or how to get the most out of your services.

Educational- and entertainment-based video content are currently the two categories to be in right now. If you can combine them, that's even better. Educational-based video content includes any content that educates your audience on your industry or something specific within your industry, your brand, or something specific within your brand, or anything similar. Entertainment-based video content should be focused on entertaining people in a way that is relevant to your industry, such as making jokes your industry's audience would understand, or purposefully using products wrong or in weird or unusual ways. Try to be as creative as you possibly can, and shoot in the highest quality you can (most smart phones shook in 4K now) while also doing some basic edits to improve your content quality. This way, you are more likely to get traction with your videos, since they will be posted alongside so many other videos that are also competing for the attention of your audience.

Context In Your Content Matters As Much As Quality Does

As our social climate changes, the way you word things matters. Online, and through most advertising mediums, there is very little room for you to give context to what you are saying or what you are creating. This means that people can easily misinterpret what you mean, which can result in your brand taking a serious hit to its reputation as well as its sales. If you are a smaller brand, this hit could be devastating.

To give you an example of how sensitive this issue may be, I want to turn your attention to a national insurance company that launched a campaign at the start of the 2020 pandemic. Their campaign encouraged people to high five over great insurance rates. The campaign was planned well in advance of the pandemic, and the high five was intended to promote a community-based feel by encouraging connection with people you care about. Unfortunately, it launched around the same time global shut downs began, which resulted in the context being entirely wrong to the current global climate at the time of its launch. The result? The brand took major backlash from many people across social media platforms.

It is important to understand that most audiences are entirely unaware of the work that goes into creating campaigns, or the amount of time it takes to get one out. Further, they are not necessarily going to interpret those campaigns accurately, and that can lead to unfortunate circumstances. Always pause, review your campaign, and look at it from as many different angles as possible. Better yet, have a group of go-to people who can review your campaigns for you to ensure there is nothing possibly harmful or negative hidden within your campaign. This way, when you launch a campaign, you know for absolute certain that you will not accidentally send the wrong message or hurt anyone in your audience due to a lack of awareness or a misinterpretation of the context of your message.

Email Marketing Campaigns Should Be More Personalized

Email marketing campaigns are still popular, despite the number of people who have suggested that email marketing has "died" over the past few years. Emails are still an important aspect of business because when you own an email list, *you* own that email list. No social media algorithm or online giant can take that list away from you or somehow destroy your ability to connect with your audience. For that reason, you should still be capturing emails and creating content for your email audience so that, in the event, something does go wrong, you still have direct access to them in a way that they are used to receiving content through.

With your email marketing campaigns, it is important that you personalize them. These days, marketing campaigns can be personalized by breaking your email list into segments and creating content for each individual segment. Most major email marketing platforms will help you create these segments, and they can be created based on the geographical location of your audience members, their unique demographics, or their activity within your emails. For example, if someone clicks on one of your links in your emails, they can be seen as someone who is more likely to engage. Therefore you can specifically send them content they can engage with. If you have people who do not click links, though, you may lighten the number of links in the email and instead offer value right there in that email to encourage them to start paying closer attention.

As you break your list up into segments, ensure that you leverage those segments in the most powerful ways possible. Write content that is highly specific to that segment, as it will feel like you are writing content for each individual member of your audience. Again, automation and personalization are two major trends that will explode in 2021, so this is an important topic to pay attention to and start mastering right away.

Interactive Content Is the Mainstream Marketing Strategy of Choice

As parasocial relationships grow and the dynamics shift, audiences in a parasocial relationship want to be acknowledged and invited to communicate with the brand or media persona of the parasocial relationship. This means that interactive content is becoming the mainstream marketing strategy of choice, and the popularity it gains continues to grow.

Interactive content means that you are cultivating content that encourages people to engage with you. Rather than being recognized or paused over while someone aimlessly scrolls, you are using call to action's (CTA's) as an opportunity to invite people to interact with your brand. This requires a three step process: you create content that encourages engagement, people engage, and you engage back. It is vital that you engage back, as this shows that you are looking at genuinely engaging with your audience, and you are not just asking for engagement to boost your algorithm. While all people may not realize that the purpose of this is often a play for the algorithm, they will realize that you are asking for them to engage but that you are not returning that energy. The lack of a two-way connection will result in them essentially ignoring your CTA because you train them that they will gain nothing from engaging.

Interactive content can be created by asking questions, starting polls, encouraging people to share specific content using your hashtag, inviting people to create videos of them using your products or services, or even asking them to leave some sort of response on your content. It is important that your request for interaction is interesting and that it leads to meaningful engagement in both directions, as this is how you can ensure your audience will respond.

When it comes time to return that engagement, be sure to respond to as many comments as you can. If people use your brand hashtag, like their posts and thank them for using your hashtag. When followers share something that features your brand, reshare their post so that you can feature them in front of your audience, and thank them for sharing content. These types of interactive posts are excellent as they really build that feeling of friendship between you and your audience, which results in them experiencing a much higher sense of loyalty to you and your brand. That loyalty will always convert into financial gains, as long as you respect the loyalty and continue to build it by also remaining loyal to your audience.

Chapter 14: The 2021 Digital Marketing Forecast

If you want to get ahead by leaps and bounds, you need to not only know what is going on in 2020, but also be aware of what trends are likely to emerge and develop in 2021. The sooner you begin researching these trends, the more you will understand them, and the sooner you will be able to get on board in a way that generates powerful results. This means you will be far more likely to capitalize on these trends and maximize your growth, well ahead of everyone else.

In the digital marketing world, audiences both want and need to see their favorite brands engaging in the latest trends before anyone else. If you wait too long, your audience has already seen it happen in other brands, and they are not particularly interested in paying attention once you do it, because it is no longer fresh and exciting. In the meantime, they may even find themselves drawn into other brands that are your direct competition because those other brands got to the trends before you did.

While we can never guarantee exactly what trends will arise in any given year, we can predict based on predictive measuring models and research collected by people who are experts in the marketing fields. What these experts have discovered is as follows.

Automation Meets Personalization, and the Balance Matters

Technology is aggressively advancing, and with it, more things are becoming automated every single year. In the past, businesses shied away from automation for fear of losing that intimate connection with their audience. Since most audiences were new to the idea and were unaware of how automation worked, or how it affected their interactions with a company, many also shied away from interacting with businesses that were heavily automated.

These days, automation is far more accepted among virtually every audience and is exploding in popularity. The simple fact is, automation provides much faster service, creates much more seamless experiences for audiences, and ensures that brands are able to capitalize on the short attention span of the average human in the modern era.

In order to successfully grow your business, you need to integrate automation strategies into your business and load those automation strategies with personalization. The key to achieving this is through how you write your content and how you target your content. Content should always be written in a way that unifies your brand with your audience, ideally on an individual level. You can also target your audience through segments, allowing you to create content that is very specific to the individual segments of your audience. For example, if you sell wellness products to women, you might segment them by age and level of fitness, then create content that caters to each age and fitness category. This allows you to heavily personalize content, while also integrating automation strategies.

Non-Linear Advertising Captures Attention

Non-linear advertising refers to advertising that does not follow any structured experience. These days, people click on what looks interesting, and they come across brands and information in all sorts of places. Previously, leading your audience through a linear purchasing experience was a great way to keep them focused and encourage them to purchase your products. These days, their attention span is way too short for that.

Rather than trying to draw your audience through a linear purchasing experience, you want to create several micro-exposure and micro-purchasing experiences that suit the non-linear behavior of most audiences these days.

Micro-exposure experiences should be focused on creating exposure to your brand or products within about 1 minute or less. These posts or campaigns should *always* point toward a micro-purchasing experience in case someone wants to learn more. Micro-purchasing experiences should be short, to the point, and easy for your audience to purchase through.

They are not going to purchase, though. Not right away, at least. Studies show that a consumer must see something at least 13 times before they decide whether or not they are truly interested in it, and up to another 13-14 times more before they actually purchase it. This leads to them seeing it around 26-27 times before they go ahead and hit "buy." Your micro-experiences, then, are focused on successfully achieving as many of those exposures as possible, all with positive associations, so your audience is more likely to purchase through you.

Keep in mind that while micro-experiences are important, you should still have at least one significant experience, or location online, where your audience can get *all* of the information. This way, when they are ready to purchase, they have access to all of the information and answers they would need in order to hit "buy." In a sense, this is automation as it automates the educational and question and answering part of the purchasing experience. Keep in mind, though; there should only be one key area where this large selling experience happens. All other exposures should be short, sweet, and to-the-point.

Marketing Automation Is a Powerhouse, and It Must Be Used Correctly

Marketing automation is a powerhouse, as it has been for at least a few years now. Previously, automation was used to drive people through lengthy sales processes that escalated them from small end purchases to large ticket items. The idea was to condition the mind of your buyer, so they would be more likely to purchase, while also proving your value at every step of the process. For example, you would sell them a $15 product and prove that it was well worth the value, which would make them more likely to purchase the $50 product you were going to sell them next. While they were being conditioned to buy, you were making money off of them.

This approach still works, but it needs to be done in an important way. The days of single-page websites with a wall of text and videos are gone. People do not have the attention span or the care to be drawn through such a lengthy experience. Instead, you need to automate your marketing so that it provides several automated micro-experiences over a period of time, as this is how you will build connections and rapport with your audience.

Automated social media posts, emails, blog posts, and even entire automated launch sequences are all powerful when it comes to digital marketing. You should also be leveraging paid advertising, which allows you to get in front of your audience without having to put in all the effort of organic marketing. While organic marketing can still get you a great deal of growth, and can explode your engagement, it can also be much slower. These days, a combined approach that is developed through smart automation is the best way to grow your audience and generate successful conversions, too.

Voice Search Marketing Is an Essential

Voice search usage is growing, especially with the introduction of digital assistants like Google Home and Amazon Alexa. Believe it or not, voice search marketing is a relevant marketing strategy, and it is becoming an essential one at that. Voice search marketing is accomplished by developing a website that directly answers questions that people are most likely to have, and that offers clear easy-to-read answers. The benefit here is that digital assistants can easily scan your website for relevant answers and read off of your website to the person who has asked such a question.

In order to get found by digital assistants, you need to use white hat SEO to optimize your page and increase your chances of being discovered. The higher you can rank with SEO, the more likely you will be to get found on voice searches. It is important that you focus on all SEO strategies, including maximizing your viewership, using proper keywords and in a proper ratio, and otherwise providing high-quality content, so your page is more likable. Increasing the social recognition behind your brand name is another great way to increase your rank and get found by voice searches, as well, as digital assistants are more likely to look for reputable sources, and they define a reputable source based on web popularity and quality of traffic.

Content Marketing Should Be Content Selling

Content marketing and content selling are now one and the same. In the past, content marketing was about gaining attention from your audience and getting your business out there. Content selling was about using that attention and credibility you gained from marketing and turning it into sales. The time is coming where both can be done at the same time.

Previously, in all industries, sales were achieved by directly advertising a product and offering the sale. These days, selling can be achieved by marketing a product and then offering a spot for someone to further explore that product on their own accord. This means that you are focused solely on creating marketing-based content, but you are always offering interested parties the opportunity to go to sales-based content if they prefer. This means that the 80/20 approach is fading and that your consumers no longer have to wait for that 20% content to arise before purchasing from you.

To successfully create the merge in your own business, be sure to have high-quality evergreen content, likely on your website, that can be used to conduct the sale. Everything else, especially on social media, should be solely based on attraction marketing strategies, and then should include the option for people to "learn more" at that link. This way, you are always marketing *and* selling, while leveraging the best attraction marketing strategies from all angles.

Hyper-Targeted Advertising

Hyper-targeted advertising is one of the best quality strategies you can use when it comes to combining automation and personalization. Hyper-targeted advertising is the same as segmenting your audience, as it allows you to focus specific pieces of content to the part of your audience that is most likely to enjoy it. This means that brands need to be focused on making content that will serve each character profile within their audience, assuming that there are many who make up your entire audience.

It may seem stressful or even irresponsible to make such niched down content, but the reality is that it is far more likely to gain traction since it has the power of being far more personalized. For example, let's say your audience contains women who are aged 35-65. You might create hyper-targeted content that is oriented for mothers for your younger demographic, while creating hyper-targeted content that is oriented for grandmothers or retirees for your older demographic. This way, you are able to actually personalize that content and make it sound like you are speaking directly to one individual, rather than to a group of individuals.

The benefit of hyper-targeted advertising, aside from maximizing personalization, is that it allows you to specify your paid campaigns to a hyper-targeted audience, too. These audiences are typically so niched that they cost far less to get in front of because it is unlikely that other campaigns are targeting for those exact placements. Of course, ensure your paid advertisements are also written in a way that emphasizes this hyper-targeted approach, as this will be far more likely to guarantee your success.

Maximizing Your Digital Marketing Budget Will Matter

As of 2020, companies who want to maintain their current position should spend 5% of their total revenue on marketing. Those who want to grow should spend 10% of their total revenue on marketing. The rest of that revenue goes into other business-related expenses.

In 2020 and 2021, you should be as close to that 10% margin as possible, if not aiming for as high as 15%. Especially for starter businesses, you need to get your company in front of as many eyes as possible, in as short of time as possible to secure excellent results.

Not only should you be spending as much as you can on marketing, but you also need to be spending that money wisely. After all, there is no point in increasing your marketing budget if you are not going to be seeing the same results from your campaigns. It is important to note that going into 2021, marketing on major platforms like Facebook and Google will change, as they are pushing for more whitehat marketing and less blackhat marketing. This means that they want you to use extremely honest, integrity-oriented marketing strategies that are considerate of their audience, and that genuinely help their audience feel good. This way, their audience is more likely to enjoy these campaigns and engage with them. At the end of the day, these platforms must focus on their audience, first, as their audience is responsible for making them big enough to be able to support their advertising programs in the first place.

It will be extremely important to read the latest marketing information on a weekly basis, at least, to know exactly what is going on with these platforms and their marketing rules, as this will keep you on track and generating massive success from your campaigns.

Streamlined Marketing Strategies Will Change the Game

Did you know the average company uses around 92 different platforms to run their marketing campaigns through? For smaller or startup businesses, the number is likely much lower, but it stands to prove that there are still many different platforms incorporated into the average business marketing strategy. This means that there are a lot of different areas that require your attention, as you need to make sure they are being optimized to deliver content on time without becoming a financial drain on your company.

Going into 2021, you need to streamline your marketing strategy as much as possible. It is no longer reasonable to have a small or startup business where you define an approach and then juggle several different platforms to make it happen. You need to have a defined order of operations and a clear system for managing your results if you are going to generate success with your business.

Starting from day one, focus on just one platform at a time and define an exact strategy for automating your marketing content, monitoring analytics, reviewing results, and then starting all over again. You should also always look for automation tools within these platforms, and educate yourself on how to leverage those automation tools for the best results. This way, you know that your approach is thorough and does not allow for anything, from campaigns to money, to slip through the cracks. If you find that any of the automation tools seem overwhelming or confusing, YouTube offers plenty of excellent videos that will show you exactly how you can use these tools in the most effective manner possible. Give yourself a few days to get used to using them before adding more automation to your plate, but make your end-goal to automize as much as possible to reinforce your streamlined approach.

It is important that you routinely double-check these orders of operations to ensure that they are continuing to serve your business. If you find at any time that your order of operations is allowing for anything to slip through the cracks, immediately change it and *write those defined changes down*. Keeping all of this written down ensures that you are always on top of things and that your system is as streamlined as possible. In the end, this is better for your audience, and this is better for your business, too.

Conclusion

Digital marketing has been around for more than two decades now, and it continues to be an incredibly powerful resource for earning an income online. Whether you want to be completely hands-on, or totally passive in how you earn an income online, you need to know how to tap into digital marketing for success in your online business.

Now that you have read *Digital Marketing for Beginners 2021,* you have access to not only all of the best information about digital marketing but also the most relevant information about digital marketing. These steps are proven, as they have already generated massive success for businesses in 2020, and they are sure to help you generate massive success in 2021, too. By following these strategies, you can do everything in a way that is up to date with modern standards, and that is going to help you really get out there and make a name for yourself, and fast.

Remember: digital marketing is all about strategy, purpose, and clarity. You also need to make sure that you are staying ahead of the curve by staying up to date on new trends so that your marketing always reflects the latest in digital marketing strategies. If you fall behind or find yourself using out of date marketing strategies, you will find that your audience fails to keep up with you because they do not enjoy following your outdated practices.

Beyond using the strategies that we already know to be successful in 2020, it can be helpful to focus on what you can do to set yourself up for success in 2021 and beyond. The sooner you start researching these budding trends, the sooner you will be able to fully understand them and effectively execute them in your own marketing strategies. As always, those who are first on the scene to a new strategy will always be the most successful with it, assuming they use it correctly.

With all of this information in mind, it is time for you to get clear on your digital marketing strategy and move forward! If you have not already, you need to identify what your income channel is going to be so that you know exactly where you are going to be earning your income from online. Then, you need to identify the best possible strategy for getting your content out there so that people know you exist and have the opportunity to shop with you. You can build your strategy using some basic research on the industry that you have chosen, and then following the map in this book. Simply identify the most popular form of marketing for your chosen industry, and then follow the "Combine _____ marketing with other digital marketing strategies" guides at the end of each marketing chapter to discover what method is going to work best for you and your audience.

Lastly, if you enjoyed this book and felt that it supported you with creating a successful strategy for digital marketing going into 2020, we ask that you please take the time to review it on Amazon Kindle. Your feedback would be greatly appreciated!

Thank you, and best of luck!

Social Media Marketing 2021

Exceed 2020, Become an Able Influencer Using Instagram, Facebook, Twitter, and YouTube with the Ultimate Mastery Workbook for Success Strategies.

Cristopher Clarke & Adam Preace

Introduction

It's safe to say that if we didn't already understand the power of social media, we do now. Following mass amounts of chaos resulting from a pandemic and social injustices, we have seen the power of social media and its ability to unite people, strengthen communities, and open doors to new opportunities.

What does that mean for your business? *A lot.*

Social media emerged back in the early 2000s, and it has proven itself to be an integral part of our modern society. Ever since its emergence, brands have been looking for ways to leverage social media and its ability to help them earn serious cash. As a result, we have seen social media expand and develop in major ways.

At one time, brands succeeded by simply marketing their brands, products, or services directly to their audiences. By plastering banner ads, popup ads, and other photo-based ads around the internet, they were able to garner the attention of their audience and earn incredible sales through their online platforms. In fact, Amazon started this way and became the powerhouse it is today from that very foundation of online advertising. Those days are long gone, though.

The idea of "make it and they will come" is no longer true on the internet. With so many people vying for the attention of your audience and earning their trust and respect, it is no longer enough to develop something and make yourself known. These days, you have to get yourself in front of your audience and give them a reason to care. You really have to sell your brand, as well as your products and services, if you are going to get anyone's attention in the first place.

When this book was first written at the end of 2019, it was already true that the community mattered most to virtually every audience across every industry. Today, as we update this title, that has become even more true than it already was.

As a result of our lives being turned upside down and dismantled from what we grew to know and feel comfortable with, many began searching for community and change in the online space. Within mere months that has resulted in consumers caring about commitment, compassion, and community more than anything else. Your audience does not just want to see you out there, flashing attractive products and attention-garnering smiles as you try to sell them the happiness they crave. Your audience wants to see that you will care about them, their safety, and their wellbeing as much as you care about your own. They want to know that you are committed to them, too, and that you will stand by them as we all face these tough and unprecedented circumstances.

Ultimately, they want the sense of community that they have lost through self-isolation and social distancing measures to be fulfilled through their online community. They want *you* to fulfill their craving to be a part of the community again. And you, as a brand, have the power to do just that.

In addition to creating excellent products, marketing those products, and attracting brand loyalty, you also need to be building a loyal and responsive community around your brand. That is the key to mastering the art of social media marketing in today's world. That is the bit that will set you apart from everyone else and have your brand coming out of this entire thing stronger than ever before. It all starts with your commitment to your consumers, old and new.

In *Social Media Marketing 2021,* we have updated the entire book to contain not only the most valuable tools for practical marketing on social media in 2020 and 2021 but also the essential steps for creating a loyal community of followers around your brand. In doing this, you increase the respect and loyalty of those who have already been following your brand. You will also attract the respect and loyalty of those who are looking for somewhere to belong during these uncertain times. The respect and devotion that you attract now will resonate with your brand for years to come, as the relationship between your audience and brand will be firmly cemented in your mutual ability to come together and overcome challenges we are all facing.

Within this book, you are going to discover everything that is relevant to marketing your business in a way that attracts immediate brand awareness and increases in your sales numbers, while also creating sustainable growth that will last for years to come. You will discover how to apply these practical strategies to all of the major social media platforms, including Facebook, Instagram, YouTube, and Twitter. This way, you can maximize your inter-social marketing strategy to develop a well-rounded approach that earns you the most growth and results possible.

To get the most out of this book, we encourage you to read it from cover to cover so that you develop a strong understanding of what it means to develop a practical social media strategy. We also want you to understand the value of all of the major social media platforms, and leverage the power of community. If you are not already on these platforms, you should follow the steps outlined in this book to get started and help get your business out there. The wider your reach, the greater your potential at developing success with your business growth. Plus, the greater your impact will be.

If you follow these strategies exactly as we have laid them out for you, you will charge your way to the top of social media rankings and become wildly successful in your endeavors. If you are ready to get to work on growing your online presence and taking your business to the next level, it is time to begin! Remember, take your time and really invest in fully understanding what each platform is for and how each strategy works so that you are clear on what needs to happen for you to succeed. This way, you are able to maximize your success on social media and knock everyone out of the water from day one.

Chapter 1: Introduction to Social Media

Let's be real: you are probably already familiar with what social media is and how it works. By this point, virtually all of us have experienced social media in one way or another and we do not really need a crash course in the very basics of social media. *However,* social media as a marketing platform is a totally different beast altogether. If you want to use social media for marketing, you are going to need to understand how social media works for businesses, what it takes to turn them into a powerful marketing machine, and what you need to be doing to set yourself up for success.

In this chapter, we are going to go beyond the basics of social media and into the hot topic of how to leverage social media for marketing. You are also going to learn about how you can pick the right niche, create a strong profile, and identify the right strategy to really make the most out of your online presence. This way, no matter what platform you choose to work with, you have the foundation locked in for a strong strategy that will earn you growth and, more importantly, profits.

How Social Media Works for Business

The purpose of social media for general users is fairly straightforward: you get on your chosen platform and begin to network with your friends and family. If you are looking to grow your network, you can add other people who are interested in similar things as you are and then become "digital friends" with them. In other words, you never actually meet them in person, but you share with them online on a consistent basis and get to know them through status updates, comments, and other social media conversations. It truly is about networking and, more importantly, *talking and sharing* with one another.

This is exactly what makes social media such a powerful platform for businesses to market their products on.

It has long been known that word of mouth is one of the most powerful marketing strategies at the disposal of any company. If you want to grow your business, having people share positive comments and experiences about your business while recommending you to others is a great way to start. Meanwhile, if they are sharing negative comments or bad experiences, that is a great way to end up running out of clients because people stop trusting you and, therefore, stop doing business with you. If you want to have success, then, you need to earn the positive comments and recommendations from people who have fallen in love with your business.

Since social media is already all about talking, sharing, and networking with others, it makes sense that this is an incredibly powerful platform to get on when it comes to marketing your business. People are already leveraging word of mouth; all you need to do is get on there and give them something to talk about. By creating a profile for your business and sharing content regularly, you give people plenty to talk about through your profile. This way, all they need to do is engage with your business and share with others so that you are being seen by those who are most likely to purchase from you.

Because of the power of social media and the power of word of mouth, an incredible modern business has evolved from this system. That is: influencers. Becoming an influencer means taking on a business model where you are at the center of conversations, and you are the one influencing what people are talking about. Essentially, becoming an influencer means that you build your popularity on social media and then begin talking about products or services that you love, thus causing those who follow you to talk about them, too. Because you are popular and they already trust you, they are more likely to purchase these products or services.

Becoming an influencer allows you to charge businesses for your endorsement, essentially meaning that you are paid a commission every time someone purchases something because you influenced them to. As a result, you can earn money solely through becoming popular on social media and then guiding people to purchase certain products or services through companies that are willing to pay you.

Both starting your own business giving something people to talk about, or running a business where you influence people to talk about certain things, are great ways to get involved in social media marketing so that you can make a profit online. In this book, we are going to talk about how you can conquer both of these models online, allowing you to build the online business empire of your dreams, no matter what that might look like.

Choosing the Right Niche on Social Media

The first thing that you need to do when you begin to leverage social media for growing a business is to find out what your niche is. A niche outlines a specific segment of your chosen industry that you are going to talk to, which is necessary if you are going to make an impact on social media marketing. Because billions of people use social media every month, and most industries are marketing to multiple millions of people, you need to have a specific segment of the market that you are talking to if you are going to be heard. Otherwise, people are going to ignore you because your information and updates do not feel personable enough for them to really relate with, connect to, and pay attention to you.

Choosing the right niche on social media is necessary regardless of where you are at in business or what business model you are using to make money online. However, there will be certain steps that you need to adjust if you are going to be developing a business online to ensure that you are choosing the niche that is going to give you the most opportunity to grow online.

If you already have a business that you have been running off of social media, choosing the right niche on social media is about finding the part of your audience that is most likely to pay attention to you in the online space. So, if your market is generally 30-40-year-old women in person, you need to find out which types of women you are marketing to the most and who is spending the most time online, and then you need to focus your marketing efforts on them.

With a business already up and running, targeting your niche online is going to be incredibly simple because you already have statistics available to show you who pays the most attention to your marketing, and your business in general. All you need to do is refine these statistics to identify who is online and what they are talking about so that you can find the right angle to talk with them online.

For example, Horace and Jasper is a leather company located in Calgary, Alberta. Their company creates belts, purses, bags, wallets, cellphone charms, wrist cuffs, and more. In reality, this company could market to just about anyone who would wear a belt or carry a wallet because of how versatile their products are. However, if they were to market to just anyone, they would not have any success in getting discovered online. Instead, they have decided to market specifically to edgy, punk rock type that is looking to shop local for products that are higher quality and backed with a more trustworthy guarantee. This way, they are speaking to a very specific segment of their possible market, which results in a massive amount of success in their marketing strategies and business growth.

Another great example of how this works is with the Honest Company. This company provides baby care and cleaning products that are cleaner, more environmentally friendly, and less harmful to your family. Ideally, they could market to anyone who lives in a house or who has young children because they are providing products that are relevant to these two segments of the market. However, they know that the people most likely to purchase their products are women who are environmentally conscious and who want to do better for their families. So, they tend to market toward women and moms who are wanting a safer alternative to harsh chemicals, which results in them having massive growth on their online platform, as well as their business in general.

Identifying your niche is less about paring down and finding one single type of person to talk to, and more about identifying the angle that you use on social media. You want to find the angle that is going to give you a specific way to talk to and share with your audience so that the ones who are most likely to purchase through you are listening and purchasing.

This is true for anyone who is just starting out in business, too. If you are starting a business to generate success online, or if you are becoming an influencer, you are going to need to find a niche so that you know who you are talking to, why, and how to reach them. This way, you are more likely to reach those individuals.

As someone who does not already have a business in place, you do face the setback of not already having statistics around who you are most likely to earn sales from, which means that you are going to have to start from scratch. However, starting fresh means that you do have the capacity to choose the niche that is most interesting to you while also having the most growth potential online, which can be an incredible opportunity to maximize your success.

If you are brand new in business, the best thing that you can do is determine what type of business model you want to follow, and then research what the latest trends are in that particular model. So, if you want to sell products or services, you need to identify what types of products or services are selling the most online. If you want to be an influencer, you need to identify what types of influencers are making the most income online. The key here is to make sure that you are looking at the right numbers. Avoid looking at industries that have the most businesses that are online, and instead, look at the industries that have the most businesses *that are actually making a strong profit* online. This is how you can ensure that you are choosing a niche that is going to be lucrative in offering you great opportunities to make money, rather than choosing a niche that is going to be saturated with businesses or influencers. If it is saturated and no one is making a decent profit, there is a good chance that you are looking at a low-quality industry.

While you look at industries that are going to offer the most opportunity, make sure that you are also looking for industries that are interesting to you. Attempting to make a go at it in an industry that you do not understand or that does not interest you is going to end with you falling flat because you are not passionate enough to really give it the type of energy it needs to grow. Instead, pick one that makes you excited because that will make it far easier to help you gain the momentum that you need to grow your business rapidly and have great success with it, too.

Creating Your Profiles and Pages Properly

Choosing your niche is only part of using social media as a marketing strategy. The next part of making the most out of social media is knowing how to set your profiles and pages up properly. Online, your profiles and pages offer a sort of "store front" for people to look at, so it is crucial that you create them in a way that helps leave a positive impression of you and your business in the eyes of your visitors.

It is important that you always approach the topic of your profiles and pages with this intention of making the best first impression possible. This way, you are looking at them with the perspective required to ensure that they are sending the right message and encouraging people to follow you, trust you, and buy from you, rather than driving people away or leaving them confused or uncertain.

Every single social media platform has fairly similar features in what is available for you to customize on your profile. Typically, you can brand your profile pictures, header images, a tagline, your username, and your wall or your personal feed. These areas can be branded to leave a very specific impression of what your business stands for so that people know as soon as they look at your profile who you are and what they can expect.

In the past, it was enough to write a basic tagline and use images that showed your logo and maybe a professional headshot of you, depending on what your industry was. These days, this type of generic approach is not nearly enough to capture the attention of people and leave them thinking about you and your services over anyone else. Instead, you need to do something that sets you apart and caters directly to your niche so that they see you, remember you, and willingly come back for more. This is where knowing your personal niche is useful: you know what type of customizations and features they would appreciate. This way, you can brand and customize your profile accordingly.

For example, if you are a realtor who focuses on the niche of first-time home buyers that are also families with children, you might make your profile picture a professional headshot where you are standing in front of a nice home that is in a family-friendly neighborhood. You may also have evidence of children in the background, such as a nearby park or playground, or some children's toys in the front yard of the home. If you are an influencer who specializes in talking to country western people who love the rodeo and western style, you might make your profile picture of you well dressed in traditional western wear standing in front of a barn or some livestock. Getting the right energy into your pictures, as well as your descriptions, usernames, and captions is crucial to really set yourself apart from other people in your industry. We are going to go into more specific detail around this on each of the main social media platforms in Chapters 3 – 6, so if you are wanting to brand specific platforms you will learn exactly how you can do that!

Identifying Winning Strategies for Marketing on Social Media

Knowing how to authenticate your chosen marketing strategies for social media is crucial if you are going to pick strategies that are actually going to help you succeed. In this day and age, countless blog posts and articles are swirling around the internet, providing all sorts of information on how you can leverage social media for business growth. Unfortunately, many of these are outdated or feature strategies that have yet to be truly tested for excellent growth. If you want to grow on social media, you are going to need to identify the strategies that help you grow *rapidly* so that you waste no time in reaching the right markets with your posts.

The best way to authenticate and validate your potential strategies is to look for other people who are using them. A strong strategy that actually works will be one that is being used by many of the major accounts, particularly those which are known for staying on top of the current trends such as brands like Nike and Sephora. Do not just focus on large brands, though, as they tend to be more resilient toward less effective strategies. Look at brands that are just a bit ahead of you as well and see if they are also using those strategies with any success. If multiple brands in all levels of success are using your ideal strategy, chances are it is a great strategy that is going to work for you, as well. If, however, you are looking at a strategy and not many people are having success with it, or it seems to be avoided or not even on the radar of larger brands, it is probably not worth your while to try it out.

In addition to looking around to see who is using these strategies and how well they are succeeding with them, you also need to authenticate the quality of the source that you have received your tips from. Receiving guidance from companies that are offering a service that is meant to help you grow, for example, may be hit or miss because they may be catering to their own services in the advice that they give. In other words, they may be giving you advice that is geared specifically toward getting you to buy or use their products to help you grow. This does not mean that it is low-quality advice, or that the service being offered is low quality, but it does mean that the advice could be biased. If you are looking at strategies or advice offered by companies looking to sell their products or services to help you grow, make sure that you validate what they are saying. If what they are saying is true and is working for other people online, chances are they are a reliable source to receive information from.

You can also validate what they are saying by looking at other people who have used their products or services and seeing how their growth is going. As well, look at their own social media platforms and strategies, and see how it is working for them in particular. Unfortunately, there are many companies out there who claim to have winning growth strategies, yet they themselves seem to be struggling to make any growth online. If you find that a company is making claims such as having the capacity to gain you tens of thousands of followers or earn you a specific amount of money, but they themselves seem to not have that same level of success on their own platforms, be wary. These types of businesses are generally making false claims and could be offering low-quality advice and ineffective services that will interrupt your success and leave you struggling.

Once you have validated the quality of your possible strategies by validating the source and validating the effectiveness of each strategy, you should be able to feel confident in whether or not these are strategies that will work. If they are not strategies that will work, or if they seem unreliable or like it may be hit or miss, avoid working with that strategy. This is likely only going to waste your time. If, however, they are strategies that are working for other people and seem to be reliable in offering growth, it is worth giving them a try to see if you can make them work for you, too!

Chapter 2: Becoming an Influencer

In one way or another, influencer marketing has existed for many generations. In the past, it was simply not paid for. People who had great popularity or pull within the community would simply endorse the companies they liked, and everyone else would agree with them and support those companies.

Over time, influencers who were popular in their industries were signed for endorsement deals to help companies grow larger sales numbers. For example, Nancy Green became famous for being the face of Aunt Jemima, where she was featured on the bottles of maple syrup with a smile and a stack of pancakes. Because of her endorsement, Aunt Jemima syrup saw a massive increase in sales.

Back in 2010, influencer marketing began to hit social media. This time, people were building entire careers around becoming influencers and endorsing products on their curated social media feeds where they would grow their popularity and promote products. This is more or less still the way it functions now, but the way that we approach influencer marketing has shifted big time since those early days.

When influencer marketing first hit social media, the strategy that influencers could use was incredibly basic. They could essentially open up a social media account and begin sharing their favorite products and find themselves growing in popularity and getting paid not long after. This is because, back in 2010, there were not as many people trying to earn money through the influencer modality. In fact, many people had no idea that it even existed in the first place and were surprised to find out that their favorite influencers were actually being paid to endorse products. This was such a big "secret" back then that there was actually a law enforced that stated that influencers had to begin letting their followers know when a post was sponsored or when they were endorsing products for companies. This way, they could not get by pretending like they were not being paid, and everything remained transparent.

In 2021, these basic and sneaky tricks are not going to help you in getting your influencer business off the ground. In fact, virtually nothing that involves hiding or creating a sneaky "behind the scenes strategy" is going to get you off the ground with influencer marketing because your followers will be able to see right through your strategy. What people want in an influencer these days is someone who is honest, authentic, and genuinely likable. In other words, people are more than happy to purchase products you have influenced them to purchase, so long as you are not treating them like a dollar sign and trying to pull in as many followers as possible in order to improve your pay. Instead, your followers want to be respected and treated like people that you actually care about and cherish.

Creating a personable, charismatic persona online is crucial if you are going to step into the influencer scene and make any money with your business in 2021. You have to be the type of person that people genuinely enjoy knowing and getting to know so that when people come across your page, they have a reason to like and follow you. This also helps them build a genuine relationship with you so that they trust in you, believe what you are promoting, and are willing to continue supporting you and listening to your recommendations. Creating this proper balance of personable and professional is the essential element in making a business as an influencer in 2021.

In this chapter, we are going to discuss what you need to do in order to set yourself apart in a way that is actually going to support you with getting ahead in your business. This way, you know exactly what you need to be focusing on and how you need to be approaching your influencer business to become a success in 2021.

Who Should Be an Influencer?

Every single business that enters the online space needs to approach its strategy to become an influencer. Even if you are not intending to become an influencer and get paid through affiliate marketing, approaching your strategy with the mindset of becoming an influencer is exactly what it takes to give your brand power. With brand power, you can feel confident that people are going to be able to recognize your brand with ease. Furthermore, if you suggest one of your new products or encourage people to buy one of your existing products, they are going to trust in you and take action because you have the power of influence that encourages them to do so.

Creating influence with your brand, even if that is not the focal point of your business model, is a great opportunity for you to create brand power and make a massive income with your business online. That being said, you should look into what it takes to be an influencer and adapt these techniques to fit your brand so that you are promoting your brand and building influence with your brand and not you personally. When it comes to influencing with your brand, you need your brand image to be the influencer itself. This way, people develop a relationship with your brand and are more likely to trust in your brand and follow the guidance you lay out for them.

If you are planning on becoming an influencer yourself, and this is your ideal business model, you need to make sure that you are prepared to do what it takes to become an influencer. You need to be willing to spend a significant amount of time online so that you have time to build up your online presence and cultivate a following. You also need to be willing to share enough of your life with your following that they are able to develop an interest in you and feel as though they are cultivating personal relationships with you. If you are attempting to create an influencer business and you are not prepared to share about your life and show up online, you need to reconsider as this may not be the best line of work for you. Although there are boundaries in how they show up, influencers are expected to show up quite a bit and really put themselves out there if they are going to make an impact and earn any type of money in their industry. We will go into more detail about what you need to be sharing and how you can create healthy boundaries, and cope with the lifestyle of being an influencer, later. This is all a part of building your marketing strategy and will need to be considered when you are building your influencer brand online.

Finding Your Unique Edge

One of the most important elements in becoming an influencer is finding your unique edge. Your unique edge is that one thing about you that you are known for, and that sets you apart from other people who are similar to you. A great way to identify your personal unique edge is to think about what you are known for amongst your friends, as this is what makes you stand out in their eyes. For example, if you are known for your sense of humor, your fascination with bugs, or your passion for helping animals, this is your unique edge. This is what sets you apart from others and makes you, you.

Finding your unique edge allows you to really share a prominent and important part of yourself with the world, while also cultivating a brand for yourself. This way, you are able to remain consistent in showing up with something that helps you stand apart from the rest of the crowd. This is the edge that you will become known for, and that will do a lot of work for you in helping you grow your business. Through this edge, people will identify you apart from others, they will determine whether or not they relate with you, and they will develop a deeper connection with you because they feel like they are being let into an important part of your life.

Once you have found your edge, you need to find a way to market it. You can incorporate it into your marketing strategy by making it *part* of your marketing image, not all of it. In other words, your quirk should not be present in every single post you make and every comment that you share, because this is overwhelming and tacky. Instead of seeing this as being a unique quirk, people are going to wonder why you keep shoving this part of yourself into their face. They may see it as inauthentic and determine that you are using it as a strategy rather than a way to share more of who you are. Instead, talk about it regularly but not incessantly. Make sure you share it often enough that people are able to identify it as being something relevant to who you are, but not so much that people see it as being overwhelming or obsessive. Ideally, sharing your unique edge about 60-80% of the time and then sharing other organic content the other 20-40% of the time is a great way to balance it out so that you are able to be identified with your unique edge, but not in an overwhelming way.

Setting Yourself Apart from the Rest

Although your unique edge is going to help set you apart from the rest of the influencers who are also trying to build a brand for themselves, you need to really take it a step further if you want to succeed in becoming a true influencer. If you look online at influencers who are already working toward establishing themselves, you are going to see a clear divide between people who are making it and people who are struggling to get anywhere with their brands. The divide around *why* this happens is also fairly obvious.

The people who are struggling are following blogs and books about becoming an influencer just a little too closely. Their posts often feel as though they have been thought through way too hard, and are littered with keywords and trending topics that appear to mean nothing to the person sharing them. When you scroll their pages, they feel excessively curated, like they have taken exactly what they were told to do and they did it, exactly. Although this approach may have worked when influencing was a brand-new thing on social media, it does not work anymore. Unfortunately, following the rules this closely in the influencer world is going to snuff out your success and leave you struggling to connect with other people.

The influencers who are generating success online clearly stand apart from the rest in that they are creating an image that is *real*. They have read the blogs and books about how to become an influencer and they have developed an understanding of what is needed in order to be successful. Then, they got creative and nurtured their uniqueness so that they stand out in a way that really suits them. They cultivate a true sense of authenticity, which leads to them being able to connect more closely with the people who will eventually become their followers. These influencers are known for showing up in a way that feels as if you could truly be their friend, which is exactly why people begin to trust in them and cultivate relationships with them.

If you want to set yourself apart from the rest, you need to avoid curating authenticity and charisma and instead nurture your authenticity and charisma. Teach yourself that it is safe to continue to flourish as you are, and then create your own image and strategy that fits who you are.

This way, you are able to really promote yourself on social media in a way that is real, honest, and likely to be connected with by others. As a result, your influencer image will stand apart from the rest and you will take off in a way that can only be achieved through organic connection.

Creating Consistency in Your Presentation

When you are showing up online, it is important that you remain consistent in your presentation. You do not want to curate your content too much, but you do want to make sure that all of your content makes sense and goes together. This way, when people land on your feed, they are not confused by who you are and what you are sharing with them. Instead, they are able to get an immediate feel for who you are and what you stand for, as well as what they can expect when they follow you.

The best way to curate a feed that does not feel too curated is to pick your favorite presentation or image and use that as your guideline for the majority of your content. Like with your unique edge, this should account for around 60-80% of all of your content so that people see it and associate you with this image. Furthermore, this is going to help people identify you and really get a feel for who you are in a matter of seconds. Then, you can use the other 20-40% of your feed to share content that may relate to your primary image but also strays away in one way or another. For example, if you are primarily sharing a minimalistic white background image, you might share maximalist colorful photos 20-40% of the time so that your feed has some diversity.

Creating this diverse image is going to help people know the core of what you are sharing, while also having the opportunity to get to know all of who you are. Moving beyond a 2-dimensional one-style image into an array of diverse images in this way ensures that you continue to come across as real and authentic. After all, no person is exactly the same all the time. We all switch up between our style, what we represent, and how we feel like showing up in the world here and there. Honoring your diversity by showing it in your pictures is a great opportunity to really create a strong brand with depth, while also helping people know who you are by avoiding the confusion that comes with a complete lack of consistency.

Ditching Marketing Gimmicks

An influencer is meant to be based on word of mouth, which means that people need to trust you in order to listen to what you are saying and be influenced to buy the products that you are promoting. If you are constantly using marketing gimmicks to try and get products in front of other people, you are going to be seen as inauthentic and someone who is just trying to make a quick buck from the online space. Marketing gimmicks are not effective for businesses, and they are even less effective for influencers.

Learning to spot a marketing gimmick is a great opportunity for you to avoid them in your own strategy so that you can use something more authentic and that cultivates connection and trust with your audience. One of the biggest marketing gimmicks that influencers fall into is trying to market in a way that represents the company more than it represents themselves. What ends up happening is their audience sees them as being fake or inauthentic and begins to lose trust and respect in that person. For example, if you were going to market a toothbrush brand and you started sharing curated pictures of you using that toothbrush with little to no reflection of your own brand, people are going to wonder if you're promoting the toothbrush just for the money. Instead of bending your own image to fit that of a company's, find a way to creatively tie together their image with your image. This is a marketing strategy that makes you more valuable in the eyes of brands because you effectively market to their audience and your audience all in one go. This means that you are going to reach people both within your immediate market and outside of your market based on who is already following that brand.

It is crucial that every piece of content that comes from you, whether it is promotional or not, is always reflective of your brand. This way, your audience knows that you are genuinely endorsing the product and that you like it, and they do not begin to wonder if you are just posting a picture for increased pay. Although they will know that you are getting paid, they will also trust that you are only endorsing products that you actually like and so they will continue to trust and respect you.

At the end of the day, your audience has cultivated a relationship with *you* and *you* are the reason they are buying any product that you are influencing them to buy. If you eliminate the aspects of yourself that attracted them to your feed in the first place, you are going to lose their interest and probably fall flat in terms of influencing. As well, if you continue to engage in behavior like this, they are going to see you as being fake or just in it for the money, and eventually, the entire reputation you worked so hard to build will be erased. Avoid this massive mistake by ditching marketing gimmicks and sharing products and services in a way that is relevant to you and your brand so that you can continue building on the success you have already begun to create.

Building Follower Relationships with Boundaries

When it comes to being an influencer, knowing how to have strong boundaries is a crucial part of the process. Many people think this is just some cautionary advice that should be thrown into the mix to help people get by, but the truth is: boundaries are an essential part of being a strong influencer. Every top-quality influencer out there has established boundaries with their audience and they adhere to those boundaries in virtually every single situation they find themselves in.

Creating boundaries with your audience serves two strong purposes, both of which are going to preserve the longevity of your brand. First and foremost, creating strong boundaries is going to protect your privacy, and your energy. Attempting to share every single thing with your audience, respond to every single person, and otherwise be excessively involved with your audience is going to get exhausting, and fast. Not only that, it leaves you vulnerable to internet bullying and abuse, as well as other damaging behaviors which can really take their toll on you as an influencer. There is nothing fun about putting your entire life out there, only to find people having negative, rude reactions to who you are and what you are sharing. Do yourself a favor and honor your privacy from day one so that as your audience grows, your privacy remains strong and you do not have to attempt to create it later on.

The second benefit of creating strong boundaries right from day one, even before you have a large audience, is that you actually weed out your audience as you go. Boundaries are going to teach your audience what to expect from you and how they can reasonably treat you, which means that you are more likely to build an audience that is respectful and loyal. People who do not do this in advance find themselves being followed by individuals who want to take advantage of them, which can lead to unreasonable demands on your time, energy, and efforts. You may also find that brands treat you this way, too, and that they are less willing to pay you properly for the work that you do. If you have strong boundaries from day one, however, you can avoid these types of behaviors and nurture relationships with your audience and your brand partners that are filled with respect and honesty.

Chapter 3: Facebook Marketing

One of the longest standing platforms out there to date is Facebook. Facebook came around in 2004 and has continued to grow in popularity ever since. Over the years, the company has shifted its platform to serve both personal connections and professional connections so that people can use it either for personal use or business use. For that reason, Facebook has also become one of the most popular platforms for marketing your business.

These days, Facebook offers many excellent features for people who are wanting to promote their business online. In an effort to diversify their platform and create more equal opportunities for business owners, while also keeping the platform enjoyable for personal use, Facebook has introduced features such as business pages, promotional opportunities, and groups. You can use all of these to market yourself or your brand on Facebook.

Who Should Use Facebook, and Why?

When it comes to getting your business online, everyone needs to be on Facebook in one way or another. Due to the way that this platform is designed, as well as the reputation that it has built for itself, everyone can benefit from having their business on Facebook. These days, people are more likely to search Facebook or Instagram for your business than they are Google, as they want to see what type of image you are maintaining with your business. Finding you on a social media platform gives your followers a greater opportunity to not only find basic information about your business, but also more personalized information about your business. More importantly, they are going to identify whether or not you are reliable, and if they are a part of your target audience.

Creating a Facebook page will ensure that if anyone turns to Facebook to look you up, they can find you. This means that you also need to maintain your page in a way that is going to give them something to look at and develop an opinion from right away, rather than having a page that is just as plain as Google's results page.

If you are using Facebook just to create a landing page, you are going to want to post at least once per week to ensure that the page looks up to date and has enough content on it to show your audience who you are. This way, people do not get the idea that your brand is inactive or inconsistent, which could lead to them not trusting in your business or losing interest relatively quickly. That being said, you can use it to turn your audience to another platform as well, allowing you to get even more viewers onto a platform that you are actually using.

If you want to use Facebook as one of your primary platforms, you can do that as well. The only difference will be that you are going to update your page more frequently so that there is plenty of new content for people to find. You may also wish to use other platforms to encourage people to land on your Facebook page, helping you to funnel more possible followers to your platform.

Leveraging Facebook in Your Marketing Strategy

As I have recently mentioned, the two best ways to leverage Facebook into your marketing strategy is to either use it as a primary platform to connect with your followers, or design it to be a landing page that funnels people to another platform. These are very basic ways to take advantage of Facebook and its reputation to reach your audience.

There are other ways that you can leverage Facebook in your marketing strategy in 2021 as well, however. These ways are going to give you the best opportunity to develop your online presence and grow your Facebook page with ease.

In the past, the best way to use your page was to simply add a profile picture and some words about your business and then update your status fairly regularly. These days, however, it works differently. One of the best ways to leverage Facebook as a part of your marketing strategy in 2021 is to use it as a platform to share your products and services with others. You can do this by completely filling out every single part of your Facebook page with information about who you are, what your business is all about, what products and services you have to offer, and where you can be located. You can even sell your products and services right there on Facebook, or offer a booking feature so that people can book a service with your company.

The number of features that are available on Facebook is massive, making it an excellent platform for people who want to sell their products. In fact, many marketing agencies are now saying that smaller businesses can run their entire online business exclusively through Facebook without the need of a website or another platform to sell anything on. This is actually a great way of putting everything online without having to spend quite as much to maintain a website and a purchasing platform.

As you learn to work Facebook into your marketing strategy, your best opportunity is to turn it either into a "hub" of sorts where people can go to do business with you. This can either be the hub that people land on after interacting with one of your more engaged platforms like Instagram or Twitter, or it can be the primary hub where people go to engage with your business in any way that they desire. You can decide how much or how little you want to be active on Facebook, but the key to making Facebook work for you is actually getting on it and creating some form of strong presence there.

Marketing on Facebook in 2021

If you want to come off on top with your Facebook marketing strategy for 2021, you are going to have to take yourself beyond the basics and really learn how to work your page. The best way to do that is to get on Facebook and get yourself acquainted with the different tabs and different features available to you as a business owner so that you know exactly what you can do to set your page up for success.

Just like in the previous years, you are going to need to create your page with a branded page name, a branded profile picture and cover image, and a custom description. You should also customize your page's username, which can be done by going to the desktop version of your browser and tapping on the "Create Page @username" under your page name. The username that you use here should be the exact same username that you are going to use on other platforms so that everyone who looks for your page knows what to look for across all platforms.

Once you have set up the basics, you can begin to customize your page. You can start this process by going to the "Settings" part of your page and then tapping "Templates and Tabs." There, you are going to get the opportunity to choose what type of page you want to have, and what customizable features you want access to on your page. In terms of templates, Facebook offers ten template options: standard, video page, shopping, restaurants & cafes, services, politicians, nonprofit, venues, business, and movies. You want to pick the one that is relevant to your business, as this is going to give you the best tab features relating to your business model.

Once you have chosen your template, you can begin to customize your tabs, or the features available on your business page. The tabs that you will have access to for customization features will depend on which template you have chosen; however, you can add or remove tabs to your template by scrolling to the bottom of the Templates & Tabs page and clicking "Add A Tab." If you want to remove a tab, you can click "Settings" next to that tab and select "Delete." You can easily re-add any tab you delete, but you may need to revise it to feature all of your business's information once again. You can also rearrange the order of the tabs by clicking on the three grey lines to the left side of each tab and then dragging them into your desired order.

After you have created your template and chosen your tabs, you will need to go back to the main view of your page in order to begin customizing each tab. From there, tap the tab that you want to customize and then select "edit" next to any feature that you want to change. You will then be walked through the process of adjusting the information in that given tab so that it reflects what you need for your business.

When you are customizing your tabs, make sure that you are considering what your customer's experience is going to be like when they land on your page. You want to make sure that it is easy to navigate, and that it is easy to find any relevant information that they may need when it comes time for them to buy through you. This means that your pictures need to be more than just an extremely basic corporate-type photograph, and your descriptions need to be more customized as well. You want to make sure that as your customer browses your page to find information, it is easy for them to find it, whether that is about products they can buy through your page, services they can book through your page, or other platforms they can find you on. The more thoughtful your presentation is, the easier it is going to be for people to find what they are looking for on your page so that they can get what they want and carry on. With online shopping, convenience and appearance is everything.

Once you have customized a tab, go back to your main page and browse that tab as if you were a stranger to your page. Get a feel for how it is to navigate that tab, whether or not you can easily find what you are looking for, and if you impressed by the overall appearance and functionality of that tab. If you are not, consider making the necessary revisions so that you can make your page more attractive and functional.

How to Monetize Your Facebook Page

Monetizing your Facebook ultimately comes from funneling people through your page to a sales page where they can purchase your products or services, or the products or services that you are promoting for another company. The key to being able to do this on Facebook is through building a presence that gets you plenty of engagement and creates loyalty between your audience and you.

In 2021, the key to really making an impact on Facebook is by having a page filled with posts that your audience wants to share or engage with. Although engagement has always been important, it is beginning to dominate as the single way to improve your visibility on Facebook. This is because Facebook is wanting to return to its roots of offering organic, authentic, enjoyable connection between friends, family, and people who are a part of the same community. Essentially, you need to get your page into the conversation by sharing as a part of your community and encouraging your followers to share your posts to their community, too. The hard part, however, is that Facebook no longer likes to show posts that say "like," "share," or "comment" in the caption. In other words, it is not ideal to actually ask people to like, share, or comment on your posts anymore because this is considered to be pushy and takes away from organic connection.

The best way to boost engagement is to share posts that are relevant to your niche and that your followers are likely going to want to share as is. You can do this by sharing blog posts or articles that are relevant to your industry, uploading pictures or memes that are relevant to your industry, and by sharing thoughtful commentary that people relate to or agree with. The more that you can focus on creating share-worthy posts that are organic and relatable, the more you are going to earn shares by your audience. This way, you are going to see your engagement ratings go up, which will result in your exposure going up, too. This increased exposure is going to pique people's interest in your business, which will result in you having a far greater chance of getting seen by the right people so that you can earn more sales.

Recently, as an effort to make Facebook community-minded once again, they have come out with an update in their algorithm that limits the number of business pages people see on their feeds. Although it is not as restrictive as it was in late 2018 and early 2019, it is still more restrictive than it once was. This means that your page really needs to perform well in order to earn an organic space on people's timelines. There are a few ways that you can encourage your own page to be the one that is seen, in addition to encouraging organic visibility from your followers through consistent engagement.

The first way that you can work with this to increase your visibility is through creating your own visibility by sharing your page as frequently as possible. Anytime you post something to your page, do not be afraid to share it to your personal profile, too, so that your own friends can see it and engage with it. You can also join groups with your Facebook page, allowing you to interact as your page rather than with your personal profile. If you can't, join groups with your personal profile but make an effort to share from your page into the groups as often as possible. Then, anytime someone likes one of your page's posts, you can invite them to like your page. This is a great way to encourage people to like your page after they have already expressed an interest in what you are sharing.

You can also improve your chances of getting found by promoting your posts. That being said, going into 2021, you really need to step your game up in order to experience any level of success with your promoted posts. Simple images with a sentence or two that sound like clickbait are no longer effective when it comes to promoting your page because they lack personality and impact. Instead, you need to share something that is going to really reflect your page positively. One great way that you can do this is by simply boosting your top performing posts so that they can perform even better, which can be a great way to reach more people. However, you can also promote specific advertisements, so long as they have personality and reflect your brand effectively.

The best way to create actual advertisements in 2021 is to create them as if you are creating a post for your page. You want them to have the same level of personality, authenticity, and honesty and you would do with your own page's posts so that the advertisement accurately reflects who you are, or who your brand is. Make sure that your chosen photographs are also reflective of your brand to ensure that they are more likely to reach the right people. This way, they captivate interest and encourage people to click "like."

Just like with everything else in social media marketing, any advertisement post you make needs to really reflect your brand's personality in the imagery and words. These days, so many tutorials exist for how you can write your advertisements complete with templates or even copy and paste messages that you simply plug in and hit "go" with. The problem with these types of tutorials is that they promote all of the same gimmicks that you already know that you need to avoid if you are going to make any progress in your online platform. Although you can certainly use other people's advertisements as inspiration for how you can create your own, you still need to use your own creative mind to design one that is going to be reflective of your business. Using anything that is too generic is only going to result in your brand being diluted as people think that you are unclear in who you are marketing to, or that you are incapable of marketing your own brand because you do not know it well enough. Get to know your brand as if you were getting to know your new best friend and use that level of knowledge and understanding to create a brand that other people fall in love with, too.

In addition to organic and paid advertisements, you can also monetize your Facebook page by using the Shop feature, or the Booking feature. Both of these features allow small businesses to sell products or book services on Facebook through their interface, making Facebook business pages a wonderful hub for small businesses.

If you want to use the Shop feature, you will need to add a Shop tab to your page. Then, all you do is visit the tab and create a custom description of what your shop offers. From there, you can upload each of your products, their descriptions, and their prices into the Facebook shop tab. When visitors land on your page, they will have the opportunity to see your products and purchase them through your Facebook page directly, meaning that you do not have to attempt to funnel them through to another page for shopping. In the world of online shopping, the fewer clicks that are required to purchase, the better.

If you want to use the Booking feature, you will set it up in the same way. You will start by adding the Booking tab to your page, then you will head to the tab and upload what services are available to book and what time slots you have available. All you have to do is keep your schedule updated in the Booking tab so that people can book with you, and then Facebook will take care of the rest! This way, if you want to book people in for your services faster, you simply encourage them to head to your Facebook page and then they can take care of the rest from there.

Chapter 4: Instagram Marketing

Instagram has rapidly grown into one of the most powerful marketing platforms for small businesses, offering some of the best features available for creating organic marketing posts for your audience. If you want to grow your brand and create a strong presence online, Instagram is a wonderful way to go as it offers you access to more than 1 billion active users per month, as of 2019.

As you may already know, Instagram was purchased by Facebook back in 2012 and has since been improved upon by Facebook's developers to become an excellent sister site to Facebook itself. This means that the platform features incredible top of the line marketing and business features, as well as excellent integration with Facebook's interface. Through these features and the integration, you can create an intricate customer experience that is unlike anything we have ever seen in the past.

Who Should Use Instagram, and Why?

Instagram is a platform that, like Facebook, is not discriminatory based on who can use it and leverage it for success. In fact, most modern influencers are using Instagram as a way to connect with their audience because it allows them to leverage graphic marketing strategies to create deeper relationships with their audience, which in turn improves their productivity.

Although Instagram is not necessary, it is an incredibly valuable platform that can provide you and your business with an excellent opportunity to take advantage of the built-in graphic marketing approach that Instagram is designed with. This means that you can show your audience how your products or services work, give them a visual idea of what they are going to receive, and even offer them ideas on how they can incorporate your products or services into their own lives. Instagram also allows you to feature customer-generated content, which is a great opportunity to boost your visibility, increase your credibility, and reach a larger audience for free.

A segment of the market that absolutely must be on Instagram in 2021 is anyone that primarily hosts their business online. If you are not on Instagram and you have an online business, you are missing out on massive opportunities to build greater connections with your audience while also offering an effortless shopping feature for your clients. Like Facebook, Instagram offers built-in shopping features, booking options, and contact options that allow your customers to buy, book, or connect with you with just one click. Again: the fewer clicks it takes to book or buy, the more purchases you are going to get from your audience. In other words, the easier you can make it, the more success you are going to have with your business.

Leveraging Instagram in Your Marketing Strategy

Adding Instagram into your 2021 marketing strategy is going to come with a learning curve due to the sheer number of features available on this platform. Having so many features available means that you can customize a more valuable and enjoyable customer experience, but it also means that you have to be prepared to learn how each of these features works. The primary goal when you are creating an Instagram marketing strategy is organizing all of these features so that they work together to create a seamless experience. You do not want all of the features disorganized or working independently of each other, as this can result in your customers growing confused by your page and not fully understanding what it is that they need to do in order to work with you or your company.

The best way to work with Instagram is to decide what exact goal you want to achieve with the platform and then use only the features that are going to help you achieve that goal. For example, if you want more people to land on your website and learn about your company, you need to ensure that all of your Instagram features are driving people to your website. Alternatively, if you want people to land on your page and shop with your company, you are going to need to encourage people to browse through your posts. When you know what your exact goal is, you can easily organize all of your features and uploads to serve that goal so that you are more likely to get what you need out of Instagram, rather than wasting your time setting everything up only to confuse people.

Some of the best features that you can use on Instagram include: Instagram stories and story highlights, IGTV, your URL, and your optional button that you can add when you upgrade to a free business account. Another great feature that you can access when you link your Facebook and Instagram business pages is the opportunity to help people shop directly from your images. This way, you can upload your products to Facebook, tag them in your Instagram post, and have people go directly from your post to the product page so that they can purchase it if they want to. Using this feature ensures that your customers have a quicker checkout experience, rather than having to go to the link in your bio and find their desired product on your website. These features can all be customized to move your audience through a custom experience, allowing you to get them to where you want them to be so that they can interact with your business and purchase your products or services.

Understand that just because Instagram has so many features does not mean that you need to be using them all. Plenty of people are not using IGTV, stories, or shopping features and they are still having great success with their businesses online. That being said, if you want to step into taking full advantage of the latest and greatest features on Instagram for your business, it may be ideal for you to set these features up so that your customer's experience on your profile is outstanding, memorable, and worthy of them returning to purchase products or services from you.

Marketing on Instagram in 2021

As I mentioned, the best features available on Instagram right now are the stories and highlights, IGTV, customizable buttons, and shopping features. Using these features as a part of your 2021 marketing strategy is a great opportunity for you to grow your Instagram, reach a larger audience, and make more money from your Instagram page. Before you can really do that, though, you need to organize them and set them up in the right way so that they flow together and create a streamlined experience on your page.

With your marketing goal in mind for Instagram, pause and consider what the best possible experience would be for your audience that would help them reach your goal. For example, if you want more people to land on your website, what would be the best way for you to get them there? Or, if you want more people to buy from you directly through Instagram, how could you set that up, so it is an easy and enjoyable experience? Consider what features could be used to get your customers to that goal, and then identify how those features would need to be used in order for them to get there. Before you begin to take any action customizing these features, make sure that you have chosen the most effective and direct method for marketing your business. Although there are likely many ways that you can get your customers toward your goal, you want to make sure that you are using one that does not waste their time or cause them to take unnecessary steps. In other words, the days of watching a 5-minute video, and then a 15-minute video, and then buying a small item before being sold on a big item are gone. People want to get to the point as quickly as possible, and the more that you can support them in this goal as you market your business, especially on social media, the more likely you are going to earn sales in your business. Ideally, your process of landing on your page to purchasing your product or service should be less than three steps, as this keeps it short, sweet, and to the point. It also gives you plenty of time to sell people on your products and services before they get to the point of purchasing so that they have a strong reason for why they should purchase by the time they land on your sales page.

After you have identified the best 2 or 3 features to use to help you get your customers to your goal point of either landing on your website or purchasing from you, you can begin to customize your Instagram features. At this point, using Instagram will become much easier because you are not attempting to master all of the features, but instead, you are only mastering 2 or 3.

To help you get started with each feature, I am going to outline how you can use them with 2021 marketing standards right away. This way, you are not only using these well-known features but also leveraging them in a next-level manner that will help you grow your business rapidly.

Instagram Stories and Story Highlights

Instagram stories and highlights are nothing new on Instagram, but how they are being used has changed completely. In the past, stories were simply used to share behind-the-scenes snapshots of upcoming products or offerings for people to have an opportunity to feel like they were getting an exclusive first-time look at what was going on in your business. This method really became popular when Kylie Jenner sold out of Kylie Lip Kits within minutes of her product going live due to this very marketing strategy that she had used. It is no secret: Instagram stories have the capacity to really offer you the opportunity to build suspense and support your customers with feeling like an exclusive part of your business. That being said, these days, the strategy that you use needs to be more transparent, honest, and catchy if you are going to leverage stories effectively. Since this feature is not necessarily new, you want to make sure that you are staying ahead of trend in the latest way that it is being used to help people feel connected with your company.

The best way for you to use your Instagram stories to help you stay ahead of the curve with marketing in 2021 is by using your stories as if they are a small television series. Stories only stick around for 24 hours, unless they are saved to a highlight, which means that you can use them to share "programming" throughout the week with your audience. By that I mean, you want to see each day's post as being somewhat like an "episode" of a show, and as you upload them, you want to remain consistent, as well as enticing.

A great example of how you could view your story feed in this way is shown in the following example: let's say that you are running an Etsy store and you are using Instagram to market your products so that people will purchase them. To help you market through stories, you could consider having "What I'm Making Monday" where you share what you are working on that week. Then, you might also have "Technique Tuesday" where you share what techniques you are using to make those products that week. You can create a customized theme for each day of the week to help show your audience what you are doing and to make them feel as though they are a part of the experience. This way, rather than having your story filled with random pictures and videos from throughout the week, you create something that is consistent and memorable. Now, your audience is going to know what to expect from you and, if they watch your stories regularly, they are going to be able to follow your process and develop a deeper sense of connection with you, your brand, and your products.

When you create these "episodes," a great way to leverage your marketing is to use hashtags that are relevant to what you are doing in each episode in your stories. For example, if you are going to go with a "What I'm Making Monday" type episode, you might use a popular hashtag like "#makeitmonday" on your story feed. This way, people who are browsing the hashtag are going to see your story and will find your feed organically.

When you are making your mini-episodes, be certain that the way you are designing each photograph or video is well-branded and enjoyable to watch. For example, do not just throw up a mediocre video or picture of you working your business and expect it to gain traction. Instead, think about how you can design pictures and videos that are going to help entice your viewers to pay attention and actually interact with you and your brand. For example, you could place your phone on a tripod and video you working on your latest project and then edit it in a simple editing app on your phone before uploading it to your story feed. These 15-30 second clips of you working can be made in much higher quality then, and they will be more interesting and enjoyable for your audience to watch. You can also use Instagram's built-in features to customize your story by doing things like adding stickers, polls, questions, or even location information or other information to your posts to make them more interactive and enjoyable. The more that you focus on making each story update a work of art, the more people are going to want to pay attention to it.

When it comes to making highlights of your stories, you can take your favorite clips of each of your daily episodes and upload them into your highlights. For example, say for #makeitmonday you take your favorite 1-2 clips each Monday and upload them into your #makeitmonday highlight reel. This way, people who are new to your page can catch a glimpse of your highlights from the past, which helps them build a connection with your brand while feeling like they are getting exclusive insight into the best moments of your past.

IGTV

Instagram TV, or IGTV, works much like stories. This feature allows you to upload up to 10 minutes of pre-recorded film to your Instagram profile, and unlike stories, they do not disappear after 24 hours so your followers can go back through your IGTV uploads and view your previous content. In a way, it works like a built-in YouTube experience, offering you your very own channel to feature your videos on.

When you are using IGTV as a part of your marketing strategy, the best way is to treat it like stories, except with longevity. Create videos that are 1-10 minutes long in a way that makes them interesting and enticing, and that follow some form of consistency. You might even tie your

IGTV in together with your stories marketing strategy by creating longer episodes on your IGTV and sharing the highlight reel of those in your story feed. Then, you can share the highlight reel of your story feed into your page's actual highlights. For example, for the #makeitmonday episode we mentioned above, you might share a full episode of you making something, or making a part of something on your IGTV channel. Then, you could share highlights of you making the said item in your story feed, and then the highlights of that story feed into your highlight reel on your page. This way, your audience can see as much or as little of the process as they desire, allowing them to decide how they want to consume your content.

Since IGTV does require more time and effort to make, and consistency is key, it is ideal that you only pick one or two days per week that you are going to upload a fuller video onto your profile. Attempting to upload a new video every single day can get overwhelming quickly, and may not be sustainable which can lead to you not being as consistent as you need to be to have success with your videos. Starting modest and working your way up is a much better opportunity for you to grow your channel effectively.

In order to really leverage your IGTV channel as a marketing strategy, make sure that you are making videos that build interest in your products or services. For example, showing you using or creating one of your products and then guiding your followers to look at your page or your website where they can find the final product for sale is a great way to use this as a marketing feature that earns you sales. Always make sure that you market your actual products or services in your videos so that when people watch them, they are watching for a reason, and that reason is one that earns you money. Since people are already curious enough to watch the video, they are also going to be curious enough to view your products and services and potentially purchase them. Use that curiosity to your advantage in marketing to boost your sales, rather than wasting it by having them lose interest after your video leaves them with nothing to follow up on.

Customizable Buttons

After you convert your profile to a business profile on Instagram, you are going to have the opportunity to add one customizable button to your page. This button is important as it offers your audience a quick way to take action with your business, ideally leading to a booking or a sale. Instagram will offer you buttons, including "Reserve," "Book," "Email," or "Shop Now." You want to choose the button that is most relevant to your business model and then follow Instagram's built-in step by step process to configure that button for your business. This way, when people land on your page and find that they are interested in your business, they can immediately take action and do something about it, which will result in you increasing your sales.

Shopping Features

Instagram's shopping features are not brand new, but they are new enough that they can still be a strong part of your 2021 marketing strategy, especially if used effectively. In order to set up your Instagram shopping features you are going to need to link your Instagram business account to a Facebook business page that has been set up with a "Shop" tab. In order to do this, you can open a Facebook business page, add a shop tab to your page, and then follow Facebook's step by step guide to add products into your shop. Once this is done, you can go back to your Instagram business page and start uploading pictures of your products in use. Then, all you have to do is tag your products in the pictures through the picture's edit screen. Once that is done, people will be able to tap the image with your products in it and follow the tag to the checkout part of your shop so that they can immediately purchase your products, right from your pictures on Instagram.

If you are running a business where you are selling products online, especially if you are a smaller retailer such as a home-based business or someone who is selling on Etsy or Shopify, this is a great opportunity to increase your sales. Through this strategy, you can improve your chances of getting found and making sales on Instagram, which will allow you to grow your business faster.

Monetizing Your Instagram Page

Once all of your marketing features are in place, you are going to have a strong funnel on Instagram that will lead your audience through the sales process so that they can book or buy with you. That being said, there are still a few additional ways that you can improve the monetization features on your Instagram page so that you can earn more from your profile.

The primary and possibly most important step in monetizing your Instagram page is knowing how to make proper posts that actually pique people's interests and leave them wanting to learn more. In 2021, people are not only scrolling their own feeds but also discovery feeds a lot more, which means that you are going to be one in many posts that they are scrolling. You need to make a post that is worthy of them stopping, tapping onto your picture, and then viewing your profile to learn more about your business. Otherwise, people are just going to keep scrolling by and will never actually discover you.

This means that you *really* need to set yourself apart from the crowd.

At this point, nearly every marketing gimmick that could possibly be used has already been used on Instagram. Viewers have seen the generic messages, stock images, and fake excitement done to the point of it becoming incredibly annoying, and they don't want to see it anymore. They also do not want to see low-quality images with captions that sound like the person does not really care about learning how to use social media, because this type of behavior dates all the way back to the early-to-mid 2000s. In other words, it is extremely outdated.

Instead, what people want to see is something that is high quality, interesting, and soul-capturing. They want to feel like you have spoken to them from your heart and that everything about you and your brand is a work of art. Your products, images, and everything you write should all be a part of your artistic process as you cultivate your social media profile and share content with your audience. This does not mean that you need to be some form of professional artist in order to really sell yourself on Instagram, but it does mean that you are willing to take down the mask and show parts of your real self to your audience. Even if you are just reselling items you purchased from wholesalers, creating this type of authentic connection is crucial in connecting with your audience and making sales through your business.

When you choose products to sell to people, make sure you choose ones that fill the need while also looking good. Believe it or not, people actually care about that type of thing, even if what they are purchasing is something that is not typically purchased based on its aesthetic. Pick products that are in attractive colors and that are made with sleek style that is easy on the eyes so that when people see images, they are immediately interested in what it does.

Then, make sure that you photograph the product well, too. Generic photographs, ones with plain backgrounds and nothing else in the picture, and other "cold" looking images do not perform well on Instagram. Instead, you want to take pictures that have attractive backgrounds that help the product stand out, with the right lighting, and at angles that give the best view of the product. A great way to set yourself apart in 2021 is to look up basic photography skills or tips that can help you take higher quality images, and then really place emphasis on learning how to do better photography. Even if you are only going to be using your camera phone, you can still use these techniques to take better pictures. Practice taking photographs of your products and really get to know what works and what doesn't, and do not be afraid to try several different shots to make sure that you find the right one. None of your photographs should be rushed, as this can lead to them being low quality and missing the mark on gaining you more attention on Instagram.

Finally, when you are sharing your pictures, make sure that the captions resonate with your audience. Some audiences are better with long captions, whereas others are better with short, so test out using both lengths with your audience and see how they respond. Use the lengths of captions that resonate best with your audience so that you know that they are reading through everything you write, rather than it just landing on deaf ears. Then, once you have the right length for your audience, make sure that you are sharing something from your heart that really sells your product. For example, rather than saying, "Check out these modern earrings I made today! I really think you should head over to my website and see if a pair suits your needs!" you could say "I was inspired to make these modern earrings after a visit to my favorite coffee shop today, and wow am I ever proud of how they turned out! What do you think? Hit the link in my bio if you want to claim them!" This gives a more personal, soulful explanation of why they were made and why you are proud of them, and really gives your audience a valid reason to go ahead and make a purchase on your products or services.

Chapter 5: YouTube Marketing

YouTube is famous for being one of the original platforms where influencers made a splash, as the rise of famous YouTubers really changed the game for influencers everywhere. These days, YouTube is still one of the best platforms for creating and sharing video content with your audience.

Unlike other platforms which have evolved to offer countless features and ways for you to market to your audience, YouTube keeps it simple. They have mastered the art of video content sharing, and they continue to focus solely on helping you share video content with your audience. Every single feature they have created helps you upload your videos into their massive search engine so that people can search and find videos just like yours. As a business owner, you can leverage YouTube as a way for you to connect with your audience through video, but it has to be done right if you are going to get into the market in 2021 and really grow your channel.

Who Should Use YouTube, and Why?

Unlike Facebook and Instagram which are great universal platforms for virtually every business that is looking to get online, YouTube has a more niche audience in terms of what types of businesses it is going to really work best for. Naturally, influencers are still a huge part of YouTube's content creators because video marketing offers them a wonderful opportunity to create a face-to-face connection with their audience. It also helps influencers demo their products for their viewers so that their viewers see how well the product works and feel more enticed to actually purchase it.

Aside from influencers, the businesses that are really going to benefit most from having a YouTube channel are those that have enough substance to really create a strong program that is going to be worth tuning into every week. Businesses that lack enough substance are going to struggle to have enough topics to create content with, which can result in them creating low-quality videos, or videos that are not really filled with enough content to make them worth watching. They may move too slowly, talk about information that is not really relevant or interesting, or share content in a way that seems like it is not worth watching. In other words, you might find yourself attempting to create videos when really a visual post with written content likely would have worked much better for the amount or type of information you needed to share.

If you have a business that enables you to feature something with substance; however, YouTube is a great place for you to market. For example, Mountain Rose Herbs uses their channel to educate people on herbology and how they can use herbs in their day to day life, which means that they have plenty to talk about while also marketing their own in-house dried herbs. The alternative to a business that has plenty to talk about already is one where you are willing to identify an angle that you can use to give you plenty to talk about while also incorporating your products or services into the mix.

For example, Hot Ones is a YouTube series where people are shown eating spicy wings while being interviewed. Although the focus of each episode is on the interview, the wings that are covered in hot sauce make the show what it is. It also gives the producers a chance to market their hot sauce at the end of each episode, encouraging people to give it a try.

If you do not have enough substance to create a channel with, or if you are unable to find a strong edge to drive your channel with, YouTube may not be the best place for you. At this point in time, each channel needs to have a very clear focus and consistency in what it shares in order to get discovered. Otherwise people are going to lose interest in your channel and go somewhere else.

Leveraging YouTube in Your Marketing Strategy

The key to leveraging your YouTube channel as a part of your marketing strategy is to treat your YouTube channel as if it were a television series that you wanted people to tune into. Imagine that you are a producer and you are producing television for people to watch, and YouTube is your platform for getting that content to the people who are going to watch your videos. This is exactly how you need to approach YouTube in 2021 in order to generate any level of success with your channel.

With your television producer perspective on, you need to stop and think about what type of series you could create that is going to capture peoples' attention and be worth tuning into over and over again. This means that the topic needs to be more about what they want to see, and less about what you want to make, since your viewers are going to be the ones responsible for helping your channel grow. You can identify some great topic inspiration by browsing for similar businesses on YouTube to see how other people are approaching their channels. Make sure that you are looking to go deeper than just the basics, as YouTube is far too mature for basic, or generic, channels to really thrive and survive on the platform anymore. For example, instead of wanting to become a "makeup artist sharing tutorials" be a "special effects makeup artist sharing tutorials about how you can look like your favorite cartoon characters." Identifying a far more specific niche that you are going to be creating videos for is essential in helping you determine what exact angle you are going to take when it comes to sharing content for your viewers.

After you have identified a specific niche, you need to get down to the basics of creating your own program. This starts with determining how long each video should be, how often they should be uploaded, and what type of edits are going to need to be made in order for your video to be top quality for viewers. These basic details are going to help you lay down the outline for what your channel is going to feature, allowing your future viewers to know exactly what to expect every time they plug into your channel.

If you have a business that has plenty of content that could be made, you might consider making a few different series that you will feature on your channel. For example, as a chef, you might feature quick vegan dinner recipes, vegan snack recipes for children, and vegan lunch recipes for work. Creating different series' like this gives you the opportunity to share more, while still retaining the same level of consistency in your channel. You should treat each series like its own show being shared on your channel, meaning that each video should have its own ideal length, day of the week that it will be uploaded, and unique edits that make it more enjoyable to watch.

After laying out the basics for how you want to create your episodes, you are going to want to then look into how you can brand each series. Pay attention to choosing titles, descriptions, and even backgrounds for your videos that are all relevant to your brand so that each aspect of your video promotes your brand as a whole. This will also make each video more consistent, ensuring that it is memorable by those who come across your videos on your page.

Finally, when you leverage YouTube in your marketing strategy, you want to make sure that it is feeding into your sales funnel in one way or another. Make sure to talk about your products and services in each video, as well as create a clear call to action in the video itself, as well as in the description that is going to help people find their way to your website so that they can buy from you. Without this proper call to action, people might find your videos and fall in love but never take any further action because they have no idea that your videos are meant to lead to the purchase of a specific product or service, which can be a massive loss for you.

Marketing on YouTube in 2021

Due to the fact that YouTube remains relatively the same as it was when it first began, the skeleton of marketing on YouTube in 2021 is still fairly simple and reflective of the platform's earlier days. The primary steps in marketing on YouTube include: making a high-quality video that has relevant content, sharing that video with your followers, sharing that video out to other platforms, and encouraging people to engage with the video. If you are selling a product or service, it will likely also include a shout out for that particular product or service so that people know what they should go purchase when they are done watching your video.

Although the process of getting your videos up and available for viewers to see is still essentially the same, the strategies required for making videos that people view as being worthy of paying attention to and sharing has changed quite a bit. These days, people want to see videos that are more or less like a television show over anything else, as I already mentioned. This may sound somewhat restrictive, but it actually provides you with an incredible opportunity to follow a tried-and-true guide that is going to help you succeed in getting your videos seen and shared amongst other people in your industry. This way, all you need to do is follow the structure while making it your own and, as long as you remain consistent and listen to your audience, you should have wonderful success with YouTube.

To create those videos and series' that people are going to pay attention to and crave more of, there are a few steps that need to be followed. First and foremost, you need to understand what types of videos your audience enjoys watching, and identify what type of personalization you could do that would make the videos your own while ensuring they remain enjoyable for your audience. In other words, you need to make sure that if you personalize something, it will be something that your audience cares about and enjoys, not something that your audience won't notice or won't enjoy. With this in mind, you can create your angle that is going to help you really design a series that is going to be powerful for leveraging in growing your business.

Once you have picked your angle, you need to start filming your videos. Ideally, you should plan out the content of 3 to 5 videos at a time so that your videos are always consistent. This way, you can see how each video ties into the next and how your series becomes a fluid experience. Like with real television shows, you want each episode to tie in together, rather than having each episode act as a standalone. Even if you are going to be talking about completely different topics in each episode, you still want to make sure that those episodes string together in a way that makes sense and keeps your viewers' interest. Attempting to bounce around from topic to topic with no clear path forward is going to be confusing for you and your viewers, and will make it challenging for you to keep anyone's interest in your show.

A great way to build even more structure into your channel is by scheduling seasons for your show to air. You can run from one season to the next without missing any time in between, but doing it this way ensures that each season can have a specific focus and that you are able to keep your show fluid. For example, let's say you run a talk show where you interview people who are able to inspire your audience. Perhaps season one is focused on interviewing people who can inspire you to overcome obstacles you are facing in your life, and season two is focused on interviewing people who can inspire you to reach for something bigger. With these focuses in mind, you can organize each episode of that season to fit your chosen topics, allowing you to have a fluid show that makes sense. Although each show may be about wildly different things, the general flow of each season will be fluid, making it more enjoyable to watch. This also improves your consistency, meaning that people will know exactly what to expect when they tune into your channel.

Once you have organized the structure of your show and identified your season topics and episode topics, it is time to get to work creating each episode. With YouTube in 2021, it is imperative that each episode is well thought out and offers high value. Your viewers either want to be entertained or educated by your videos, which allows them to feel like their time was well spent watching the videos you have shared with them. In fact, if you entertain or educate them well enough, they may even spend an afternoon or two binge-watching your episodes and turning into loyal followers of your channel.

With that in mind, be really clear in what you want to achieve with each episode and plan it accordingly. If you need to book guest speakers or find certain equipment to make your show work out, do so. Never film an episode before you have everything in order, unless you can make a reasonable and high-quality adaptation to ensure that your episode still comes out as higher quality. If you film an episode and anything is left incomplete or seemingly sloppy, people are going to stop paying attention to what you are making and look elsewhere for entertainment or educational value. Take your work seriously so that your viewers see your dedication, and in return they will offer you dedication back.

Aside from these important steps when planning and creating each video, the other steps required to achieve successful YouTube marketing campaigns are the same as they were in years' past. You need to have high-quality filming equipment, great lighting, and you need to have both yourself and your environment well put together so that when people see your video it looks clean and polished, rather than sloppy and poorly created.

In addition to making your videos into a YouTube series, you can also market through your descriptions, and through your channel design itself. For years now it has been common knowledge that when you get on YouTube, you need to upload a branded channel photo and channel art, as well as create a branded description of what your channel is. In 2019 it also became mandatory for all channels to have a high-quality channel "trailer" which is a 30-60 second clip showcasing what your channel is all about and what people can expect to see on your channel when they land on it. Naturally, all of this should be completed for your channel in 2021 as well. However, you can also take it a step further by really leveraging these sections for marketing purposes.

In 2021, creating a channel description filled with personality is just one of the ways that you can get people to pay attention to your channel. Another great way is to make it a marketing pitch where you leverage your description to help people get to know you, your business, or your product, while really promoting the benefits of you, your business, or your product. Then, at the end of the description, you can create some form of memorable call to action that will leave an impression on the person who is reading your channel's description.

If you choose to use your description to create a marketing pitch, you are going to need to create a pitch that is clever and that actually encourages people to pay attention to what you are sharing. This way, people are going to be likely to read all the way through. If you create a pitch that is generic or that is clearly a pitch from the first line, people are likely going to disregard it and it will be a wasted space. The best way to turn it into a pitch is to create a description that clearly describes who you are and what you are doing, and then encourages people to join in by either visiting your website or following your YouTube channel. Creating your pitch this way ensures that it is personal and enjoyable to read, ensuring that people are far more likely to read it all the way to the end.

Finally, another great way to market with your YouTube channel in 2021 is to brand the actual appearance of your channel. On YouTube, every channel is laid out the same, but you can still brand your channel by customizing your thumbnails and organizing your channel in a way that effectively shows of your brand. To do this effectively, you are going to need to conceptualize an ideal appearance for your YouTube channel and then create that appearance through your thumbnails and through how you organize your videos into playlists. There are two great ways that you can customize the appearance of your videos based on what you want your channel to actually look like.

The first option is for channels which are only creating one series for their channel, and it works by having the same thumbnail template but drastically different images uploaded into that template as you go. To get started, you can design your template with a program like Canva, and upload all of your branded colors and symbols, such as logos, onto that template. Then, all you have to do is change the actual image itself for each episode so that people can see what the different episodes are about. You want to make sure that the actual images that you are using are different enough from episode to episode to ensure that people can see what makes each episode different from the others. If you have the same image or similar images for each episode, people are not going to stay on your channel for very long because everything looks the same and there is nothing to really draw them from one video to the next. If you take pictures that are unique and feature elements that advertise the specific topics of that episode, then you give your audience more information to gather from the image alone. This way, they can visually see what draws their interest, and then read the title and description to see if they actually want to watch it.

If you are going to have multiple series on your YouTube channel, you should create different thumbnails templates for each series. That being said, your different thumbnail templates should all be uniform in terms of what colors and symbols are featured on them so that they flow together. This way, when someone watches one of your series on YouTube, if they see a thumbnail for another, they immediately know it is also one of your own series. Since you have already got them watching one of your videos, as long as they enjoy it, this is an easy way for them to find your other series as well. Again, you want to make sure that the actual images taken for each episode's thumbnail is different so that when people find each new series, they can immediately determine which episodes they are going to be interested in, and which ones they may not be super interested in.

Finally, in 2021 most people are going to be watching YouTube channels with series, but they are not necessarily going to be watching these episodes in order, nor are they going to be watching every single episode. Although you may have some viewers who watch every episode, most are going to watch the episodes that seem interesting or relevant to them and they are going to ignore the rest. For this reason, you want to make every single episode a complete stand-alone episode while also tying it into the series. To do this, you want to have each episode have its own plot that helps you get through one thing from start to finish in a single episode. For example, if you are a talk show, one episode will be one entire interview with one host. Or, if you are a DIY channel, one episode will be one entire DIY project from start to finish. This way, when people watch your channel, they see everything they need to see in order to gain value from your video, making it worth their while. However, as you go through the episode, you might reference other videos you have made in the past so that you can "advertise" them in your video. For example, say you do a DIY on how to make a custom cabinet and you are using a painting method that you showcased in another video. You might skip over sharing every element of that painting method in your new cabinet video and instead direct people to your other video. This way, people who already know how to do that method or who are going to use a different method do not have to attempt to skip the instructional to get back to the cabinet making. For those who are interested in learning the modality, however, they can click through to your other video, which will begin the process of them finding more content on your channel for them to enjoy.

Creating a fluid experience that can also be enjoyed as a stand-alone experience takes practice, but once you begin to put your videos together in this way, you will find that it becomes a lot easier. As well, it helps significantly when it comes to sharing your content with your followers, making it an excellent opportunity for you to organically market the other videos on your channel.

Monetizing Your YouTube Channel

Having the right strategies for designing your channel and helping your videos flow together with ease is imperative. These are going to be the primary way that you advertise on your page and help grow your channel so that more people can find you and enjoy your content. That being said, there is plenty more that you can do to monetize your YouTube channel so that you can begin to earn a significant profit off of your channel. The strategies I mention below are going to be helpful both for your retail or services business, or for your influencer business.

The first way that you can really earn a profit off of your channel is by selling something directly through your videos. If you are a retailer or a service provider, naturally you will want to talk about your products or services in your videos so that people can go ahead and purchase from your company. In order to effectively sell in this way, you want to show the products or services in use throughout the video and then offer a way for people who are interested in gaining access to those products or services themselves. This way, they develop an interest as they are watching and then they are offered the opportunity to get their hands on that product or service, which ultimately results in you leveraging their curiosity for sales.

If you are an influencer, this is how you can showcase products of companies that you presently have affiliate deals with. A great example of this is how makeup artists will use makeup products from the company they are affiliated with, or how chefs will use cooking tools or appliances for companies that they are affiliated with. By showing the product in action and then later offering the opportunity to get those products for a discount, you are giving people the opportunity to act on their interest that you have built with them throughout the video.

Affiliate marketing is not just for influencers, either. On YouTube, plenty of people who run their own businesses will become affiliated with other brands so that they can earn even more money online. If you are running your own retail or service business, you might consider becoming an affiliate with companies that you are using in your own business to help keep you running. For example, you might become an affiliate with your web host or your accounting program so that you can earn money from other entrepreneurs who are in need of the same services. Affiliate marketing can be adapted to serve anyone looking to earn even more money, especially through YouTube, so do not be afraid to look into options that may be available to you based on the model of business that you are running.

Another way that you can monetize your YouTube channel is by becoming a sponsored page. On YouTube, there are businesses that will sponsor your page in exchange for you shouting out their company in each video. This model works similarly to affiliate programs, except the company will often subsidize your YouTube channel in terms of what equipment you need to make high-quality videos, and will possibly pay you a salary, in exchange for your endorsement. This is typically something that individuals with a larger following will do, so once you have increased your exposure on YouTube, you might consider reaching out to sponsors to help you run your page. Sponsors can be found through simple Google searches, and they can help you out with monetizing your channel in big ways.

Finally, the most popularly recognized way for monetizing your YouTube channel is through running advertisements on your videos. The key to making money through advertisements on YouTube is to place them effectively and to choose the types that are most likely to earn you money. On YouTube, you have the opportunity to choose which style of advertisements you want to use and where you want them placed in your video, both on desktop and on mobile. Placing your advertisements effectively is crucial in helping you actually make money this way. If you post too many advertisements, you are going to lose the attention of your audience because they will be clicking away from your video to get away from the excessive advertisements.

The best way to place advertisements in 2021 to make an income this way without driving your audience away is by creating an advertisement that goes at the beginning of each video. For longer videos, such as those that are 15+ minutes long, you can also consider adding an advertisement halfway through. For incredibly long videos, like those that are 45+ minutes long, you might consider placing an advertisement every 10-15 minutes throughout the video. This breaks up the video and gives your viewers the chance to take a break from the content you are sharing, while also allowing them to check out a new product or service and potentially earn you some income.

Another way that many YouTubers are leveraging advertisements to earn an income is a way that is said to be on the uptrend and that will likely become a massive way to monetize your YouTube channel in 2021. This way is by using your YouTube channel as somewhat of a tripwire that encourages people to purchase from you. There are two ways that you can use YouTube as a strong tripwire, allowing you to earn even more from your page.

One way includes advertisements, and the other way includes strategically made "incomplete" videos.

To leverage advertisements as a way to make even more money on your YouTube channel, you can offer your viewers the opportunity to gain access to your content *without* advertisements by buying it from you directly. For example, say you are making motivational videos for people to watch or listen to so that they can feel more empowered and confident in their lives. You might offer the full talk available as a video and an audio download without any advertisements in it for a low price. This way, viewers can watch the video without advertisements, or even listen to it in their earphones or their car for that added benefit of being able to take your content on the go with them. Keeping the price of these downloads low ensures that people are more likely to purchase them because they are not being charged too much to do so.

Another great way to leverage videos on YouTube is to offer some incomplete videos that have advertisements in them. This really encourages people who are enjoying the videos to buy your products because they want to see the end of the video and they want to have an experience that is free of advertisements. If you use this method, it is important that you do not overdo it on your channel or people are going to start seeing your channel as a cash grab. While people will likely want to financially support you so that you can keep making videos, you want to start by gaining their interest and their commitment to your channel. You can do this by offering videos that are high quality and that are completely uploaded from start to finish, and then offering some that are incomplete. This way, you have plenty of videos encouraging people to see the value in your channel, as well as plenty other videos encouraging them to purchase your "premium" videos so that they no longer have to watch advertisements *and* they can see the end of your premium content.

Applying one or all of these methods to your YouTube channel is going to massively support you with growing an income from your YouTube channel in a relatively short time. As long as you remain consistent in applying these strategies and apply them in a way that offers massive value while also encouraging people to purchase from you or view your advertisements, you are going to have an effortless time earning money from your YouTube channel in 2021.

Chapter 6: Twitter Marketing

Twitter has been a highly controversial platform in the past, with many claiming that it is becoming "irrelevant" or that it is too challenging for smaller businesses to use. Some have even gone so far as to claim that Twitter is not ideal for certain industries, discriminating against companies that have younger, older, or more eclectic audiences than the average company. In fact, a common myth that was passed around for much of 2018-2019 is that Twitter is only beneficial if you are a politician or a white collar business person. Many believed that its sole focuses were stocks, politics, business, and relevant news articles.

Believe it or not: none of this is true, and knowing this may just make Twitter your best tool for growth in 2021.

Twitter has actually been proven to be one of the most effective platforms for businesses to get on, offering a whopping 80% click-through rate, where 80% of visitors on your profile are actually going and visiting your URL, too. People on Twitter are highly active, love to check out new businesses, and believe that if a business is on Twitter, it is a business worth knowing about. In fact, in 2019, a study showed that 85% of Twitter users said that they believe it is crucial that a business is on Twitter, particularly so that they can offer customer support. Clearly, Twitter is an incredible tool for business, no matter how large, small, or niche your business may be.

Who Should Use Twitter, and Why?

Getting on Twitter in 2021 is crucial, no matter who you are. In the past five years, many influencers and small to large businesses have harnessed the power of Twitter by getting on, getting involved in the conversation, and being available to offer support to their clients as needed. Adding your business into the mix, whether you are retail or service based, or if you are an aspiring influencer yourself, is crucial. You need to get involved in the conversation and start growing your platform in 2021 if you want to harness the power of this underrated beast and grow your business massively in the coming months.

For many businesses on Twitter, they have discovered that they actually gain more followers faster on this platform over any other platform. Where other platforms may take a couple of months to build into the hundreds of followers or beyond, with minimal effort your Twitter platform can grow to multiple hundreds or thousands of people within just a couple of weeks. People on Twitter *love* to engage and connect, and they are believed to be some of the most active and hands-on social media users on the net to date.

If you are running a business and wanting to grow in 2021, Twitter needs to be on your radar. Using it at all is going to give you a massive boost in your exposure and growth, but using it effectively is really going to help you take off. Not only will Twitter help you grow on that platform, but it will also help you grow on your other platforms and really extend your audience reach. Using this platform properly can be life-changing for your business, and is well worth the somewhat complex learning-curve that comes with surviving and thriving in the "Twitter-verse."

Leveraging Twitter in Your Marketing Strategy

The marketing strategy that you use on Twitter is going to largely depend on how big your business is and who your audience is. Unlike Instagram, which relies largely on topics and trending hashtags, Twitter actually also relies on proximity as a valuable tool in helping you grow your audience and increase your impact. By using proximity, you can leverage the power of local, national, or global audiences to grow your platform and get found. The key is knowing what size your business is, who your audience is, and who is going to be the most likely to care at each point in your platform's growth.

If you are a smaller business, or you are just starting out, you want to focus on a close proximity to you. Getting on Twitter and targeting local trends is a great way for you to begin to get found on the Twitter platform, as this way, you are not attempting to target too large of an audience. When you target local trends and local groups of people, you give yourself a greater opportunity to get found because you are not competing against so many people who are trying to speak to the same audience as you are. Whereas a larger business with a bigger name may have an easier time getting found in the larger audiences, you as a smaller business and with a smaller reputation will have a hard time. This is truly the key to getting your foot in the door.

As your audience begins to grow and your business begins to grow as well, you can start targeting larger audiences. You can do this by looking into your national audience and targeting national trends. Although smaller businesses can do this too, you should avoid doing it too frequently as a smaller business to avoid being drowned out by the rest of the people speaking to your audience. Alternatively, as a smaller business or a transitioning business, you can combine national and local trends to improve your odds of being seen by your target audience.

Once your business begins to get larger and more well-known, you can start targeting international and global trends. This way, you have a larger built-in audience that is already going to be communicating with you through their timelines, which will actually improve your odds of being seen in the trending topics by people outside of your existing audience. Using this approach will help you grow even larger so that you can get found by a greater number of people, allowing your business to grow even faster. If you are a small or medium business, or if you have a small or medium audience on Twitter, you can still use global trends, but you should avoid using them as your primary focus. Instead, either use them from time to time while focusing primarily on your local or national audience, or use them in addition to a local and national audience in a single post to increase your chances of getting seen.

Speaking to the right *size* of an audience on Twitter is crucial, as this is how you are really going to get found online. Again, attempting to speak to too large of an audience when you do not have a strong enough reputation or recognition to support you is only going to cause your brand to get drown out amongst all of the other voices. Really knowing how big of an audience you can reasonably speak to is crucial in helping you get the word out there and grow your platform more rapidly. As you begin to grow your business, you can begin to grow your reach, too, allowing you to get even further out there.

If you are a business that deals primarily with a certain audience, such as a local business that deals primarily with local people, or a global business that deals primarily with global people, following the aforementioned strategy is still important for you. Even though you might not be targeting your exact audience at all points, you will be growing your popularity and visibility, which means that your target audience will be more likely to see you. The larger audience, even if it is outside of your typical sales audience, will increase your perceived value, making you more likely to sell products or services while also making it easier for you to sell your products or services at a higher price tag. This way, you can leverage your audience for improved profits, not just for improved visibility and discoverability.

Marketing on Twitter in 2021

When it comes to marketing on Twitter in 2021, you are going to want to first identify the size of your existing audience. If you are brand new on Twitter, chances are you do not have a very large audience and so you are going to need to start off targeting smaller audiences. If you have been on Twitter for some time and you are looking to upgrade your strategy, you may already have a fairly decent sized audience. For the purpose of this book, we are going to group Twitter audience sizes accordingly: small audiences are any audience with 0-5000 followers, medium audiences are any audience with 5,000 – 15,000 followers, and large audiences are anyone with 15,000+ followers. This counts for organic, active followers, and not followers that were purchased through a platform like Fiverr or Upwork. Once you have identified where your audience size lies, you can begin applying the following techniques for marketing with your Twitter account in 2021.

First, you are going to want to modernize the branding on your profile. In 2018, branding was largely centered around an incredibly clean and polished appearance, complete with stock images or images that looked like stock images. These photographs were created to give a clean, professional, and modern look into what your company offered or represented, and was said to be appealing to the eye. This is, in fact, true, and supported many businesses in growing through 2018 and 2019. That being said, trends are changing since 2020. Studies have shown that the number of brands misusing stock images to create low-quality high-profit brands online has grown, causing consumers to become wary when they see profiles filled with stock images or overly polished photographs. Although they do want to see images that are high quality and professional, more and more people are wanting to get away from the stock image appearance and start seeing something more personal, artistic, and inspirational.

As you create the imagery for your profile, you are going to need to create with the idea of being more personable in mind. You want your profile to have character, to represent a brand that stands apart from the generic click-and-build brands of 2018 and 2019, and to be worthy of earning people's attention so that they decide to follow you and engage with your content. This means that your pictures should continue to be high quality and with a clear focal point, but that they should be personalized to feature characteristics that are representative of your brand. Furthermore, these characteristics should be of high quality and artistic in a sense. If you are not the artistic type, a quick browse around other Twitter profiles can help give you an idea of how other people are customizing their profiles, simply pay closer attention to the ones that are more personalized and authentic.

On Twitter, the focus is less on graphics and more on verbal marketing, so you have less space for your images on your profile. That being said, avoid having "busy" images which are going to take away from the quality of your profile. Attempting to be artistic while creating images that are too busy for your audience to really know what they are looking at is actually going to minimize the quality of your profile, and therefore the number of people who find you and follow you. Instead, find a way to be artistic while using details sparingly in your images. For example, if you are a clothing designer, rather than having a picture of you posted in front of clothing racks, which would look incredibly busy in a small image, have a picture of you posted in front of a store window wearing the clothes that you designed. This way, you are able to show off your character without overwhelming the image and making it difficult for your audience to really know what they are looking at.

In addition to your graphics, you need to brand your bio and your link. Again, roughly 80% of the people who land on your page are going to visit your link, so having a relevant and high-quality link that leads people directly to an opportunity to purchase or work with you is important. This way, you can take advantage of those 80% of people and drive more traffic to your website, another platform, or an affiliate link where you are going to earn more money than you might on Twitter.

Creating your bio on Twitter in 2021 needs to be simple, and filled with personality. One liners are still incredibly popular, with brands creating a single sentence that summarizes their entire brand, including its personality, in just a few words. You can also add a sentence to discuss any upcoming points of interest that you may have to share with your audience. For example: "Take your cheese habit to the next level with unusual and unique cheese flavors. New flavors launching 05/10." Remember that you only have 160 characters to write out your bio, so you need to choose something that packs a punch and gets the message across as quickly as possible. This way, people get an immediate feel for who you are, what your brand represents, and what they can expect to find on your page. When you are done, add a link to your bio area so that people can find that, as well.

The next way to leverage Twitter for marketing in 2021 is to pay close attention to the trends. Twitter is one of the most well-known platforms for spotting and following trends online, as it has an entire page catered toward highlighting trending topics that are collected from the platform itself, as well as news platforms and gossip columns. Using Twitter specifically to learn about trending topics is a great opportunity for you to grow your platform, while also gaining insight into how you can grow on other platforms, too. This way, you can stay relevant and your audience is more likely to keep up with you and pay attention to what you are posting.

Remember, you want to focus on trends and topics based on what proximity is going to be most reasonable for your audience size. If you have a smaller audience, look to find the trends that are currently growing in your local area so that you can get on board with talking about those trends, or even incorporating them into your products, services, or sales. For example, if you have a local celebration going on that celebrates something in specific, you might consider creating products, services, or even a special sale to celebrate with your local area. This is a great opportunity to get more local eyes on you, helping you expand your reach and grow your audience. If you have a medium sized business, focus on national trends, and if you have a large sized business, focus on global trends. Continue paying close attention to the trends relevant to your business size, while also playing around with trends that cater to other audience sizes from time to time, too. This way, you are always marketing toward an audience that is going to be large enough for you to grow in, but small enough for you to get found in.

Using these trends is not only going to help you tap into your audience and choose a marketing strategy, but it can also serve as a guide for how you run your business going forward. For example, if you find that your local community celebrates a specific day every year, you might begin to prepare for that day in advance in future years, allowing for you to stay ahead of the curve. So, not only will following these trends help you reach out to your audience now, but it can also prepare you for having an even more impactful reach in the future.

Although trend-following has always been a popular marketing strategy on Twitter, it is growing even more popular in 2020. This is why following the approach of using the right proximity for your audience size is so crucial, as this is how you are really going to leverage this feature in 2021 to get in front of your audience. In previous years, it was believed that just marketing to your industry was enough, but as Twitter continues to grow, it has shown that this may not be the most effective way to grow your profile. You do still need to have a primary focus on your own industry, but focusing on your industry, niche, *and* appropriate proximity is really going to help you grow faster. This applies no matter how large your existing audience already is, and no matter how long you have already been marketing on Twitter.

In addition to creating a strong profile, leveraging your bio and URL, and taking advantage of trending topics, Twitter also offers you the opportunity to market by creating a way for you to converse with your audience. This platform has always been centered around real conversation, and it continues to maintain this focus going into 2021. That being said, we are starting to generate an even deeper understanding of what this means and how it affects businesses going forward. The primary key is realizing that, no matter what size your business is, Twitter can be used as a powerful opportunity to improve your customer service and offer an even better shopping experience with your brand.

First and foremost, you need to start getting involved in organic conversations with your appropriate target audience on Twitter. This means that the same trends you are posting about, also need to be the trends that you are conversing about on other peoples' posts. Showing that you are willing to get involved in these conversations, particularly in a meaningful way, really helps showcase your brand and get your name out there. People love seeing brands that partake in meaningful conversations, and share their opinion in a way that actually engages and moves the conversation, rather than just sharing a generic sentence or two about the topic. Although it will take more time to genuinely engage in these conversations, doing so will offer you the benefit of showing that you care, while also giving your potential audience insight into who your brand actually is. This really creates that opportunity to have the deeper and more meaningful connections that you know are a cornerstone for all marketing strategies in 2021, which is why it is so important on Twitter in the coming months, as well.

When you do engage in these conversations, make sure that you are still being mindful about what you are talking about. In the past, many brands clung to generic responses because they made it easier to avoid looking ignorant or misinformed, or otherwise sharing an opinion that may deter your audience from wanting to actually follow you. In other words, they were playing it safe to avoid losing their audience over something they said. Especially on Twitter, where we have seen many businesses at the forefront of scandals for various unprofessional displays on the platform, it can be easy to be concerned about how your responses may be taken. Still, none of this means that you should be sticking to the safer, generic response to avoid stirring the pot. Instead, you should offer genuine, authentic, and polite responses that offer your opinion. However, you need to do it in a way that ensures that your responses are educated, polite, and considerate toward the people you are talking to, as well as anyone else who might be reading your posts and responses. In other words, you can and should offer authentic and thoughtful responses; you just need to make sure that you are representing your business in a positive way while you do it.

Lastly, if you really want to take advantage of your Twitter account for marketing, you should use Twitter as your own personal "news station" for your brand. Because Twitter has gained popularity for being a professional platform that is largely focused on news and trending topics, you can leverage this reputation in favor of your own brand. To do so, you can promote your Twitter as being the "first place" for people to learn about important news relating to your company. For example, this might be the platform where you announce sales, new products, or other exciting and relevant news regarding your company. This way, people want to follow your platform because they know that this is where they are going to get the first wind of anything that is going on with your brand. In other words, you give them an incentive to follow you, while also using the platform's reputation to your own benefit.

Monetizing Your Twitter Page

Monetizing on Twitter requires a special approach, particularly because Twitter is more focused on "we" rather than "me." On Twitter, the brands that are having the best success are the ones that are more focused on everyone, rather than just themselves. For that reason, if you attempt to grow or monetize your page using verbiage like "look at *my* new product" or "look at *our* new product," you are unlikely to get much response. Instead, you want to focus on ways to point your marketing terms outward with words like "you," "us," "together," and "we." This way, people are more likely to engage because you are partaking in the community-oriented mindset that largely exists all over Twitter.

Aside from making sure that you are using the right vocabulary to get your audience's attention, you also need to make sure that you are using the right strategies to actually earn money with Twitter. This way, you can make sure that those intelligently worded posts are actually getting you somewhere on this platform.

The first and possibly most obvious way to monetize your Twitter account is to turn it into a part of a sales funnel. Because Twitter does have such a high click-through rate, you can feel confident that people who land on your page are going to also click through to take a look at your website, or whatever you have linked in your URL. To really take advantage of this, you want to make sure that you are organizing your page, and posts, in a way that encourages people to visit your profile. The key here is to be sparing in how you are doing this to avoid making it look like every single post is just trying to draw traffic to your website. Creating too many posts that are obviously attempting to drive traffic to your profile or website is actually going to lose your audience's attention because they will feel like you are just attempting to capitalize on them. Again, although your audience understands that you are a business that wants to make money, they want to feel like they are more than just a number in your bottom line. Instead, they want to feel like they matter, and like you have truly given thought to how they perceive and experience your brand.

A better way to make posts that encourage people to visit your page is to create posts that are relevant so that when people find your posts, they are more likely to click through to your profile to see if you post anything else they might like. This is a natural behavior of people on Twitter as they want to learn more about the people they are following, and ensure that they are following people that they will actually resonate with. So, in 2021, rather than creating overwhelming "buy this!" posts for your Twitter, you can simply focus on having organic, enjoyable conversations about relevant topics, trusting that this *is* a strategy that will draw traffic to your profile.

Once you have accumulated a healthy number of non-promotional posts, you can begin to post the occasional promotional post that features obvious promotions. The key here is to make sure that these types of posts never become the primary form of post that you are using on

Twitter. The general rule of thumb in the past has been to use an 80/20 approach, which is still the most effective strategy as long as you are using it properly. In 2018 and 2019 it has largely been promoted that this 80/20 approach should be used on a day-to-day basis, when in reality it is better to focus on using this as a part of a week-to-week approach, or even a month-to-month approach. In other words, instead of posting 4 non-promotional posts and 1 promotional post per day, you should focus on posting a promotional post 1 or 2 times a week, or 6-7 times a month. This way, you are posting enough that you are getting attention on your specific promotions, but without seeming like all you can talk about is what you are promoting.

The best part about using this form of the 80/20 approach in 2021 is that it offers more room for a greater number of promotional posts closer to special launches. So, rather than posting 2 promotional posts and 3 non-promotional posts per day, which would reflect the 60/40 rule on a day-to-day basis, you would post 2-4 times per week, or 12-14 times per month leading up to a launch. This offers you far more promotional room, without coming across as spammy during important launches. Remember that in addition to these posts, you can always leverage paid advertising on Twitter to help get the word out there even more, ensuring that your promotions are seen, but not to an overwhelming degree.

Finally, another great way to monetize with Twitter in 2020 is to take advantage of their pre-roll ads. This actually launched in 2016, but it is becoming increasingly more popular as more people are uploading video content to Twitter now and going into 2021. Monetizing your profile is relatively easy; all you have to do is join Twitter's Media Studio platform and begin creating, posting, and sharing videos from here. Twitter will automatically add promotions to your creations, and pay you for those promotions.

Unlike other platforms which are requiring a certain follower count and level of popularity in order to monetize your videos, Twitter is now allowing anyone to monetize their videos, meaning that you can begin earning with Twitter right away. That being said, if you do begin to add advertisements to your videos right away, people may not take your page or brand seriously. They may think that you are just attempting to monetize your profile, which can lead to them feeling like there is no strong reason to pay attention to or follow your platform. This can not only stunt or permanently sever your growth on Twitter, but it can also lead to incredibly low earnings due to no one watching your videos. Instead, you should wait until you have a much larger following of 15,000-25,000+ before monetizing your videos so that your audience is already committed and engaged and know that the content is worth watching the advertisements first.

Chapter 7: Mistakes You Must Avoid

As social media marketing begins to mature, we are starting to learn more and more about how effective this marketing strategy actually is. We are also learning about what needs to be done in order to make it work, and what types of strategies are preventing people from experiencing any success through social media marketing. We know that you want to make sure that you are using only the highest quality approach so that you can achieve 2021 growth right now in 2020, which is why we want to highlight mistakes that you *must* avoid if you are going to succeed with social media marketing right now.

Many of these mistakes are actually incredibly subtle, and therefore incredibly common. Brand new businesses, or brands that are not yet experienced with successful social media marketing, seem to make these mistakes regularly and find themselves really struggling to get ahead in marketing their businesses as a result. The reason why these mistakes are made often comes from a lack of awareness that they even exist or need to be avoided in the first place, which is why simply knowing about them is going to set you so far ahead in the first place. Take time to acquaint yourself with these mistakes and to understand what they look like in use so that you can avoid making them in your business, allowing you to bypass many rights from the start.

Not Being Personable Enough

As you have noticed, one of the overarching trends in this very book has been the importance of how personable and authentic you are being in your marketing in 2021. Naturally, that is because this is going to be a foundational element of marketing going forward. We have already given you plenty of excellent tips on how you can be more personable, so now we want to point out what you need to avoid when it comes to being personable online.

The best way to get a feel for what *not* to do when it comes to being personable online is to get on social media and take a look at some accounts. Pay attention to small-to-medium businesses that are not growing well, ones that are, and larger businesses that are thriving on social media. You will quickly notice how different these businesses sound from each other, as businesses that are not thriving will sound completely different from those that are growing and those that are thriving. The ones that are struggling to grow will either lack personable communication altogether, or will sound as if their personable communication is fake or generic. This type of language can only be spotted by reading the content that people are sharing, as you will quickly get a feel for whether or not they are being genuine.

Studying the difference between genuine and generic posts will help you pick up on the subtleties of what sets success apart from failure online. You will begin to notice the nuances and phrases used by companies that are forcing their personability, versus the natural flow of language used by companies that are genuinely being personable with their audience. Through this, you will get a clear vision of what to do, and what not to do when you are sharing your updates with your audience.

Thinking You Don't Need A Strategy

One of the biggest flawed mindsets we have seen in the day of social media marketing is the idea that you do not need a strategy. This could not be any further from the truth. Business and strategy go hand in hand, and just because social media marketing can be incredibly easy does not mean that this platform comes without the need for strategy. If you attempt to get online without any clear strategy of what you are going to be doing online, you are going to find yourself struggling to make any type of impact with your business on social media.

It is extremely apparent when businesses have failed to make a strategy before getting into the world of social media marketing. The telltale signs include a business that does not seem to have any clear direction in what they are posting or sharing, one that seems to constantly be behind on trends and, ultimately, one that is struggling to get in front of its target audience. More often than not, if your numbers are not growing consistently, it is because you have failed to make a strategy, or you have failed to make a strategy that *works*.

In this book, you have identified several strategies for how to market your business in 2021, and in chapter 9, you are going to discover how you can turn all of this knowledge into an actionable strategy. We strongly advise that you *do not* overlook the part of turning it into a real strategy if you want to grow your business rapidly and successfully in the coming months.

Not Targeting Your Audience Effectively

As you begin marketing your business online, it can be easy to be fearful of what might happen if you attempt to be "too" specific in who you are talking to. Many new businesses worry that if they speak to a very specific audience, no one will pay attention or want to engage with their business. They feel that they will be irrelevant, or that they will completely miss the mark with a larger audience. This leads to them making the huge mistake of not being clear in who they are talking to.

The truth is, when you do talk specifically to your own audience, you are going to be irrelevant or unlikeable for many other audiences. *That's the point.* When you are marketing on social media, you want to be talking directly to the people who are more likely to purchase from you, while also avoiding the people who won't. This way, you are not wasting your time trying to cater to an audience that is never going to actually purchase from your business.

When you begin marketing your business on social media, get clear in who you are talking to, and keep talking to those people. Do not be afraid to be your authentic self, and do not be afraid to speak your opinions that are relevant to your business. The more relevant that you can be to the specific audience that you do want to sell to, the more likely they are going to pay attention to you and, more importantly, buy from you. Worry less about the people who are not going to appreciate what you have to say, and more about the people who will. Leave the larger audiences for the massive corporations that have millions of dollars to invest in talking to a larger audience than you can reasonably talk to in your business.

Improper Management of Negative Feedback

If you are in business, you are going to receive negative feedback. Period. Every single business experiences some form of negative feedback or criticism at one point or another, both from people who have done business with you and people who have never experienced your business before. This is completely normal.

People online like to have opinions, and they will share their opinions about everything. It is important that when you do come across people with negative feedback or criticism, that you handle it properly to avoid destroying your own business reputation alongside that negative feedback or criticism.

When it comes to negative feedback, there will be two types of people offering it: those who can have their minds changed, and those who can't. You can sort through who is who quickly by saying something simple like: "We're sorry that you feel this way, can you please message us with your concern so we can help you resolve it?" This type of comment shows that you are willing to support the person offering negative feedback. Those who are willing to change their minds can then communicate with you so that you can resolve their concerns and, hopefully, earn a loyal follower who respects your business. Those who are not can simply be ignored, as they are unlikely to have anything kind to say toward your business, regardless of how polite you are to them. When it comes to business, taking the high road in sticky situations is *always* the best choice.

Using Promotional Tools in a Poor Manner

The more that social media matures and social media marketing evolves, the more tools are being provided to businesses so that they can make marketing online even easier. The selling feature for many is based on passive income: the more that you can automate or simplify your processes, the more time you have to do other things while your business stands by making money for you around the clock. Wanting passive income or time freedom is certainly not a bad thing, but it is imperative that you take the right action in turning your business into a passive income stream if you are going to be successful with it.

If you want to have success with online marketing, you need to be able to remain personable and approachable at all times. This means that if your business is too automated, people are going to catch on and they are going to lose interest in and respect for your company. As well, automating your business too far into the future can lead to you being irrelevant, or uploading content that does not effectively serve your market any longer. You need to use these tools effectively if you are going to have any success in reaching your audience through your social media marketing efforts. Otherwise you are just wasting your time.

When it comes to automated posters, make sure that you are always uploading relevant content, that the content still sounds incredibly personal, and that you are not uploading too far in advance. Do your best to only create enough content for one week to one month at a time to ensure that your content continues to remain relevant and personal for your audience. This will not only help your content remain meaningful and valuable, but it will also make it easier for you to make necessary adjustments in your approach or include important pieces of information along the way. If you automate too far in advance, it can feel like a hassle to make any changes or shift your approach because you will feel like you are wasting a massive amount of time that was spent creating unnecessary content.

Another type of automation you need to be cautious with is bots. Bots can be incredibly useful, but they can also work to the detriment of your company. Many businesses have created bots for platforms like Instagram, only to have their bots sending out messages or comments that make no sense, or that come across as spammy by posting the exact same comment on far too many different profiles. If you do choose to use a bot in your marketing strategy, make sure that the comments are authentic and genuine, and that they are not being over posted. It also can't hurt to be honest in your message by introducing your bot and letting your followers know how they can get in touch with a real person for support or inquiry if they want to. This way, while you are getting the benefits of a bot, you are also not losing parts of your audience who may prefer more personalized attention.

Posting Low-Quality Content to Meet Quantity Goals

Content calendars are in just about every blog post and marketing book these days, and they have long been seen as a tool that is necessary to help keep you consistent with your posting. Since consistency *is* key, this tool was designed to help people who are not used to posting regularly get their content out there consistently enough to be recognized by their audience. Unfortunately, for many people, all these calendars have done is place an incredible amount of stress on the shoulders of new social media marketers who are trying to produce more content then they are used to producing.

Following a marketing calendar can be effective, but it is not worthwhile if you are going to be attempting to post content that is low quality just to meet your content calendar's "needs." At the end of the day, no matter how consistently you are posting, if the content is low quality, people are going to perceive your brand as being low quality and they are not going to want to follow you or do business with you. It is much better to skip a post here and there and wait until you have something more inspired or meaningful to say than it is to attempt to come up with something to say when you are not really clear on what it is that you want to say.

Instead of following a content calendar day by day, set the goal of uploading a certain number of posts per week, organize what the goals of these posts need to be based on how you want to be marketing your business, and then go from there. This way, rather than attempting to push yourself to post when you are not inspired, you can simply post later when you have something more meaningful to say. Trust us on this one; your audience is not going to abandon you because you did not post anything on Tuesday at 2 PM.

Not Focusing on Your Analytics

Creating a strategy is virtually pointless if you are not going to focus on how your strategy is holding up. When it comes to running a business online, it is crucial that you pay attention to your statistics and analytics and use them as a means to determine what is working, and what is not working.

Using your analytics to serve as a guideline for what you need to do to better serve your audience is the single most important step in reaching your audience effectively. Reading your analytics is simple: you want to review your analytics consistently, ideally weekly, bi-weekly, or monthly. Then, you want to use the information you gain to identify what marketing trends or strategies are working, and which are not. The ones that are working will have higher engagement ratios, while the ones that are not working will have lower or virtually non-existent engagement ratios. Naturally, you want to nurture the ones that are working and adapt or let go of the ones that are not.

Chapter 8: Tips to Guarantee Your Success

Running a business does come with a certain level of expected risks, but there is a way to minimize these risks as long as you are willing to do whatever it takes to succeed. If you are not educating yourself and developing a deeper understanding of how you can succeed, you are going to find yourself failing. The only way to guarantee your success is to educate yourself, take action, refine your plan as needed, and constantly apply effort in the right areas to achieve your goals. In this chapter, we are going to cover four necessary steps you need to take to help guarantee your success in social media marketing in 2021.

Take Advantage of Video Marketing

First things first, if you have not already you need to get on board with video marketing. As all of the trends have shown in the past three years, video marketing is one of the most popular ways to get in front of your audience online, and it continues to be the best way for you to do so. It is likely that you have already heard about the importance of video marketing, so rather than repeating facts you may already know, we are going to give you some great tips on how you can step into next-level video marketing for 2021.

One of the best tools that you can use in video marketing is live streaming. Virtually every popular platform has a live streaming feature at this point, and for a good reason: people love watching live streams because they are more personal and enjoyable. Live streaming can and should be used in these three ways going into 2021: live streaming important events, live streaming Q&As, and live streaming demos.

When you have an important event going on in your business, whether that is a huge launch, a display at a trade show, an important visitor at your store, or anything, live streaming the event is a great opportunity to show off to your online audience. You can use live streaming to increase visibility, recognition, and your reputation all by live streaming important events to raise awareness and interest in your brand.

Live streaming Q&As is a great opportunity for you to have a one-on-one connection with your audience in a way that was previously not available for online businesses. As an effort to make your business more personable, offering these Q&A streams is a great opportunity for you to hear about what your audience is interested in, answer them in a personable way, and further represent your company.

Finally, live streaming demos is a great opportunity to generate interests in your products or services and show people why they should be purchasing from you. When you show people how your products work or what your services do, you answer one of their most important questions: "Why should I buy this?" This way, they have a more meaningful reason to take the leap and purchase from your company.

Get More Social with Your Audience

2021 is all about putting the "social" back in social media, and starting now while most businesses are still locked into the behaviors of stock images and automated messages is a great opportunity to set yourself apart. Getting social on your social media means that you are going to take some time every single day to communicate with your audience and cultivate a deeper sense of connection and closeness between your audience and your brand. When you take the time to actually be social with your audience, you give them a reason to pay attention to your brand and interact with you: because you are paying attention to them and interacting with them.

The days of social media being a place where you can sprinkle posts and suddenly earn massive amounts of income are gone, as too many people have attempted to use this strategy and their customers have caught on. Nowadays, real people are out there communicating with your audience, building relationships with them, and earning their loyalty and sales. They are the ones earning the income that you want to be earning, and they are the ones having success with their businesses. If you want to be successful online, you need to pound the pavement so to speak and put the work in to actually establish meaningful connections with your audience. If you don't, someone else will, and you will be left in the dust as your brand struggles to regain your audience's attention.

Research Your Market Frequently

No matter how well you get to know your market over time, you need to make sure that you never become complacent with who they are and what they want. At the end of the day, your market is exposed to a lot in their lives and they are inevitably going to evolve and have different wants and needs over time. Learning how to identify who your market is and stay adaptable to meet their needs is crucial if you are going to have success with online marketing.

You should be focusing on researching your market and following their trending behaviors consistently if you are going to be successful with online marketing in 2021. Pay attention to what they want and need, and make sure that anytime these wants or needs change you are listening and adapting your company as needed. If you are not listening and making the necessary adaptations, you are going to find yourself falling into a state of irrelevancy rather quickly.

Research your market by socializing with them online, following what they are following, and paying attention to the news and current events that they are paying attention to. Do your very best to put yourself in their shoes, and educate yourself on what is going on in their lives. You will find that this makes understanding them and serving them far easier because you know what you need to do in order to support them to the best of your ability.

Highlight Your Products on Social Media

Your social media presence is being built primarily for your business, so do not be afraid to promote and be "business-y" online. Although we have placed a large emphasis on not *over* promoting your business in generic ways online, there is nothing wrong with promoting your business and letting people know what you have going on. In fact, it is necessary! If you are not promoting your business on social media, people are not going to realize that you have a business and they are not going to be able to purchase from you. The key here is not to avoid business promotion altogether, nor is it to be too stiff in when and how you are going to post your business promotions. Instead, it is to ensure that your promotions are relevant, meaningful, high quality, and posted in a ratio that is not overwhelming.

You *should* let people know when you have a new sale on, or a new product being launched. You *should* talk about it often enough that people know what is going on and are able to take advantage of your new sales or launches when they happen because they have heard about it. You *should* be promoting yourself regularly. In fact, every single post you make should be seen as promotional because it is helping your audience get a feel for who your brand is and what you have to offer.

That being said: you do not need to be posting content about your sale or launch every couple of hours. You do not need to be bombarding your audience with information about when your launch is, how much your sale is for, or when it all ends. The excessive promotion will be to the detriment of your business, as it will cause people to get annoyed as they feel like they have already read that same post before, about a thousand times.

Instead, when you post about promotions, make sure that you are doing it consistent enough but not so frequently that people are getting annoyed. The best way to make sure that you are promoting at a reasonable rate is to determine how far out you are from an important date, and how important the date is to your audience. For example, say you have a sale for 25% off in two weeks. You could post about it once every other day or every two days in the first week to 10 days, once per day in the last 4-7 days leading up to the sale, and then each day during the sale. You may even post twice about it on the day the sale starts, and twice again on the day the sale is going to end. Then when the sale ends, go back to normal 80/20 marketing. This way, your frequency is not *constantly* high, so people do not become annoyed with reading about your business and your sales.

Chapter 9: How to Create Your Strategy

The final part of this entire process is you creating your own social media strategy so that you can have success with your marketing efforts. Building a social media strategy is easier than it may sound, and it is also a highly necessary step for you to have success with social media marketing. Remember: no matter how easy it seems or how simple your business model is, you need to have a strategy for how you are going to get that business to your audience. If you don't, you are going to find yourself struggling to get in front of anyone, which will lead to the failure of your business. In this chapter, we are going to cover the 4 steps you need to take in order to create a strong social media strategy for 2021.

Outline Your Brand and Goals

The first step you need to take in creating your own business strategy is to identify what your brand is and what your goals are. Having a clear understanding of who you are and what you are trying to achieve is going to help you create a strategy to get from where you are now to where you want to be.

Start by identifying what your current brand identity is and where you are at in your business. Make your brand identity simple: write down the name of your brand, the personality type it has, and the way that it shows up in the world. Write down important information like what you sell, why, and what your overall business mission is so that you have a clear understanding of what the whole purpose is for you. This is going to help you have a clear sense of "self" when it comes to your business, which is necessary to avoid you straying off course due to a lack of understanding of what image you are attempting to market.

Once you have identified your brand's identity, you need to identify what your current goals are. Since you are focused on marketing for 2021 right now, you might want to set goals towards the end of 2020, as well as for the entire year of 2021. This way, you have short term goals and longer-term goals to keep you on track with your business. Your goals can be anything from having a successful company launch to improving your sales by 10% or more. Create goals that are realistic for you so that you can feel confident that you are going to be able to reach them.

Lastly, you need to identify who your audience is. Once you know who your brand is and what you are trying to achieve, it will be easy for you to identify the audience that is required to help you achieve these goals. Make sure that you authenticate your audience by doing the necessary research to validate that they are, in fact, relevant to your industry and likely to spend the type of money that is needed to be spent in order for you to reach your goals.

Create the Bridge Between Your Audience and Goals

Next, you need to create a bridge between your audience and your goals. Remember, your audience becomes your clients, and your clients are crucial for your business to succeed. Without your clients, there will be no money to circulate through your business to keep you running. Instead, you will just have an expensive hobby that is not really getting you anywhere.

If you want to have a business that reaches its goals and serves its clients, you need to find a way to build a bridge between your audience and your goals. In other words, you need to find a way to position yourself and nurture your audience so that they are likely to take the actions that are necessary to help you reach your goals.

This is where social media marketing comes in. You need to identify what platforms your audience spends most of their time on, what platforms are going to be best for you to market your products on, and how you are going to use those platforms to create sales. The techniques in this book outline four significant platforms that you can use and how you can position yourself on them to begin to make sales through your business. You can personalize these techniques and strategies by choosing the step-by-step method that you will take and then adapting those methods to fit the image and goal of your brand.

A really powerful tool that you can use when creating a business strategy is to draw a map on a piece of paper and place yourself at one end and your goal at the other end. Then, identify the steps required to help you get from where you are now to where you want to go. All you have to do, then, is follow those steps to achieve your goals.

Begin to Take Action

Results don't come without action. Once you have hashed out your plan, you need to start taking action on it. This is where having a map is incredibly handy: you can focus on one single step at a time on your map, allowing you to keep your focus clear and simple. This way, you are not getting ahead of yourself or trying to do more than what is reasonable for you and your business.

For example, if you are starting on a YouTube channel, start by getting the first video up and sharing it out. Create a method for how you film, edit, upload and share your videos. Review and revise your method as often as needed until you find a way that works and gets your video into the eyes of as many people as possible. Then, follow that method over and over again, building on your success each time. This way, you are taking action and getting viewers, effectively growing your channel. You can use this exact approach for any platform you are on, and any strategy that you are using to market your brand on social media.

Review and Revise Your Approach as Needed

As you continue to apply your strategy to your social media approach, it is crucial that you always keep "review and revise" as an important step in your plan. As I mentioned in chapter 7, paying attention to your statistics and analytics is crucial if you want to succeed as these will tell you exactly how you are doing in your business. Through your analytics, you are going to find out what is working, what is not working, and what can be adapted to work better. You *must* pay attention to this information if you want to retain and grow your audience in a substantial way.

After you have created your strategy and begun to apply each step to the process, you need to set out a schedule for when you are going to review your strategy. Most larger companies review their strategies every quarter, but smaller companies should focus on reviewing their strategies every month since they do not have as much customer loyalty or experience backing them up yet. Reviewing your strategies every month will help you ensure that each month you are applying the best techniques toward your business and growth so that your 2021 social media marketing is effective, efficient, and able to earn you an incredible profit.

Chapter 10: The Power of Paid Advertising

If you are a new or small business, you might believe you can get away without paid advertising for a while as you rely solely on the power of organic marketing. For many budding businesses, the idea of adding the cost of paid advertising to their expense list, on top of all of their startup expenses, may seem overwhelming or unattainable. Despite this, it is important to understand that the "build it, and they will come" mentality is no longer effective in marketing, especially online marketing. These days, if you are reluctant to invest in your business advertising, you are going to find yourself struggling to get in front of the audience you need, and the audience you deserve. After putting all of that work into your business, it is important that you do not let your growth fall flat because you are afraid to invest in your marketing. It is also important that when you do take the leap and start investing in your marketing, you do so in a way where it actually pays off. Otherwise, you might find yourself wasting a lot of money on advertising methods that do not work. A lot of the information out there contradicts how paid advertising should work when it should be incorporated into your business plan, and how you can leverage paid marketing across multiple platforms to develop a well-rounded campaign that gets you results. Let's clear up some of the confusion and help you get started or kickstart fresh growth from a strong foundation of understanding and knowledge around paid advertising.

Paid Advertising Leads to Rapid Results

No business generated success by shying away from paid advertising. Yet, so many self-proclaimed experts will advocate that you should aim for organic growth first, and then move toward paid advertising. The idea is that this gives you an understanding of who actually interacts with your brand, allowing you to use your advertising money to create high-impact results from day one. The problem with this approach is that it can take an incredible amount of time to actually get anyone to pay attention to your page. Part of this is because you are brand new and so social media algorithms don't know where to place you, and part of this is because you have no social proof. You have to tell platforms where to place you, then generate proof by accumulating as many followers as you can through high-quality, well-targeted promotions. Even if you have already been running your business for some time, this more aggressive approach will guarantee impressive growth and turn you with much better profits in the end.

Ideally, marketing money should be incorporated into your brand's budget right from day one and should continue to be replenished every single month. This way, you have enough to continually get your brand in front of a new audience, remind your existing audience that you exist, and let everyone know about excellent deals and promotions you have running. The wider you can get your reach, the more of an impact your sales will have, and, as a result, the more you will earn through your business.

If you have a hard time justifying placing money toward your advertising, I must ask you this: can you name one single brand that was developed using an entirely organic, word-of-mouth strategy? You can't, because one doesn't exist. Every single brand invests in their marketing because that is how they generate results. Most brands invest in campaigns such as online advertisements. Some brands get away without that, but don't fool yourself into thinking that they have not invested in their campaigns. They invest in graphic designers, videographers, actors and actresses, and possibly even affiliates to get their "word of mouth" marketing strategy going. No marketing was ever successful when it lacked the money to back it, and yours won't be either. You *must* invest in paid advertising if your brand becomes a success.

Targeting Your Paid Campaigns

Getting the most out of your campaigns starts with knowing how to target your paid campaigns. Targeting advertisements can be intimidating, as there are so many different factors that go into defining a demographic. If you have never engaged in paid or targeted advertising before, you might be overwhelmed with where to begin, or you may worry that you get your demographic wrong and end up losing money. Firstly, do not worry about losing money. The money you do spend will pay off in the end as it helps you clarify who your audience is, *and* you can cancel social media promotions before their expiry date if you are unhappy with their results so you will not be out hundreds of dollars with anything to show for it. If you do it right, it is a low-investment way of clarifying your audience so you can turn out high-performing results much faster.

The best way to start targeting your campaigns is to look at your direct competition or the people in your industry who are doing precisely what you are doing. Identify who their target audience is, and use this as a basis for where you set your targets. Use your competitions audience to define your audience's likely age, gender, location, and interests. You may also want to include educational background, career, and family information if this is relevant to your industry.

Once you have mirrored the audience of your competition, you can plug that information into your paid campaign. Whenever possible, define your goal as being either "brand awareness" or "reach" as these are the best ways of getting your business out there for everyone to see. You will then design the ad creative for your advertisement, which we will discuss in the next section, and launch your campaign.

If you have not yet defined who your audience is and you are using advertisements to get there, it is a good idea to start with a relatively low budget and timeframe. You will want to carefully monitor your results over the first three days of your campaign. I suggest you start at $5 per day, over 3 days. Do not just resolve to look at your campaign in three days; have it actually end in three days. This way, the platform you are promoting on will generate your "results" page, which will allow you to see who saw, engaged with, and responded to your campaign the most. This will go a long way in helping you create stronger campaigns going forward.

Whenever it comes to targeting new campaigns, always use a combination of what you already know from your existing audience *and* what you are discovering from other people in your niche. For example, your demographic may remain the same as far as gender and age group, but you may discover that there are new trending interests that pop up that are relevant to your desired audience. You can find these trends by paying attention to your competition and jumping on board the moment you notice a trend rising. Targeting your campaigns to include these new interests or trends will help you maximize your reach even further, and attract an audience of engaged, active followers who are far more likely to actually purchase from your brand.

Creating A Cross-Promotional Campaign Strategy

Targeting your audience will be virtually the same across every single platform, but how you deliver your campaign will change from platform to platform. For example, on Facebook and Instagram, photo-based or video-based campaigns with compelling captions work best. On Twitter, photo-based and video-based campaigns are also great. On YouTube, video-based campaigns are the only ones that work.

Despite the fact that photo-based and video-based campaigns are best, there are many things you need to consider when launching your campaigns on each platform. For example, on Facebook, photos perform best when they are not covered with too much text.

Alternatively, Instagram thrives with a small amount of text in each picture. Twitter can go either way. YouTube works best when your videos are educational, entertaining, or otherwise designed to perform like a commercial that is presented before video content, such as what you would see on cable TV.

A truly effective campaign strategy will have the same promotion being promoted using similar metrics across all of your active platforms, but they will be modified to fit that platform specifically. This means that each campaign should have the same focus, message, tone, color-scheme, and general design theme. However, the exact format of the design for each platform will be adjusted to ensure it suits that platform and the strategies that work best on that platform.

An example of what I mean is, let's say you were promoting t-shirts. Your cross-platform campaign might look like:
- Facebook: a photograph of two people wearing the t-shirt and smiling at each other, with a compelling caption of 1-2 sentences.
- Instagram: a photograph of someone wearing the shirt with 1-5 words on it, drawing attention toward the shirt or promotion.
- Twitter: someone putting the shirt on and smiling at the camera, with a compelling caption of 1 sentence.
- YouTube: someone handing another person the shirt, that person is putting the shirt on and adjusting it. Then they wink at the camera, followed by an image of the brand logo and a few details on the promotion, as well as where and how

to buy the shirt. Wording should be minimal and shown long enough for the viewer to follow the call to action.

On all platforms, the same shirt should be used, the same promotion should be talked about, and the same tone and types of words should be used. However, you should be talking in a way that directly communicates to that specific part of your audience. This consistency yet subtle adjustment means that your campaign speaks directly to your audience on that platform *and* that anyone who follows you on multiple platforms will not tune the advertisement out as soon as they see it because each one is different and fresh. This way, they immediately remember the cool content you had shared and the promotion you were talking about, and they absorb each new exposure to that promotion, making them more likely to interact with it. You will be far more likely to get effective results if you do this.

Monitoring the Performance of Your Ads

Anytime you activate a promotion on social media, you should be prepared to monitor the performance of your ads. There are a few different guidelines you should follow when it comes to monitoring the performance of your ads, and they vary based on how familiar you are with your target audience and how long your campaign will be running for.

If you are brand new to paid advertising and are generally unfamiliar with your audience, you should be checking on the performance of your ads every few hours. Do note that the first day or so can be relatively ineffective as your ad is just starting to warm up, but by day two and three, you should begin to see it pick up. If you notice your ad is not performing at all or has barely picked up, pause and cancel the ad so you can try again. At this point, you can try retargeting your audience or adjusting the design of your ad campaign. Only make one adjustment before trying again; otherwise, you will not know which adjustment helped you improve your reach, which means you will not know how to replicate those results later on.

If you are familiar with your targeted audience and you are running a short, time-sensitive promotion, you should check on your campaign every 12 hours, or every morning and night for the days it is running. On those days, look to see how far your reach is and how much interaction you are getting with your reach. Ideally, you should see it steadily pick up over the first 1-3 days, then maintain high-performance from there on out. If you don't, you will want to pause the campaign and adjust either your target audience or your campaign design. Again, only adjust one thing before trying again, so you know which adjustment was responsible for your improved results.

If you are familiar with your targeted audience and are running a long-term or ongoing campaign, you can check in every day or every other day, after the first three days. For the first three days, pay attention to make sure your performance picks up enough to make the campaign worth it. If you reach your desired bid amount per impression and interaction, and you are happy with how your campaign is running, checking in every day to every other day is plenty. Once you notice the campaign is no longer performing as well as it was, you can cancel it and create a new campaign with the same audience but a new design. This way, your campaigns do not become stale and result in your audience no longer paying attention because they have grown bored with your imagery.

Using Your Results to Amplify Your Performance

Your results will tell you everything you need to know about how to keep your campaign running. There are two times when you should look at your results to amplify your campaign performance. The first time is if you decide to cancel a campaign because it is not performing the way you thought it would. The second is if a successful campaign ends, and you are ready to look at how it performed to help you gain insight now on how to run an even more successful campaign next time.

If you have to cancel an advertisement because it does not offer the performance you were looking for, you can troubleshoot why by first looking at which demographic was most engaged with your advertisement. Chances are, your low-performing advertisement was only seeing a very small percentage of engagement from part of your target audience. This likely means that your target audience overlaps with the audience you defined and that you were not quite on the mark with defining who your actual target audience is. You can adjust this by creating a brand new campaign with the same design and targeting the audience that was most interactive with your campaign the first time around. This way, you are directly targeting those who are most likely to engage, rather than accessing them through an overlap between them and the audience you originally targeted. For example, if you targeted people who are between 20-65+ who like cooking, baking, and beekeeping, and you find that the people primarily responding were women between 45-65+ who like baking and beekeeping, you need to adjust your audience to reflect that specific group of women. This way, you are far more likely to get in front of your engaged audience and turn results from your campaign. Once you have fixed your audience, you can go ahead and renew your campaign. If you find that you get engagement but not enough engagement at this point, you should adjust the design of your campaign (the graphics and the wording) to better target your proven audience. Then, you should start getting better results.

If your successful campaign ended, do not make the mistake of ignoring the results and assuming that replicating the campaign at a later date with new graphics is enough for you to create the impact you desire. You must always look over the results of your campaign to see who was actually paying attention to your campaign, and how much. Write these results down and keep track of them. This way, every time you launch a new campaign, you can look over your historical results and use that to help you effectively target, design, and launch your campaign so that you get the best results right from the start. You will likely notice that your results slowly change over time, and this is completely natural. Keeping track will help you better understand your audience and produce not only better-paid advertisements but a better business strategy overall. The results you gain from these campaigns is invaluable, so do not overlook the results or ignore their ability to help you expand your business and grow your profits.

Chapter 11: The Need for Community-Oriented Brands

These days, if you want your brand to get noticed, you *must* prove that you are community-oriented. More than ever before, consumers are developing a greater awareness around the fact that brands hold great power, and they are urging brands to use that power for positive forces by voting with their dollar. In fact, studies have shown that 57% of consumers say that human connection would increase their brand loyalty. 58% say that human connection would increase their likelihood of spending money with any given brand.

To develop a real sense of human connection in your brand, you must be aware of what is going on in the world and have the ability to position yourself within the community. This does not mean that you need to be at the forefront of activism, or that you need to be blazing trails for your audience, although those certainly have the power to produce results in our current economic climate. For the average brand, though, developing a sense of compassion, empathy, and loyalty to your customers and their concerns is exactly what they are looking for. At the end of the day, your consumers want to know that you are aware of the issues, that you support the resolution of those issues, and that you will create a safe and welcoming space for them within your brand.

Creating a community around your brand is the ultimate power move when it comes to effective branding in 2020 and beyond. This is key. You are not just creating a recognizable brand or a brand that engages in one-sided loyalty where you expect loyalty from your consumers and, in exchange, offer them plenty of products or services to buy. You are creating a community around your brand, where you mutually help each other through the power of your connection, your voice, and your choices. There are six powerful steps you can take right now to start building a community around your brand, which will inevitably help you generate massive success in marketing your business. And yes, getting on social media and leveraging social media for this purpose is one of them.

Step 1: Recognize That Building A Community Takes Time

An effective community includes the emotional investment of everyone involved in that community, and developing that investment takes time. You need to earn the trust, positive attention, and respect from your audience, and that comes from consistently showing up and offering up everything your audience needs in order to experience a lasting connection. The best brands have the ability to fill a void within their audiences' lives and become a sort of friend and trusted source for their audience. Do not try to rush your audience into developing a connection with you, as they will feel that and begin to wonder why you are applying pressure in the first place. No matter who you are, being pressured to do something is never fun and will virtually always result in you beginning to avoid said thing. Maintain a pressure-free zone and develop a sense of community while also cultivating patience so that your audience has time to develop that sense of connection with your brand.

Step 2: Start By Building A Community Within Your Team

If you have ever spent any time observing human behavior, then you know that people are more likely to copy the actions of another individual, rather than follow their verbal instructions. If what you are asking for and what you are offering are not one in the same, your audience will copy what you are offering, and not what you are asking for. This means if you are asking for your audience to join in a community with you, but you are not cultivating a strong sense of community within your brand, your audience will recognize that discrepancy and be far less likely to engage with your brand in a positive, lasting manner.

At the same time, as you work toward developing a community around your brand through your connection with your audience, you need to be working on developing a community within your brand through your relationship with your team. If you are a small or medium-sized business that has employees or contracted workers who are a part of your team, this means adjusting your approach so that you have more meaningful relationships with these individuals. Truly cultivate a sense of community within your employee-base, encourage them to reciprocate, and share that with your audience. As you build this sense of community, do not just do it for the marketing aspect of things. People will be able to tell, and the facade will break down eventually. Instead, genuinely work toward developing this sense of community because it improves the quality of your team, the relationships you share together, and the work you create. Pursue it for all the right reasons, and you will get all the best results.

If you are a solo person running a business by yourself, you can still create a sense of community. Consider the people who inspire you, motivate you, and support you with getting to where you want to be as being the very people who are a part of your team. Although they may not be employed by you, and you may not be paying them, they are integral parts of your business and they deserve to be recognized. Nurture those relationships, showcase them, and add value to those relationships in as many ways as you possibly can. What you give to these relationships will always give back to you in the long run. Plus, as your audience sees you developing this sense of community within your company, they will want to be a part of that community, too.

Step 3: Passionately Embrace A Relevant Social Cause

As I mentioned, consumers care about the world around them. They want to see that the brands they support care, too. You do not have to be a leading activist, nor do you have to be on the forefront of change, but you do have to be committed to giving back in some way through your commitment to making the world a better place than you left it. This matters.

Brands with high social impact that help the larger community are effective both in their ability to create a community and in their ability to have a tangible impact on effecting change in their chosen cause. As people see your brand working toward something positive, they will join you in their shared passion to effect change, too, and will see you as a part of their community. You become an ally, and that becomes an incredibly positive thing for your business.

When choosing a social cause, be sure to choose one that is relevant to your brand, that you actually care about, and that you can realistically involve yourself with. Then, look for ways to give back as much as you possibly can, either through donating proceeds toward the cause, directly involving your workers in volunteering for the cause, or otherwise getting involved. Showcase your commitment to your audience and encourage them to step up and make a change, too. This will result in them investing in your business, and in the cause that you care so deeply about.

Step 4: Use Video To Involve Your Customers

Video is a powerful way to involve your customers in your community and to make them feel recognized and cherished for being a part of your community. There are many different ways that you can include your customers through the power of video, from inviting them to be models for your brand, to encouraging them to partake in a video-based challenge that results in them uploading home videos to your company tag.

If you want to involve your audience in your community using videos that you make for your brand, there are two different steps you can take. The first one is to invite members of your audience to an official filming experience where they are essentially hired as volunteer models to be a part of your campaign. The second option is to have your audience submit videos of themselves doing something specific, such as modeling how they use your brand's products or services, and then you can use those videos as a part of your campaign. Ensure that your audience understands that they are submitting videos for you to use so that you do not run into copyright issues later on.

Running video-based campaigns or challenges is a wonderful way to get your audience involved in your brand because it allows you to leverage the power of user-generated content. A great example of how you might do this would be to decide on a specific type of video content you want to see, material that would adequately reflect your brand and market it in a positive light. It will invite your audience to share videos using a specific tag. For example, let's say you are running a local gym, and you want to have your users create video content for your social media. You could invite them to share a 30 clip video of their workout in your gym and use a specific hashtag as well as tag your brand so that they can be featured in the challenge. To encourage participation, there are a few steps you can take. One would be to reshare the best videos to your primary newsfeed to showcase all of the excellent videos that have been submitted, while also celebrating your audience. If you have multiple short clips uploaded, you might even create one longer video with all of these shorter videos in them to upload on a platform like YouTube or Facebook. This way, you can show off your audience's talent and create peer-backed evidence that your company is an excellent company to work with. Another way you could encourage engagement would be to turn it into a contest, where users are entered for a chance to win something, such as a free one month or one-year membership, or something similar.

Once you begin to accumulate user-generated content, it is vital that you actually use it. Doing so shows that you really do value your audience by giving them direct, individual attention every time you acknowledge their videos or share their posts. If you will not be able to share every single video, make sure you like and comment on those videos and thank them for participating. This attention is all an essential part of using video content to create a sense of community. And, by the way, video content is non-negotiable in 2020, so you *must* be getting on board with some form of video-based advertising and outreach.

Step 5: Drive Your Social Media Presence with Value

In the past, advertising was largely about creating a focus on your products and letting your audience know just how much these products would enhance their lives. Newspapers were full of photographs of interesting products or people talking about their services, billboards were plastered in the same, and even bus stop benches, magazines, posters, and brochures were full of similar types of advertising. In fact, even when the internet first launched, advertisements were primarily pictures of products or services, just as they were in print advertisements, just placed on the internet. Back then, this worked.

These days, people have become so bombarded by this type of advertising that they actually tune it out. Research has shown that most people don't even see or register these types of advertisements anymore because they have grown bored of them, and because many grew to realize that the products were not always things they needed. As people become more mindful of how they spend their money, and purchase with purpose rather than curiosity, advertising strategies have changed. You can no longer throw up a picture of your product with colorful lettering that showcases the promotional pricing and a few vague details about how the product works. In fact, on social media, marketing has very little to do with talking about your products or services *at all*. Instead, you can build a sense of community and build brand-loyalty by minimizing the time you spend talking about your products or services and maximizing the amount of time you spend offering free value to your audience. This value should come in the form of a tangible, useful, and meaningful offer that can be redeemed right there through the post. It can be a post offering education on a topic specific to your niche that is largely relevant to your audience. It could be a how-to video or a link to a free eBook that educates people on how to learn a specific skill or better understand something of interest to them. These types of content provide massive value to your audience and result in them being more drawn to you because they do not feel like they have to pay you for everything they get from you.

This brings up the idea of your brand being friends with your audience, in a sense. Would you hang out with someone who constantly asked you to buy them things or spend money on them, while they did nothing in return? No. You would hang out with someone who offered you excellent value, too, so that when they did ask for something in return, you felt fine giving it to them. The relationship feels equal, balanced, and like you are mutually benefitting. This is exactly what people want to experience from your brand, too.

Studies have shown that social media personas who offer 80-90% value and only 10-20% sales are far more likely to make money off of those sales because they are participating in a healthy back-and-forth relationship with their audience. By the time they get to advertise what they have for sale, their audience is so engaged that they have no problem reading through the advertisement and taking action on it. Of course, there still needs to be a sense of value within the advertising post itself, but the fact that it is centered more around advertising than free value is far more acceptable to your audience in this circumstance.

It is also important that, while following the 80/20 rule, you ensure you have evergreen content that describes what you have available for sale. Evergreen content, or content that is available at all times, can be posted on your website, pinned to the top of your page, or shared somewhere else where your audience can easily find it at any time. The purpose of this evergreen content is this: as you give away value-based posts, people are naturally going to be interested in who you are and what you have to offer. If they benefit from the value in your value-based posts, they will quickly become interested in learning about what you can do if they actually pay you. Naturally, they become curious about what you have for sale and how they can find your products. Many are already sold on your products or services before they even learn about them because they enjoy your content *that* much. Yes, this happens, and no, it is not uncommon. That is the value of high-quality content. Having evergreen content about your products or services posted in an easy-to-find location means that people will have a much easier time finding what you have for sale. This way, they are able to find those posts at their leisure and buy on their own time, rather than waiting for you to loop back around to the 20% promotional materials portion of your marketing strategy.

Step 6: Develop Educational Content For Your Audience

Educational content is extremely important when it comes to building your audience and developing a community. To understand this, let's talk about the psychology of relationships for a moment. In a relationship, if you want to bond with someone, an excellent way to do so is by learning something new with that individual. Learning something new with that individual allows you to understand each other better. Together, you will be faced with stress, overwhelm, uncertainty, confusion, and exposure to brand new things that neither of you are familiar with.

If you want to take it a step further, have one person teach the other person something. This way, you have to learn about how to communicate with each other and how to work in a way that allows one of you to teach the other person something, and one of you to learn something from the other person. The dynamic creates for unique situations that can ultimately create a much stronger bond, particularly if it is created in a positive and meaningful manner.

As a brand, if you want to increase your sense of community, take on the role of teaching by educating your audience through educational content. Videos, pictures, posts, recipes, and other guides are all excellent forms of content because they allow you to have a positive experience while sharing something important with your audience. The result is that you begin to create a deeper bond because you start to better understand how your audience learns, and your audience discovers that they can rely on you to teach them new things. From your perspective, this means you develop a deeper understanding of how you can talk to your audience, what they like to learn about, what helps them learn best, and how you can help them get the most out of whatever you are teaching them about. In many cases, you could be teaching them about how to use products like yours, or how to get the most out of your products when they buy them from you. This is extremely valuable information that allows them to thoroughly understand their new products while also feeling like you care about them enough to help them maximize the value they gain out of the products they purchased through you.

For your audience, they realize that you care about them enough to continue supporting them even before and after they have purchased from you. This makes them feel like your focus is not just to make money by selling them products, but to actually help them out in some meaningful way while using your products as a tool to do so. They appreciate the fact that you are about more than just the money and, as a result, they become loyal followers and purchase more through you, while also recommending your company to all of the people in their lives who may be interested in what you have for sale.

As you make educational content, always place emphasis on helping your audience get the most value as they can, regardless of where they are at in the purchasing life cycle. The more you can emphasize this value-based approach, the more they are going to remain loyal to you and shower you with all of the benefits of their loyalty.

Chapter 12: The Latest Trends in Social Media Advertising

Being able to follow trends is one of the most important things a brand can do. Trendspotting and trend following allows you to create content that is directly in alignment with what your audience is already interested in and already talking about. This is the absolute key to staying relevant, making marketing as easy as possible for you, and turning your business into a major success. It is important, however, that as you follow trends, you look for opportunities to uniquely and creatively fit the trends into your existing brand so that your brand maintains its integrity and continues to serve your audience in a powerful and meaningful way. Swaying away from your core brand in an effort to chase every trend will make your brand look weak, difficult to follow, and even fake or insincere

Ephemeral Content Is Expanding In Popularity

Ephemeral content, or content that disappears after a short period of time, is expanding in popularity throughout 2020. Instagram or Facebook stories are excellent examples of this type of content, as they exist for 24 hours and then disappear. Since people's attention spans are short in the modern world, this type of content is excellent as it often shows up in short 15-30 second clips and then disappears soon after. The benefit is that you capitalize on their short attention spans, *and* you create exclusive content that disappears after a short period of time. This means if you don't see it, it's gone forever. This exclusivity is excellent for developing brand connection and loyalty.

Niche Social Platforms Are Gaining Popularity

While mega-platforms like Facebook, Instagram, YouTube, and other similar platforms have been dominating for years, we are starting to see a change. In 2020, niche social platforms have massively expanded in popularity, creating new opportunities for marketers to connect with their audiences. Platforms like WhatsApp, WeChat, QQ, QZone, Tik Tok, OnlyFans, and Reddit are starting to become extremely popular platforms where marketers can connect with their audiences, offer unique content, and generate money off of that content, too. Not every niche platform will work for every brand, so if you do take this approach, ensure that you choose a niche platform that makes sense to your brand.

Video Content Is A Non-Negotiable Marketing Tool

For years now, video content has been gaining in popularity. We have seen it come up and become wildly popular, capturing the attention of audiences and creating unique opportunities for them to connect in a more face-to-face way. These days, video content is a non-negotiable tool. In 2020, if you are not using video content, you are not doing yourself any favors in developing or maintaining relevancy. Further, you are actually hurting your success by failing to connect with your audience in a meaningful way. Video content absolutely must be a part of your 2020 marketing strategies, and all of your marketing strategies from here on out.

Social Media Is Often Used For Customer Service

Social media has become a powerful tool when it comes to managing online customer service. Rather than paying to have a chat app installed on your website, brands can use inboxes on Facebook, Instagram, Twitter, or other apps as an opportunity to provide quick and personalized customer service to their audience. Platforms like Facebook now offer chatbots as well as automated FAQ hosted directly within the chat itself, which makes communication between brands and their audiences even easier than ever before. If you are not already, you need to incorporate social media into your customer service strategy.

Personalization Is The Key To Success

As I've already mentioned, people are no longer okay with having unemotional, flashy advertisements of products or services thrown across their screen. This method may have worked in the past, but it no longer works now because most individuals are desensitized to this form of advertising. Further, people assume that you are a low quality or possibly scammy company if you use this approach. They want to feel like your advertising considers them, values them, offers value to them, and directly benefits them. The more individualized your approach, the stronger your campaigns will be as they will work toward nurturing the "friendship" between your audience and your brand. This is the only way to be a successful marketer in 2021, is to recognize this relationship and nurture it through your marketing strategies.

Social Media Communities Are On The Scene

As community-oriented brands claim the preference in modern-day social media marketing, it is no surprise that social media communities are on the scene and thriving more than ever before. Throughout 2020 we have seen many social media communities built, particularly through Facebook groups, that have allowed for people with similar interests to come together and partake in a social experience built in the online space. These communities are similar to old school forums, except they are developed through social media profiles instead of self-hosted websites. Though, self-hosted forums seem to be making a comeback, too, through apps like Tap A Talk. Brands who host their own communities are at the center of these experiences, giving them excellent exposure and allowing them to leverage the development of that community for their own professional growth. If your audience is not large enough to reasonably sustain a group, you can start by joining other social groups on Facebook. This will help your page, as it gets your name out there and leverages the power of organic marketing to grow your influence. Make sure you join groups that are relevant to your brand; otherwise, your efforts will be misplaced and poorly received.

Local Targeting Is Gaining in Popularity

Previously, brands were attempting to leverage the global market by getting their brands across to global audiences. Paid advertising strategies, in particular, were targeted at anyone, anywhere who was interested in things that were relevant to the brand itself. These days, these audiences are not performing as well as they once did because most individuals prefer engaging with local brands as a part of the shop local movement that has been gaining traction. Geotagging your posts and stories, as well as using local hashtags or tagging local businesses and targeting your paid advertisements to local audiences, is an excellent way to tap into this new trend and maximize your local growth. Another benefit to local targeting is that if you choose to participate in local events or local businesses, such as by joining a local conference or consigning your products at a local store, you already have an audience built up in your area. This means you will gain far more traction, and your business will grow with more success.

Social Listening Is A Strategy You Must Be Using

Social listening is a practice brands use where they monitor keywords and mentions so that they can better understand their audience and their general industry. This listening means they can create a responsive brand that allows them to more directly serve the needs of their audience, effectively expanding their audience and increasing their sales base. Within their existing audience, social listening helps brands understand what encourages engagement and what types of things those same people are currently interested in, which may be relevant to their industry. This way, they can continue creating content that attracts engagement, while also staying fresh and on top of the latest interests of their audience. Within their future audience members, this allows brands to better track where those individuals' attention is so they can target campaigns toward those trends, which allows them to see improved results from their campaigns.

User-Generated Content Is A Marketing Powerhouse

User-generated content has always been a powerhouse in marketing, as it provides you with social proof that you are a trustworthy and reliable brand. Previously, "regular" brands used influencers to provide social proof by paying them to promote their products to their audiences. Because of how marketing worked when modern influencers first became popular, most people blindly trusted the influencer and would purchase said product solely based on the influencer's ability to make it sound exciting or worth investing in. These days, consumers realize that not everyone is marketing high-quality products, which means they are more skeptical about investing in things that are being recommended to them. User-generated content, then, is as important for brands as it is for influencers. Encouraging users to generate content surrounding your brand and then sharing that content so your other followers can see it improves your social proof, effectively increasing your traction, trustworthiness, and sales numbers.

Chapter 13: The 2021 Social Media Forecast

With 2020 already halfway done, forecasters are starting to predict what the 2021 social media trends will look like. Going into 2020, they were extremely accurate, which means they will likely be highly accurate for their 2021 predictions, too. So far, we can expect to be seeing a lot of advancement between automized systems as well as a need for personalized content. This will also bring with it a variety of changes to the way platforms and businesses are regulated.

Regulatory Control and Legal Scrutiny Continues

Changes to the way social media works, and to the way marketing is occurring through social media, means that social media is starting to see a lot of regulatory control and legal scrutiny. Some of this is pressure coming out of the government as they attempt to keep social media free of any fraudulent advertisers, and some of it is coming out of the head offices of these platforms' as their programmers attempt to do the same. Going into 2021, this will continue, and it may lead to some changes in how the platforms work and in how business owners are allowed to use the platforms for marketing their products. It is important to routinely look into legal changes and platform algorithm changes to ensure you are marketing your business in a way that is within regulation.

Influencer Marketing Continues to Rise in Success

Influencer marketing has been wildly successful for the past five to ten years, and we expect that trend to continue upward. We have not even come close to seeing the peak of influencer marketer advertising yet, according to forecasters, which is excellent news for anyone who wants to engage in influencer marketing. Whether you are an influencer yourself, or an aspiring one or you are a brand wondering if now is the right time to invest in influencers, you can be confident that there is still plenty of power left in this marketing strategy.

Social Commerce Continues to Expand

Social commerce or commerce that is hosted directly through social media websites is expected to expand over 2021. On Facebook, marketplace and shops hosted directly through business pages were introduced in the past few years, and we are starting to see businesses take greater advantage of these options. On Instagram, shoppable posts have been introduced and are skyrocketing in popularity as brands realize they can sell directly through the platform. While you may still need a website to complete the transaction through, depending on what model you are using, the majority of the sale is conducted directly through the social platform.

Voice Search Is Becoming Increasingly More Popular

Voice search has been a feature on phones for nearly a decade, but as the software behind it becomes more reliable, people are starting to rely on it a lot more. It is important to ensure that your content is compatible with voice search by ensuring that your text is conversational in nature. When you write content, write it in a way that directly answers a question someone might ask, while also using the exact keywords they are likely to use, too. This way, you are far more likely to appear in voice searches where users with Amazon Alexa, Apple HomePod, or Google Home may be searching for something using their voice. This is relevant for both your social media content and your self-hosted website content, which will be most favored by these machines.

Intuitive Content Is Skyrocketing

Intuitive content refers to content that directly addresses an issue that people might be having before they ever even really look it up. This content is then already available when they go to search for it, or it appears across their timeline, reminding them that they were wondering about it in the first place. A great example of intuitive content marketing that happened in 2020 was when stores began to sell out of bread yeast, and many self-sufficiency and food bloggers recognized this and immediately began to post alternatives such as sourdough recipes. Posting intuitively like this is a powerful way to shorten the time it takes for you to answer your audience's questions, which increases your relevancy and makes you the go-to source for information they are seeking.

AR And VR Are Finding Their Way into New Industries

Augmented reality (AR) and virtual reality (VR) systems are finding their way into new industries. These two technologies have been rapidly expanding over the past couple of years, and brands are now starting to really see the power these features have when it comes to marketing and creating an immersive experience for their audience. Previously, AR and VR was almost a taboo subject, as in it was usable only by large brands who could afford it, and most of their customers had no idea how to use it. We are arriving at the point now, where this is becoming more mainstream, which means it is easier for brands to get into using AR or VR, and their audiences will be far more likely to take advantage of these experiences.

Company-Specific Device Apps Will Be Trending

Company-specific device apps have been a possibility for quite some time yet, like with AR and VR, it took a hefty investment to create an app that would be high enough in quality for followers to download it. Over the past five or so years, many low-quality apps have been designed by small to medium brands who tried to capitalize on this opportunity, without realizing the sheer investment it would require to create a high-quality app. These days, as apps become more mainstream, the cost of creating one is becoming less and less, meaning we are starting to see these become far more trending. Having your own app is a great way to create a custom digital "world" for your audience, right on their smartphones, while pushing notifications every time you have a great update for them. It is an excellent marketing strategy for anyone who has a strong enough app idea to back the strategy up with.

Conclusion

Social media marketing is rapidly changing. In the past 6 months since 2020 started, we have seen the projected trends come in full force and create powerful shifts in the way social media marketing works and the necessary action brands must take to stay relevant. Compounded by the worldly events we have all experienced, we have seen even more changes than many expected. Alongside these changes, we have seen an increasing demand – and need – for community-oriented brands that seek to build a community while also building the communities they are a part of. Consumers want to see that brands are committed to the wellbeing of everyone in the community, and are expecting their favorite brands to step up and play a key role in helping everyone get through these tough times. Brands are recognizing this need and emerging into these positions are expanding rapidly, while those that are not are quickly being forgotten about.

These days, marketing is all about give and take. Consumers no longer care about product-oriented ads plastered with fancy colors and "salesy" words that attempt to illicit sales. They care about the specific relationships they are building with the brands they invest in, and they want to see these relationships being cared about and nurtured by the brands themselves, too. The more value, compassion, and service you can offer to your audience, the more loyal they will remain to you and, in turn, the larger your sales will be.

Social media marketing is now a two-pronged marketing strategy that requires both practical efforts and emotional or social-based efforts. Cheap manipulation plays that worked in the past no longer work, as most people are largely immune to them and will even "cancel" brands that are continually pulling these plays. As a marketer, this means your number one focus needs to be on creating an authentic brand that genuinely cares about its audience, while also leveraging practical techniques to get in front of them to develop your sales base.

As marketing continues to change, we see the increasing demand for community and personalization growing going into 2021, despite the fact that we are also seeing growing trends for more automation and artificial intelligence-based approaches. Finding the proper balance between intuitive, personalized marketing and automated systems will be necessary if you will effectively serve your audience in a timely manner and create the results you desire.

As long as you can strike this balance using the strategies and tools provided in *Social Media Marketing 2020,* you should see great success in your ability to get in front of your audience and turn results through the rest of 2020 and beyond.

Finally, if you liked this book and felt that it helped you create a stronger marketing strategy for the coming months, I encourage you to please leave a review on Amazon Kindle. Your honest feedback would be greatly appreciated.

Thank you, and best of luck in growing your business for 2021!

Made in the USA
Coppell, TX
14 May 2021